Fitting the Facts of Crime

Chad Posick, Michael Rocque,
and J. C. Barnes

Fitting the Facts
of Crime

An Invitation to
Biopsychosocial Criminology

Foreword by John Braithwaite

TEMPLE UNIVERSITY PRESS
Philadelphia • Rome • Tokyo

TEMPLE UNIVERSITY PRESS
Philadelphia, Pennsylvania 19122
tupress.temple.edu

Library of Congress Cataloging-in-Publication Data

Names: Posick, Chad, author. | Rocque, Michael, author. | Barnes, James C.
   (James Christopher), author. | Braithwaite, John, writer of foreword.
Title: Fitting the facts of crime : an invitation to biopsychosocial
   criminology / Chad Posick, Michael Rocque, and J. C. Barnes ; foreword
   by John Braithwaite.
Description: Philadelphia : Temple University Press, 2022. | Includes
   bibliographical references and index. | Summary: "This book applies
   findings from neuroscience, behavioral sciences, and evolutionary
   biology to persistent issues in criminology to show how the
   biopsychosocial approach extends and complements traditional
   sociological theories of crime and approaches to crime. John
   Braithwaite's facts of crime serve as a longstanding agenda for
   macro-issues in criminal behavior"— Provided by publisher.
Identifiers: LCCN 2021023007 (print) | LCCN 2021023008 (ebook) | ISBN
   9781439919804 (cloth) | ISBN 9781439919811 (paperback) | ISBN
   9781439919828 (pdf)
Subjects: LCSH: Criminology. | Biopsychosocial criminology. | Criminal
   behavior—Psychological aspects. | Criminal behavior—Genetic aspects.
Classification: LCC HV6025 .P646 2022 (print) | LCC HV6025 (ebook) | DDC
   364—dc23
LC record available at https://lccn.loc.gov/2021023007
LC ebook record available at https://lccn.loc.gov/2021023008

Printed in the United States of America

9 8 7 6 5 4 3 2 1

Contents

Foreword

When I was invited to write this foreword, my first reaction was that it was an easy task to decline because what I know about biological criminology can be written on the back of an aspirin with a crowbar. Yet that is also somewhat true for experts in biological criminology because the unknown is so vast compared to the known. And it is true for me with respect to macrocriminology, in which I consider myself well read. Few things are more complex than the neurophysiology of human brains. While I genuinely admire the brilliant people who do research on brains, my practical philosophy has tended to be that a deeply valuable understanding of how human brains work is not something that will be accessible to me in my lifetime.

This goes to the first strength of this book that it is very accessible. I did learn a lot from it, and I expect this will be true of other nonexpert readers. Criminology is richer for it. This is evocative writing that challenges readers with clarity of analysis. Chad, Michael, and J. C. successfully persisted and overcame my resistance because they used the same method I used in the 1980s when writing *Crime, Shame and Reintegration*. They persuaded me because I was pleased to see colleagues do this. I still think that when we work in a field where most questions are unsettled, unknown, or unknowable, there is virtue in asking what are some of the consensually known facts of the field. And then we must keep modifying the theory to improve the fit of the theory to that list of facts. Of course, that is far from the only good method for theory development, but it is a useful method for shaping the process with explanatory discipline. That discipline is impressive in this book.

You do not have to be a feminist to think it is a weakness of a criminological theory when it fails to give an account of why, in all times and places we know about, men commit much more of most kinds of crime compared to women. We learn from the book that in mammals, but perhaps not in bees, mother/infant bonding is an adaptation necessary for survival. Moreover, "certain protective behaviors of mothers toward infants 'appear to be hard-wired and not at all learned.'" We learn that the human brain evolved to facilitate important interpersonal skills that are useful for relationships.

There are big implications for understanding how our work can contribute to a better world by grasping those deep structures of human beings as relational animals—indeed, as storytelling animals. For me, for example, it motivates an interest in restorative relational justice and a decentering of the formalistic in justice. It can help us understand why men do the majority of the talking in formally legal courtrooms while, in restorative justice circles, according to Sherman and Strang's (2007) Reintegrative Shaming Experiments (RISE), the actors who occupied the most speaking time were mothers of the defendants.

This book teaches us that work on mammals reveals a neurological component to "pair bonding" in adults as well. Life-course criminology, in the hands of practitioners like Robert Sampson and John Laub, suggests that marriage may be a primary factor in encouraging desistance from crime. For feminists, this goes to why biological criminology—indeed, why any criminology—is a dangerous game. Whatever we think about these biological foundations, mothering and marriage are burdened by gendered social and political overlays that enable one sex to dominate the other. Marriage is patriarchally structured in so many ways that privilege men. Men cannot breastfeed, but that becomes a foundation for lumping women with an unfair share of all manner of caring obligations toward children that need not be sexed.

Biological criminology here becomes a dangerous game from a feminist perspective. Yet feminism and biological criminology do a service in this because all criminology is normatively dangerous. The risk of biological essentialism simply makes that more visible. The law is always dangerous because it bans certain activities, including certain kinds of marriages, and because it provides for serious second-order deprivations of liberty in the way it responds to breaches of the law. So good theory in criminology must be integrative of normative and explanatory considerations. Another strength of this book is that it does this, and does it deftly.

This book is appropriately cautious—normatively—about the biological. Not only is it normatively hedged, but it is hedged in the explanatory sense by being a book on biopsychosocial criminology rather than biological criminology. That is, the book brings the biological back in (as it was in the nineteenth and early twentieth centuries) instructively for illiterates like me while not excluding psychosocial explanations. Chad, Michael, and J. C. do not set out to privilege biology or argue it is a better lens than others. Too much emphasis on the biological is as limiting as too much emphasis on the psychological or sociological. A great strength is the way the book introduces interactions among biological, psychological, and social explanations. It also considers toxins like lead that shape class variation but are not purely biological, psychological, or social; rather, they shape and are shaped by all three.

The book does not test a theory in the sense of an ordered set of propositions against the 13 "facts." Rather, it persuasively explores the framework that a combination of the biological, the psychological, and the sociological will do better than one of these alone. It does not go far on applying the framework to crimes by organizations like states or corporations, as opposed to crimes by individuals. It does not consider the relevance of the biopsychosocial to even more macro questions, such as that raised in Robert Reiner's 2020 book that social democratic societies perform better at crime control and justice than neoliberal capitalist or authoritarian capitalist societies.

The book's discussion of the work of Terrie Moffitt (1993) and Gerald Patterson (2016) reveals the practical and liberating use of biopsychosocial explanation. For example, neurological difficulties help us understand why some infants do not bond early with their parents, thus engendering thorny personalities. Parents become exasperated, relationships with the infant become strained, and multiple problems follow from the strained bond. Explaining this interactive complexity to mothers can help liberate them from their own, their family's, or their friends' simplistic explanations, such as "I am a bad mother" or "He is a bad child." We learn that meta-analyses of relational parenting programs show that interactions between parents and children can be improved, thereby improving well-being and self-regulation.

While most all of my 1989 "facts" have stood the test of time well, I look back on one as ill founded even then. This is that "crime rates have been increasing since World War II in most countries, developed and developing. The only case of a country which has been clearly shown to have had a falling crime rate in this period is Japan." Within three or four years of that being written, as this book points out, most developed economies had falling crime rates. Also, most former communist countries and most of Latin America and the Caribbean had rising crime rates during the ensuing decades.

Through the work of historical criminologists like Manuel Eisner, we see that England, the United States, and other countries have periods in their history where the homicide rate is 100 times as high as it is at other times. At any one point in time within one country, there are spaces that have crime rates 100 times as high as in other spaces. Biological differences give a poor account of why different spaces and times in the same country can have hundredfold differences in crime rates—and, indeed, why one country can have 100 times the homicide rate of some other countries when intercountry biological profiles (by sex, for example) are more similar than different. Actually, not only does biological criminology make a poor fit of this explanatory challenge, but so do all extant criminologies. The facts of variation across time and space are not as clear as I posited them in 1989. If we are to build a more potent biopsychosocial criminology, it must look the challenges and complexities of these facts more clearly in the eye than it currently does in the Global North.

The book also makes a good case for adding some new facts for which the evidence has become ever stronger in the past 30 years, such as that child maltreatment is associated with subsequent crime.

This book was a pleasure to read and a treasure of learning for this reader. I congratulate the authors and wish you, in your reading, this treasure and this pleasure.

John Braithwaite
Australian National University

Preface

Back in 2009, two of us (Posick and Rocque) entered graduate school at Northeastern University in Boston, Massachusetts. We became fast friends. One of the things we had in common was our love of criminological theory (some of the others were scotch and baseball—but theory always seemed to come up). Nights were often spent discussing different theoretical perspectives, their strengths and weaknesses, what we liked and did not like. We both leaned toward control theory perspectives—likely furthered by our relationship with Chet Britt, who had become the chair of our department. But while we saw much in the control perspective, we also discussed, at length, what might be missing in those theoretical approaches. One of our go-to books to start to fill in these gaps was *The Criminal Brain* by Northeastern faculty member Nicole Rafter. We quickly grew to advocate for a biosocial perspective to the explanation of crime and were honored to help Nicky write the second edition of that book. What we really honed in on was how biosocial perspectives did not "replace" theories of criminality but enhanced them, made sense of them, and directed interventions.

As we integrated biosocial perspectives into our theoretical discussions and into our academic writing, we became familiar with the major theorists working to promote biosocial criminology. We were fascinated by the work Anthony Walsh was doing on evolutionary perspectives on crime and justice (Walsh, 2000). Adrian Raine's work on the brain and behavior was groundbreaking and opened a whole new world for criminological thinking (Raine, 2013). The molecular and behavioral genetic work being done a few years before we got to graduate school by Terri Moffitt, Kevin Beaver, and John Paul Wright gave us a new way of approaching explanations of violence and antisocial behavior (see Beaver et al., 2008, 2010; Moffitt, 2005).

Along with these leaders in the biosocial field, there also appeared to be a new cadre of young criminologists doing innovative work in biosocial criminology. In particular, we began reading the work being conducted by J. C. Barnes (at this time, for example, Barnes & Beaver, 2012; Barnes, Beaver, & Boutwell, 2011). His work sparked our interest in biosocial topics even more than it was already, and we continued to pursue biosocial criminology in our own work. And as we came to find out, while J. C.'s work was strong and interesting, he would also become a great friend of ours.

When one of us (Posick) began to discuss the idea for this book with Temple University Press and Ryan Mulligan, it was clear that collaborating with Mike and J. C. would be the best approach—if they agreed to it. Luckily, both did and were enthusiastic about the project. Thus, Mike, J. C., Ryan, and Chad began to develop this book. We are proud of our final product, which is really a collaboration not only between the three of us authors but others as well whom we would very much like to acknowledge and thank.

We owe a lot to Ryan for being patient as we completed the book. Mike and Chad went up for (and thankfully received) tenure during this time. J. C. became the interim director of the School of Criminal Justice at the University of Cincinnati. And we all went through—and continue to go through, as of this writing—the global COVID-19 pandemic. We thank Ryan for continuing to push and have faith in the project.

We also want to thank others who influenced us and assisted us on various parts of the book. First, we are thrilled that John Braithwaite, a foundational criminological scholar whose work is used extensively in the book, has written the foreword and added richness to the setup of our project. John provided very thoughtful comments and has added more than he knows to our final product.

We want to thank K. Ryan Proctor, who provided very useful comments on parts of the book and also discussed with us his work on mechanistic criminology, which was incorporated into several chapters. We are certain his work will be integral to a biopsychosocial perspective in criminology.

A set of anonymous reviewers commented on our work throughout the process. While we do not know their names, they all deserve to be thanked and acknowledged for their peer review, which has undoubtedly strengthened our work.

This book, no matter how rich the source material, could not have been completed without the support and love of our families. Chad would like to thank Lulu, Silas, and his "COVID-19 pod family." Mike would like to thank Andi, Teddy, and Cam. J. C. would like to thank Sara and Trey.

Fitting the Facts of Crime

1

Introduction

*The Promise of Biopsychosocial Criminology
for Explaining the Facts of Crime*

On June 12, 2016, Omar Mateen opened fire on patrons of the Pulse nightclub in Orlando, Florida. When the gun smoke cleared, 49 people were dead and another 53 injured. Less than a month later, on July 7, in Dallas, Texas, military veteran Micah Johnson ambushed police officers, killing 5 before being killed by return fire. The following year, on October 1, 2017, in Las Vegas, Nevada ("Sin City"), Stephen Paddock killed 60 people and injured over 500 others when he used a semi-automatic gun to shoot concertgoers from a hotel window. Early the next year, on February 14, 2018, a gunman—Nikolas Cruz—walked into Stoneman Douglas High School in Parkland, Florida, killing 17 people and injuring 17.

These are just a few of the more than 100 mass public shootings in the United States that have occurred in the last 50 years, in which individuals have shot and killed at least four victims in one event (see Duwe, 2020). What could push an individual to take a loaded gun into a public space and unload round after round into innocent men, women, and children? Mental illness? Becoming stressed to the point of no return? There is no consensus in academia or in the public. However, three major issues have come to the forefront of discussions about this issue: (1) mental health, (2) gun availability, and (3) toxic masculinity.

Proponents of the mental health explanation argue that mass shooters suffer disproportionately from mental illness. The act of gunning down innocent people must involve some mental break with reality. Indeed, individuals with mental disorders are more likely to commit a host of antisocial behaviors compared to those with no history of mental health disorders (Silver, 2006). A sizeable proportion of mass shooters have a history of either documented or suspected mental illness (Duwe, 2020). Some critics have taken issue with this assertion, stating that if mental illness led to mass shootings, the United States would have higher levels of mental illness compared to other nations where mass shootings are rare; however, the data show no more mental illness in the United States than other wealthy countries (Kessler et al., 2009).

Alongside the mental health argument—a biopsychological perspective—are broader, more sociological or societal arguments for mass shootings. For instance, a number of commentators have noted the ease of obtaining guns in the United States compared to other countries. Statistics produced by Adam Lankford, an expert on mass shootings, indicate that while the United States 90 mass shooters from 1966 to 2012, no other country had more 18 mass shooters (Lankford, 2016). The United States has many more guns than most other nations, according to Lankford. Could it be that individuals who want to cause harm to others can do so more easily in the United States than in other countries? Perhaps the United States does not have more mentally ill people, but these illnesses coupled with easy access to deadly weapons produce the high level of mass shootings we now see. Figure 1.1 shows the trend in mass public shootings in the United States since 1976, which shows an increase at an elevated rate since the early 2000s.

Finally, the idea of toxic masculinity to explain violence has flooded intellectual and public spaces alike. Toxic masculinity refers to the identity men adopt under a patriarchal societal structure that promotes violence, manipulation, and control. Syed Haider (2016) specifically applied a toxic masculinity framework to the Orlando shooting mentioned previously. He concludes that Mateen's masculine identity turned toxic when he became disillusioned with violence. This disillusionment made Mateen not just angry but enraged, which led him to take lives in great numbers. Is it the patriarchal society in the

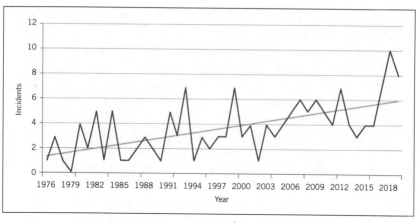

Figure 1.1. Mass Public Shootings in the United States, 1976–2019 (*Source*: James Alan Fox, Grant Duwe, and Michael Rocque as part of a project supported by a grant from the National Institute of Justice [2018-75-CX-0025].)

United States that breeds violent (mostly male) killers? Our contention here—and throughout this book—is that a confluence of factors (a proverbial stew) intertwines to create violence.

Criminologists, unfortunately, do not have all the answers to questions about what causes violence. Behavior is tricky, particularly in humans. However, we now have some pretty good ideas about why people do what they do. The evidence, as presented and discussed in this book, indicates that behavior is the result of a combination of biological, psychological, and environmental factors. Despite debates on how to best measure the specific combination of factors and attribute behavior to either genetics or the environment—or interaction between the two—study after study has supported the idea that genes combine with the environment in causing antisocial and violent behavior (Tuvblad & Baker, 2011; also see Polderman et al., 2015 for a massive review of studies). While it might not be easy to neatly separate genetic and environmental factors and their relative contributions to any trait or behavior, the important idea is that both genes and environments matter . . . and our job is to figure out how.

Criminology as a scientific discipline has traditionally progressed with a singular focus. Initially, in the late 1800s, when researchers began to examine crime with a scientific bent, they paid attention only to biology (Rafter, 2004). Italian military psychiatrist Cesare Lombroso almost solely concentrated on biological factors responsible for behavior—at least until later in his career (Rafter, Posick, & Rocque, 2016). The tracks shifted in the twentieth century when criminology became synonymous with a sociological focus on the environment as the primary cause of behavior (Laub & Sampson, 1991). In this view, it is not the person but his or her environment that drives behavior. Both perspectives offered important, if at times outdated, views on the origins of criminal behavior (Rocque & Posick, 2017).

In recent years, criminology has reached a new junction that merges both these separate tracks. Biosocial criminology and biosocial criminologists focus on the environmental and biological factors that contribute to antisocial behavior. Importantly, they do not view these two domains as separate parts of an equation but as pieces of the same puzzle that fit together into a complete picture of the causes of crime/antisocial behavior. Environmental factors such as social stressors, relationships with antisocial peers, friend and family bonding, and drug use are among the most supported environmental mechanisms associated with poor behavior and are often the focus of biosocial research (see Beaver, Barnes, & Boutwell, 2015). Biological factors such as genes, hormone levels, neurotransmitters, and operation of the central nervous system are often a focal point of biosocial research and have been linked to various delinquent and criminal behaviors (see Raine, 2013).

Recently, researchers have begun to unravel the intricate ways that environmental and biological factors combine (or do not combine) to produce certain behaviors. For example, abuse and neglect are among the most powerful predictors of subsequent delinquent behavior; however, this relationship has been found to be dependent on the presence of a certain variant of the MAOA gene (Caspi et al., 2002). The relationship between having a criminally involved father and participation in the criminal justice system is robust across studies. But this relationship might be contingent on whether a child has a particular version of the DRD2 gene (DeLisi et al., 2009). Biosocial criminologists call these patterns gene-by-environment (GxE) interactions because they exemplify the many ways nature and nurture work together and are far from opposed to one another.

Along with direct genetic and environmental contributions to behavior, environmental factors have been found to lead to behavior via indirect routes through the brain. The brain, of course, is the only thing that directly influences behavior. Without it, we cannot act (indeed, we cannot live). Contrary to earlier beliefs, we now know that the brain is plastic, or still changing, through adolescence (Steinberg, 2014). This means the environment shapes the brain not only in childhood but through much of the first three decades of life. While it is true that the brain is not "infinitely plastic," or malleable, to the same extent throughout life, there are some periods where the brain appears more receptive to change than others. This is important because adolescence has often been considered a time of "storm and stress," with many changes in the teenage environment, including the growing importance of peers (Brown & Larson, 2009). How might the brain be differentially affected by the environments people encounter throughout their life? A very fascinating biopsychosocial question!

The questions of violence that criminologists seek to answer are not restricted only to explanation but also apply to intervention. We are learning more and more each day about how stressful environments can negatively influence brain chemistry, which provides additional information about why crime seems to be concentrated in certain people and particular places (McEwen, 2012; Rocque, Posick, & Felix, 2015). Yet this is not all bad news; it shows us how we can *help* people become more restrained and responsible throughout life. In criminology's early years, when the focus was on biological factors, the prevailing wisdom was that there was little we could do to address the causes of crime short of unethical and inhumane policies such as eugenics (see Rafter, Posick, & Rocque, 2016). After all, so the logic went, if genes are responsible for much of behavior, and those genes do not change or vary over time, what else can be expected to reduce crime but incapacitation? Similarly, when sociological research came to dominate criminology, policies were single-mindedly focused on changing environments. Little attention was paid to why particular people react differently to different environments or what biological information may help design programs to reduce offending (Rocque, Welsh, & Raine, 2012).

Thankfully, the new era of biosocial research recognizes that both the environment and the body matter, and they matter in ways that are mutually reinforcing (see Vaske, 2017). Thus, to understand why crime occurs, and what to do about it, both the environment and the body must be taken into account. New and exciting discoveries are regularly being made that enhance our understanding of crime and, importantly, how to reduce it, relying on both environmental and biological information. This approach is also in line with "mechanistic criminology"—the acknowledgment that explanations for crime must understand proximate causes for how behavior is produced—which is inherently integrative, multilevel, and multidisciplinary (Proctor & Niemeyer, 2019). In this vein, the label "biosocial criminology" is increasingly being replaced with the perhaps more accurate "biopsychosocial criminology." In fact, a new division was developed within the American Society of Criminology under that name in 2017. Accordingly, we use that term throughout this book.

With this in mind, biopsychosocial criminology may hold the key to answering some of the most pressing questions in the field of criminology, a relatively new discipline that has accumulated a substantial body of research and established a few "facts" of crime and antisocial behavior. These are not the same as scientific facts from physics or chemistry, where the evidence is considered perfectly consistent across time and space. Rather, the "facts" of crime should be considered recurring themes that are observed across studies, throughout time, and over a wide range of geographic areas but without perfect harmony. We suggest that a biopsychosocial perspective must be used to explain the "facts of crime."

In chapter 3 of his seminal and influential book *Crime, Shame and Reintegration*, the criminologist John Braithwaite (1989) describes 13 "facts" of criminology. These, he states, are "the strongest and most consistently supported associations in empirical criminology" (Braithwaite, 1989, p. 44). Any theory, according to Braithwaite, ought to account for these 13 facts. While biopsychosocial criminology is not a theory per se, it is a perspective on studying crime and criminality that may help move the field closer to accounting for the empirical findings Braithwaite carefully describes. As shown throughout this book, traditional criminology has offered some answers to these facts, but questions remain. Overall, there is little dispute in criminology regarding the existence of these facts; explanations for them are another matter. What do the facts mean, and how can we explain them? The purpose of this book is to illustrate how a biopsychosocial approach to criminology addresses these questions and gets us a bit closer to answering them. In addition, it has been over 30 years since Braithwaite wrote his book, so we offer some updates to particular facts to bring them in line with recent research.

Plan of the Book

The 13 facts of crime are dealt with in this book one chapter at a time, with some inevitable overlap and, for clarity, some facts being combined or condensed into the same chapter. We hope to show how the biopsychosocial perspective in criminology is a profitable, and very powerful, tool of explanation. It is also our intention to highlight that biopsychosocial criminology should become the standard for criminology in general. We briefly introduce these facts here along with empirical research that supports these findings. In subsequent chapters, we use evidence from biopsychosocial criminology in answering these facts. At the conclusion of each chapter, we discuss outstanding questions—what we still do not know about the facts of crime.

First among Braithwaite's facts is that "crime is committed disproportionately by males." Regardless of the time and place, males commit far more crime—especially violent crime—than females. From serial killers to terrorists to run-of-the-mill delinquents, males get in more trouble than females. This finding cuts across time and place. Sociological theories contend that the disparity in offending is due to such things as the types of peers one hangs around, patriarchy, masculinity, and the different activities in which males and female engage (Hagan, Gillis, & Simpson, 1985; Messerschmidt, 1993; Warr, 2002). These theories are useful but seemingly incomplete. That males are more antisocial than females across time and place suggests something more than social context may be at play.

Notably absent from these explanations are the many biological differences between the sexes. Differences in behavior have emerged from evolutionary forces and genetic differences that control hormone processing and neurodevelopment. Sex hormones—such as testosterone and estrogen—have significant links to behavior, and other neurohormones, including dopamine and serotonin, function differently depending on biological sex (see Walsh & Vaske, 2015).

Physiological factors, such as heart rate, also appear to play a role (Choy, Raine, Venables, & Farrington, 2017). As will be seen, a person's biological sex often moderates the association between neurological function and behavior. A more powerful approach to understanding the gender gap in offending is a combination of biological, psychological, and sociological perspectives. We consider these points in the following chapters.

The second fact presented by Braithwaite is that "crime is perpetrated disproportionately by 15-to-25-year-olds." From some of the earliest research on crime and criminality through contemporary developmental theories of behavior, researchers have noted a robust "age-crime curve" across cultures and across time (Gottfredson & Hirschi, 1986). To be sure, toddlers are often the most antisocial and "violent" in their own right (see Tremblay et al., 1999), but individuals between the ages of 15 and 25 commit the most crime as defined by the law. Early onset criminal behavior often begins in the early teen years and peaks in the late teens and early 20s. Following the mid-20s, there is a precipitous decline in criminal behavior. Since the publication of Braithwaite's book, criminologists have focused on this decline in crime with age—called desistance—with increasing rigor (for example, Rocque, 2017).

Several theories in the 1980s and 1990s sought to explain peak offending in late adolescence. Theorists argued that changing social environments were the cause of increases and decreases in criminality while others pointed to changing peer groups and routine activities. Youth in their late teens are increasingly seeking independence but remain trapped in a position of dependence and lack of freedom. Some sociological scholars have argued that this context provides the foundation for the peak in offending in late adolescence/early adulthood (Agnew, 2003; Greenberg, 1977). Developmental researchers highlighted changes in pushes and pulls toward crime in life domains and turning points in life that would protect against antisocial behavior.

More recently, neuroscientists have offered biosocial explanations that combine neurocognitive development with changing social environments. One such theory suggests that the adolescent brain is composed of two systems that develop on different timetables, resulting in adolescents experiencing heightened attraction to risk without heightened levels of self-control (Steinberg, 2010). Other explanations have similarly relied on physiological factors, such as hormones, to better understand the age-crime curve.

The next fact recognizes that "crime is committed disproportionately by unmarried people." Research in the 1980s showed a positive relationship between being unmarried and engaging in criminal activity (West, 1982). More recent research focused on this marriage effect concluded that being married is a protective factor for individuals (King, Massoglia, & MacMillan, 2007) and larger communities (Rocque, Posick, Barkan, & Paternoster, 2015a). A strong marriage can also act as a turning point where previously deviant individuals change course and desist from offending (Sampson & Laub, 1993; Sampson, Laub, & Wimer, 2006). From an environmental perspective, marriage may reduce crime for several reasons ranging from social control to cutting a person off from his or her potentially antisocial peers.

However, of late, some research has begun to question whether marriage has a causal effect on criminal behavior (Skardhamar, Savolainen, Aase, & Lyngstad, 2015). Instead, it appears that changes occurring prior to marriage may be more influential (Lyngstad & Skardhamar, 2013). A biopsychosocial explanation may help us understand what those changes are and why they make people (1) more amenable to meaningful romantic relationships, and (2) less likely to commit crime. Moreover, some biosocial work has indicated that marriage suppresses genetic effects on crime (Li, Liu, & Guo, 2015). Other research has suggested a link among marriage, divorce, and testosterone—marriage is found to reduce testosterone, which is linked to aggression (Mazur & Michalek, 1998). Clearly, the social control effect of a "good marriage" is not a sufficient explanation for why this institution appears to be associated with a reduction in crime.

Braithwaite's next fact is that "crime is disproportionately committed by people living in large cities." When considering street crime, people in urban areas contribute the most to crime rates. The "fact" that certain areas are disproportionately plagued by violence has been a long-standing criminological finding—one that was most elegantly illustrated by Shaw and McKay (1942). Many sociologically oriented theorists and theories locate this issue within the context of city life. Sampson, Raudenbush, and Earls (1997) argue that sections of the city are marked by disorganization, which makes trust and collective action difficult when crime occurs, resulting in more crime and disorder.

Others, such as Anderson (2000), put forth arguments that explain violence as a reaction to street codes harbored by inner-city residents while others put the brunt of the blame on gangs and delinquent group activity (Matsueda & Anderson, 1998). Yet these sociologically oriented theories ran into difficulties when confronted with the reality that not all (or even most) people in urban areas are antisocial. Biosocial theories can reveal why particular people are most affected by their local environment. For example, an early study found that a combination of living in an urban area and having a criminal parent predicted antisocial behavior (Gabrielli & Mednick, 1984). Others have recently posited biopsychosocial perspectives to explain crime in cities—particularly through the lens of delinquent subcultures and brain chemistry (see Rocque, Posick, & Felix, 2015).

The fifth fact is that "crime is committed disproportionately by people who have experienced high residential mobility and who live in areas characterized by high residential mobility." This fact is tightly associated with the previous one. When individuals move around the city at high rates and very frequently, it is difficult—if not impossible—to establish close ties with neighbors. Therefore, residents do not feel ownership of their neighborhood, do not consider their neighbors as friends and thus are not concerned with their well-being, and are not particularly invested in what goes on in the neighborhood they will likely leave in the near future. Collective efficacy, as Sampson and colleagues (1997) hypothesize, is low in these areas, resulting in high crime rates. Residential mobility is linked to poverty as well as to negative cognitive outcomes (Roy, McCoy, & Raver, 2014) and adverse childhood experiences (Dong et al., 2005).

Biopsychosocial research is also relevant, with genetics and selection effects helping explain residence in particular areas (Domingue et al., 2014; Sampson & Sharkey, 2008). To date, selection effects (a staple in evolutionary biology) have largely been ignored in criminology. However, there are various strands of research that can provide insight. One comes from evolutionary psychology, which has revealed an association between neighborhood context and individual-level traits and behaviors that are relevant to reproduction and survival. Interestingly, Daly and Wilson (1997) identified a correlation between structural signals of violence and the choices made by individuals in those areas concerning mating strategies. More violent areas—meaning life expectancy is lower—tended to also have earlier timing of first births, suggesting individual-level mating decisions are (albeit almost certainly subconsciously) affected by the contextual conditions in which people live. Genomics/genetics research may also be relevant, as there is evidence to suggest that genetic markers linked to educational success are associated with social status and social mobility (Belsky et al., 2018). Although there is still a need to better integrate this work with sociologically focused explanations (e.g., Sampson & Sharkey, 2008), we believe the evidence is suggestive that biopsychosocial research can provide insight into the mechanisms that may underlie neighborhood selection/sorting.

The sixth fact is that "young people who are strongly attached to their school are less likely to engage in crime." When young people are attached to their schools and care what their teachers think of them, they are less likely to jeopardize those bonds by engaging in poor behavior (Hirschi, 1969). Research shows that when students enjoy school and get along with their teachers, they are less likely to act delinquently (Agnew, 1985). From a sociological perspective, these relationships can be explained by social control or strain. When students like their teachers, they have incentives to act in prosocial ways so as not to jeopardize their relationships and futures. Failure in school may also induce the stress of not obtaining—or anticipating not obtaining—desired goals.

Biopsychosocial work can help us better understand why particular individuals are more likely to be attached to their school as well as become more fully engaged in that environment (Jacobson & Rowe, 1999). One particularly influential theory was put forth by Moffitt (1993; 2018). She argued that certain individuals are "life-course-persistent" offenders—in other words, they have difficulty relating to others throughout life. They are more likely to be irritable and impulsive early in childhood and act out in many contexts. Clearly they are not bonded to schools and also engage in antisocial behavior. In this case, neuropsychological difficulties might explain both crime and lack of school bonding. Cognitive ability is also a biosocial factor that can help illuminate the relationship between school attachment and crime (Sniekers et al., 2017). School may be challenging and aversive for someone with developmental problems or delays.

The seventh fact states that "young people who have high educational and occupational aspirations are less likely to engage in crime." When adolescents and teenagers have something to look forward to and aspire to get a job and earn a living, they are, again, less likely to jeopardize those dreams by acting in ways that could get them in trouble, arrested, incarcerated, or injured. Individuals who do not aspire to much in life do not have much to lose and therefore are relatively uninhibited when it comes to engaging in criminal activity (Hirschi, 1969, 2004). Part of the idea of aspirations, which traditional sociological views do not recognize, is linked to the psychological concepts of present orientation and future discounting. The idea is that people who are more concerned with the "here and now" and less concerned with what the future will bring are more likely to act on temptations and seek gratification, often via criminal conduct (Nagin & Paternoster, 1994). A biopsychosocial view allows us to link this idea to aspirations—delinquents may tend to have lower aspirations for a reason (see DeLisi, 2015). They have less concern for a future they do not think about, and this orientation has much to do with how the brain is activated in certain situations.

The eighth fact is that "young people who do poorly at school are more likely to engage in crime." Similar to the last few facts, those who are attached to school and their teachers are protected from engaging in crime. Those who do poorly, get bad grades, or eventually drop out are more likely to engage in crime (Hirschi & Hindelang, 1977). This link can also be seen in the recent rise of punitive discipline—such as suspension and expulsion—that increase offending (Mowen & Brent, 2016). If adolescents are not in school, there is a good chance they will replace school activities with deviant activities, including crime and violence.

The ninth fact is that "young people who are strongly attached to their parents are less likely to engage in crime." One of the most replicated findings in the criminological literature is that individuals who are strongly bonded with their parents are less likely to be delinquent (Hirschi, 1969). This association has even been found in several cultures across the globe (Posick, 2013; Posick & Rocque, 2015). Hirschi (2004) posits that strong associations with parents are inhibitions that individuals carry with them in their daily lives and that act against poor behavior. In that sense, parents can act as supervisors of behavior when they are present and can be ingrained in a child's conscience even when they are not (what Hirschi [1969, p. 88] called being "psychologically present").

Gottfredson and Hirschi (1990) argued that parenting is the key to developing childhood self-control; those with stronger social bonds will have higher self-control and lower levels of criminal behavior (Hirschi, 2004). This is a purely sociological take that draws on social control and social learning perspectives. Yet biopsychosocial research has questioned just how much parents influence children in general (Harris, 2009), in particular with respect to pouring self-control into their prefrontal cortexes (Beaver, Ratchford, & Ferguson, 2009; Wright & Beaver, 2005). Parents, it turns out, might only be able to do so much for instilling impulse control into children via the environment—they may have already set the pace with the genes they passed on. Further, some research has found that social control measures interact with gene variants to explain antisocial behavior (Guo, Roettger, & Cai, 2008). It may be the case that parents are close to children because of factors that also influence their children's behavior; in other words, it is not *only* the parent-child relationship that is protective against crime (see also Christakis & Fowler, 2009).

For his tenth fact, Braithwaite states that "young people who have friendships with criminals are more likely to engage in crime themselves." Mark Warr's (2002) *Companions in Crime* presents a considerable amount of evidence that associating with delinquent peers increases one's own criminal behavior. In Akers's (2009) formulation of social learning theory, he suggests that peers can reinforce and motivate delinquent behavior. However, both Warr and Akers overlook *how* people are motivated and what it is about peers that has such a strong impact on behavior. Learning processes are strongly affected by brain structure and function. For instance, genes in the dopamine system (DAT1, DRD2 and DRD4, and COMT genes) substantially impact receptiveness to rewards (i.e., reinforcement) and punishment (Hahn et al., 2011). Clearly, then, to fully understand the learning process, social and brain science must be joined.

Eleventh, "people who believe strongly in the importance of complying with the law are less likely to violate the law." People who believe in the legitimacy of and need for the law are more likely to follow the law. The work of Tom Tyler throughout the 1990s provided substantial support for this proposition (for example, see Tyler, 2003;

see also Jackson et al., 2012). When people believe the law is unfairly applied, unjust, illegitimate, or ineffective, they are not likely to follow it. On the other hand, the reverse is true. People follow the law when they see it as fair, legitimate, and effective in reducing crime and keeping people safe. The notion of belief in the law was also a part of Hirschi's (1969) social control theory, suggesting that legitimacy acts a social restraint.

Readers may wonder how a biopsychosocial model can be applied to this fact of crime—but we will address this very underdeveloped issue in a separate chapter of the book. Recent work, for example, has shown that psychopathic traits (linked to biology) are related to feelings about procedural justice (Augustyn & Ray, 2016). As Anthony Walsh (2000) has shown, a sense of justice can be traced to our evolutionary origins. Feelings of being discriminated against can contribute to biological problems, including premature aging (Chae et al., 2014) and excessive inflammation (Brody et al., 2015). These factors contribute to crime through a process some have described as "criminal energetics" (Vaughn & DeLisi, 2018).

The twelfth fact is that "for both women and men, being at the bottom of the class structure, whether measured by socio-economic status, socio-economic status of the area in which the person lives, being unemployed, being a member of an oppressed racial minority (e.g., being black in the US), increases the rates of offending for all types of crime apart from those for which opportunities are systematically less available to the poor (i.e., white-collar crime)." Support has been garnered for the link between low socioeconomic status (SES) and crime, but not without controversy. However, it should be fairly obvious by now that violent crime is concentrated among those who live in impoverished areas. Regardless of sex, race, or age, individuals who live in poverty are more exposed to violence and more likely to participate in delinquent activities (Weisburd et al., 2004). Poverty may be related to antisocial behavior for a variety of reasons. Traditional sociological theories have focused on mechanisms such as an inability to attain the American dream (Merton, 1938) or frustration resulting from efforts to achieve middle-class standards (Cohen, 1955). Yet such theories often cannot explain the intermediary linkages between violence and poverty. Biopsychosocial perspectives can help us understand the effects of poverty on such things as brain development (Barkan & Rocque, 2018; Johnson, Riis, & Noble, 2016) and emotion regulation (Kim et al., 2013). Those in poverty are also exposed to harmful environmental toxins to a greater extent in both urban and rural areas (Nevin, 2000; Thatcher et al., 1983). In addition, poverty may be related to toxic stress and adverse childhood experiences (ACEs), which are also related to later antisocial behavior (Poole, Dobson, & Pusch, 2018).

Thirteenth, and finally, "crime rates have been increasing since World War II in most countries, developed and developing. The only case of a country which has been clearly shown to have had a falling crime rate in this period is Japan." Since Braithwaite's 1989 book, crime rates have seen a surge and then a dramatic decline. In particular, since the early 1990s, crime dropped in the United States and other nations precipitously in ways we still have not been able to fully explain. The crime decline has been the subject of numerous debates, and scholars have suggested several factors that may have contributed, such as a booming economy, better policing tactics, and greater use of incarceration—all social/external forces (Zimring, 2007). Because of this crime decline, we amend Braithwaite's thirteenth fact to cover crime trends in the twentieth and twenty-first centuries generally. We focus on how biosocial criminology can explain macro-levels inclines and declines of crime and violence over time and across places. For example, one fascinating possibility is that the decline in crime may be tied to a decrease in environmental lead levels, which have been linked to cognitive development and antisocial behavior (Sampson & Winter, 2018).

Given the evidence in support of these 13 facts, Braithwaite states that "most of the entries on this checklist would be uncontroversial to those familiar with the criminological literature" (1989, p. 50), and we agree. The debate is not on the existence of these facts but around why these facts have emerged. What is the etiology behind these facts? In other words, what explains the origins of these facts? We contend that traditional criminological (and, in particular, sociologically based criminology) only reveals part of the answer. Biological and psychological factors add another vital piece to this puzzle and cannot be ignored if we are to account for these facts with theory. Thus, our intent is to use biopsychosocial criminology as a unifying framework to enrich our understanding of the most robust, empirically based findings in the field of criminology.

The book is organized in the following manner: Chapter 2 begins our foray into applying a biopsychosocial lens to the 13 facts. This chapter explores how biopsychosocial work can help us understand gender/sex differences in criminal behavior and criminal justice outcomes. Importantly, we differentiate gender and sex, which helps illustrate where the biopsychosocial work applies compared to traditional sociological perspectives. Chapter 3 moves on to fact two, showing how a biopsychosocial perspective can help us understand the relationship between age and crime. We discuss why young people are disproportionately involved in crime but also consider why crime declines into adulthood.

Chapter 4 moves on to consider disadvantage and crime, from both individual and macro perspectives. Fact twelve is most relevant here, as it deals with disadvantage in terms of socioeconomic status on an individual and geographic level. Why does disadvantage lead to crime? How do the pressures of poverty push individuals, from a biopsychosocial perspective, into deviance? Chapter 5 addresses fact ten, which states that individuals with delinquent or criminal associates are more likely to engage in crime themselves. Generally, this finding has been explained via social learning theory. However, social learning has been criticized for ignoring selection, described by the saying "birds of a feather flock together." Biopsychosocial perspectives may help us understand why these birds flock together. Chapter 6 addresses social bonds, incorporating facts three, six, seven, eight, and nine. Typically, social bonds have been utilized in a social control framework. While this is a sociological perspective, biopsychosocial work can help us understand why people may be naturally inclined to deviance and why social connections may restrain us from doing so.

Chapter 7 deals with stress and antisocial behavior. While a social-psychological approach, general strain theory, has often been applied to understand this connection, new research utilizing biopsychosocial information can provide more insight into how stress affects the body and subsequent behavior. This chapter applies to facts four and five, which consider stressful environments or situations and their influence on behavior. The last substantive chapter, Chapter 8, considers the influence of the police and crime trends. Police can affect crime via legitimacy, which applies to fact eleven, and crime trends applies to fact thirteen. Fact thirteen may be one of the more difficult to explain from a biopsychosocial perspective, as it deals with long-term changes in crime rates, but here we will show how environmental changes, which affect the body, can impact crime rates. Chapter 9 offers some conclusions and predictions for what the future holds with respect to biopsychosocial criminology.

It should be noted here that several of the facts of crime can be discussed in multiple chapters in this book. We organized the chapters the way we did because it made sense to group certain theoretically related facts together, and other times we grouped the facts because we thought it was best for readability. In any case, it remains that biopsychosocial perspectives can address issues related to the facts of crime—and can do so broadly and comprehensively.

To close, it is worth revisiting a story told by Robert Hare (1993) in his book *Without Conscience*, in which he describes two twins who differed like "heaven and hell." Despite both having a supportive family and growing up in a supportive environment (not to mention sharing the womb), the two sisters could not be more different. The catch? They were fraternal twins—sharing 50 percent of their DNA instead of 100 percent like identical twins. The origins of most behavioral traits—from depression to happiness to antisocial behavior—lie in a complex web of genetic and environmental (often unshared or unique) causes. To get to the bottom of people's most perplexing behaviors, we must examine this web—and find out how to disentangle it.

The three of us believe this book is needed and can inform both academic work on the etiology of human behavior and practical approaches designed to reduce crime and make society healthier and safer. In these ways, it is intended to be read (and used!) by students, scholars, practitioners, and the general public. We hope this book sheds light on the factors related to criminal and antisocial behavior as well as exactly *how* those factors are related to behavior. Thus, each chapter concludes with a section on how the pieces of the crime puzzle fit together and which pieces remain missing. We also hope our discussion on violence prevention and intervention is useful to practitioners and academics alike who are interested in effectively addressing violent behavior and subsequent negative outcomes. Our intentions are to provide the best ways we know to study criminal behavior and intervene for the best chance to reduce violence in society.

2

Sex Differences
in Criminal Behavior

From 1590 to 1610, a serial killer was on the loose in Nyirbator, Hungary. While the exact number varies, the killer murdered over 80 people—and some say as many as 640. Accounts of the murders were grisly. It was said that the killer stripped the victims naked and made them withstand freezing Hungarian nights until they died of hypothermia. Others told of savage beatings, burning, and mutilation at the hands of the killer (McNally, 1983). If you are wondering "his" name—you will never guess. The murderer here is Elizabeth Bathory, the famous serial killer who has become legend for having bathed in her victims' blood to preserve her youth (among other heinous acts, as mentioned). In addition to their depravity, Bathory's acts stand out, as do those of other female serial killers, such as Aileen Wuornos (depicted in the movie *Monster*), because female killers are so rare. In fact, some estimates have suggested that as much as 93.3 percent of serial killers are male (Fox, Levin, & Quinet, 2012).

It is not just serial killing, an extreme form of criminal behavior, in which gender differences emerge. In fact, males commit more of almost every single type of crime by an average ratio of 3:1. Using the most recent data from the 2015 Uniform Crime Report Program, males commit about 73 percent of all crime while females are respon-

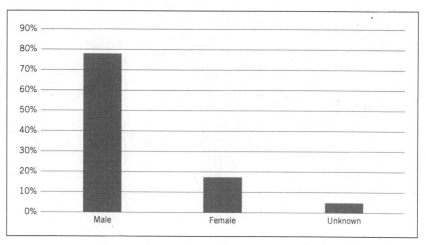

Figure 2.1. Violent Crime in the United States by Sex, 2019
(*Source*: Federal Bureau of Investigation, Crime Data Explorer,
https://crime-data-explorer.app.cloud.gov/explorer/national/united-states/crime.)

sible for the remaining 27 percent. The discrepancy, though, is largest for violent crime. Males commit the bulk of rapes (97 percent), murders (88 percent), and robberies (86 percent). They are also nine times as likely to be arrested for carrying a weapon. Even in crimes that are not typically "gendered," such as embezzlement and theft, males are arrested at greater percentages (51 percent and 57 percent, respectively). One of the few exceptions to this rule is arrests for prostitution, of which about a third are male. Figure 2.1 presents some of these data in summary form for 2019.

Of course, these are official crime rates, which include only those offenses known to the police. But the trend also exists for self-report data not only in the United States but around the globe and for youth. Data from the second International Self-Report Delinquency Study (a study of school-aged individuals) reveal that males commit more crime than females for all types of offenses across the 30 countries included in the study. Table 2.1 shows the results for one violent crime type, assault, and one nonviolent crime type, shoplifting, for six countries. While the gap is smaller for nonviolent crime, both types are dominated by males. This is just one more example that at all places, and at all times, males commit more crime than females.

TABLE 2.1. THE PERCENT OF MALES AND FEMALES COMMITTING
ASSAULT AND SHOPLIFTING BY COUNTRY

Panel 1. Assault for Males and Females by Country

	Denmark	Estonia	Germany	Russia	U.S.	Venezuela
Males	2.6	0.5	6.7	1.7	2.8	1.6
Females	0.8	0.3	2.2	0.5	1.5	0.4

Panel 2. Shoplifting for Males and Females by Country

	Denmark	Estonia	Germany	Russia	U.S.	Venezuela
Males	27.5	26.7	26.7	6.3	20.8	5.6
Females	23.6	23.3	23.4	5.1	20.4	3.2

Source: International Self-Report of Delinquency Study-2

Finally, this male/female difference in the commission of crime extends to victimization and also holds over time. With respect to victimization, males have higher odds of being attacked than females (except for rape/sexual assault) (Sampson & Lauritsen, 1994; Posick, 2013). In addition, the gender/sex discrepancy in crime has been found throughout history. One of the earliest statistical analyses of crime, by Adolphe Quetelet, found similar differences. Using French court data from 1830, he found a ratio of 100:23 male to female criminals. The ratio was higher for property crimes, interestingly. Quetelet hypothesized that women are "especially restrained by the sentiment of shame and modesty as to moral qualities, by her state of dependence and more retiring habits as to opportunity, and by her physical weakness as to her ability to act" ([1831] 1984, p. 48). We see that in terms of crime—across culture, across time, and even for victimization—males are at a greater risk than females. This is not in dispute. The question is why.

Gender versus Sex

At the outset of this chapter discussing differences between male and female crime rates, it is important to understand our terms. Gender is typically understood to be related to but somewhat distinct from sex. Sex refers to physical and biological differences between males and females. Primary sex characteristics include genitals (e.g., penis, testes, vagina, ovaries), while secondary sex characteristics are those distinguishing features that have no reproductive value (e.g., facial hair, differential musculature) (Barkan, 2011). In other words, sex encapsulates the differences we are born with as well as those that accompany puberty. It also is important to note that while typically and normatively there are two sexes (male and female), there are other variations included under the category intersex. Intersex individuals are born with primary sex characteristics of both males and females (often not in equal proportion). In medical terms, this is called a disorder of sexual development (DSD) (Viau-Colindres, Axelrad, & Karaviti, 2017). In her controversial piece, Anne Fausto-Sterling (1993) argued that, in fact, there are five sexes. Sex as a category would also include things such as brain structure and function, hormones, and physical features that separate males and females (and other groups).

On the other hand, gender is a social construct. By social construct, we do not mean it is entirely unrelated to biological realities. Gender is linked to biological and historical differences between men and women. But it is socially constructed because it is composed of a set of social expectations not solely *determined* by anything biological or historical. These expectations vary by social context and over time. For example, certain societies that have been studied seem to hold gender norms opposite to those popular in the West (Cuddy et al., 2015; Mead, 1963). Sometimes gender roles and norms are clearly socially constructed, such as dress, fashion, and hairstyles. Others are seemingly more tied to evolutionary and historic social contexts, such as expectations that males will be aggressive and females will be more nurturing. But just because something may be related to historical social situations or biological differences does not mean it is cemented in stone—this is what we mean by socially constructed.

Braithwaite's first fact that a theory should fit is that "crime is disproportionately committed by males" (1989, p. 44). A theory, therefore, needs to explain this finding. He shows that official reports and self-reports of crime and victimization overwhelmingly indicate that males are more involved in just about every type of crime and that this is true almost everywhere in the world. Often, he notes, theories and perspectives focus almost solely on why males commit crime and do not focus as heavily on why women do (or do not) commit crime. We contend that a biopsychosocial perspective can explain both very well.

When explaining differences between males and females in crime rates, or trying to understand why females commit crimes (criminology has historically been concerned with male crime/criminality), traditional theoretical approaches have tended to focus on gender and social structure. These explanations, including traditional sociological theories, are discussed first in this chapter. We find many of these approaches to have merit, but they are incomplete. To expand, we then turn to how biopsychosocial approaches can help inform both gender and sex differences in crime and criminal justice experiences. Our argument is that biological and biopsychosocial perspectives can help us understand how both the social environment (including gender expectations) and underlying biological differences combine to explain variation in criminological outcomes between males and females. Biological and evolutionary perspectives can also help us understand how culture and context are molded, in turn impacting behavior.

Traditional Theoretical Approaches

Traditional criminological theories that attempt to account for the gap in criminality between males and females are notoriously incomplete. Generally, sociologically based theories of crime have not attempted to account for the gender gap but rather have focused nearly exclusively on males (however, this has been a focus of recent research—see, for example, Savolainen et al., 2017). Early theories, such as social disorganization, status frustration, and control theories, utilized nearly all male samples (for an infamous example, see Hirschi, 1969). This is understandable because, as we have mentioned, males commit the vast majority of all types of crimes. However, using male-only data, and constructing theories to account largely for male criminality, makes it difficult to explain why males have higher crime rates than females.

When it became apparent that it was folly to ignore gender in traditional theories of crime, when the gender gap became something to explain, criminologists began to wonder whether their theories could explain why males seem to misbehave more. Some thought that the same pressures and motivations cut across gender lines but differentially affect males. When these pressures and motivations came to affect more females (for example, with the rise of economic equality), you would begin to see more equitable rates of crime between males and females. This was essentially the argument of two land-mark books published in 1975: Freda Adler's *Sisters in Crime* and Rita Simon's *Women and Crime*. Both these seminal books argued that female criminality was on the rise due to changes in the social structure that offered more equality for women. As women came to have the same rights and privileges as men, they would be exposed to the same pressures and motivations that led to crime (as argued, for example, by strain theory; see Merton, 1938), and thus their crimi-nal behavior would come to resemble that of men's. In essence, these theoretical views see men and women as basically the same biologi-cally but simply located differently in the social structure—that is all there is to explain gender differences in behavior.

Adler's and Simon's prophecies did not come to fruition, either because of theoretical inaccuracies or perhaps because women's equal-ity has not advanced as much as they thought it would. However, that does not mean traditional theories are unable to explain both male and female criminality. In fact, in an illuminating study, Doug Smith and Ray Paternoster (1987) explored whether traditional theo-ries such as differential association, strain, social bonding, and deter-rence perspectives are equally applicable to male and female decisions to participate in marijuana smoking and the frequency with which they smoke. In large part, they found few differences in terms of ef-fects of the variables. They regard this as suggesting that the under-lying processes influencing deviant behavior are the same for males and females and that sex- or gender-specific theories are a waste of time. Whether social bonds predict crime for both males and females is a different question, though, than whether social bonds can explain the gender gap in offending (see also Kruttschnitt, 2013).

Certain traditional theories in criminology purport to be "gener-al," by which we mean they can explain all crime by all people across all contexts. These theories include self-control theory and general strain theory, among others. These theories suggest that the same causal mechanisms affect both males and females but at different levels and (in some cases) in different ways. For example, self-control theory (Gottfredson & Hirschi, 1990) views crime as a consequence of low self-control. Parental socialization is the key mechanism that instills self-control in children. Thus, any difference in criminality between males and females is a result of differences in parental socialization, which creates different levels of self-control by sex. Research on this score is not supportive. Parenting is not the sole source of self-control, and it does not explain any large portion of the gender gap (Botchkovar et al., 2015; Botchkovar & Broidy, 2013), but self-control may account for a small portion of the gap in some instances (Burton et al., 1998; Tittle, Ward, & Grasmick, 2003).

Research on general strain theory—which argues that strain, or being treated as you do not wish to be treated, leads to negative emotions and, in some cases, criminal behavior—has also been examined in terms of the gender gap. Broidy and Agnew (1997) argued that males do not commit more crime than females because they experience *more* strain but because they react to it differently and experience different types of strains. Some evidence provides limited support for this theory, particularly as it pertains to males externalizing frustration and females internalizing it (Posick, Farrell, & Swatt, 2013). Again, research is suggestive but not conclusive that the theory can account for the gender gap (Hoffman & Cerbone, 1999; Mazerolle, 1998; Piquero & Sealock, 2004).

Some feminist scholars have taken issue with this sort of assessment and argue that there are gendered pathways into and out of delinquency. That is, males and females differ in how they become criminals in the first place and how they desist. Feminist criminologist Kathleen Daly (1994) argued that a typical pathway for women to become traditional offenders begins with their own victimization or abuse. This victimization tends to happen within their own families and forces them into the streets. Once there, a lack of resources leads to hardships and, eventually, crime. Research on the gendered pathways hypothesis is somewhat equivocal, with some work finding both males and females have similar routes to delinquency and others finding that females respond differently to abuse (Kruttschnitt, 2013). In addition, according to Kruttschnitt (2013, p. 301), while the traditional correlates of crime may apply across gender, "the mediators of these experiences, which may include opportunities for reacting to these stressors, may not."

Finally, some theories have been constructed specifically to account for the gender gap. These include John Hagan and colleagues' (1985) power control theory. Briefly, power control theory suggests that there are two ideal types of families—patriarchal and egalitarian. In the former, males exert more control and influence on the families, and boys are less controlled than females. This encourages boys to take risks and get into trouble. In these families, there is a larger gap between the genders in deviance. In egalitarian families, men and women share similar influence and socialize boys and girls similarly. As a consequence, in egalitarian families, there is a small gender gap in crime. Research is mixed on the theory (De Coster, Heimer, & Cumley, 2013), again raising doubts about whether a traditional sociological theory is sufficient to explain the gender gap in offending. There are also questions about how males and females appraise familial situations in the first place and are ultimately deterred from committing crime (Blackwell, 2000).

One theory, rather than focusing on the unique experiences of females to understand the gender gap, has attempted to shine a light on male socialization. Masculinities theory suggests that boys are socialized to be risk takers, independent, and aggressive. James Messerschmidt (1993) calls this situation "hegemonic masculinity," which operates to maintain male dominance over women in the workplace and at home. Proving one's masculinity is itself conducive to crime (as the previous chapter highlighted with the Pulse nightclub shooting), but for Messerschmidt, the types of crime men commit are determined by their social location and access to resources. Thus, crime is "structured action" in which people perform their gender in varying ways according to the social situation. Messerschmidt's theory has been critiqued for a variety of reasons, including not representing female crime well and being tautological (e.g., crime is masculine "because men do it," Hood-Williams, 2001, p. 45; see Miller, 2002).

Of course, there are other treatments of gender and crime in traditional and sociologically oriented theories. Each provides important insights into why men and women offend at different rates and in different ways. Our discussion here is necessarily cursory and brief but demonstrates at least three things: (1) traditional theories of crime and delinquency have illuminated the differing ways males and females experience the social world and are influenced by the social world; (2) traditional criminological theories have not fully accounted for the gender gap—questions remain unanswered, such as why the gap is largest for violent crimes (Agnew, 2009); and (3) by and large, these perspectives have ignored the role of biology and the body in producing differences between males and females in crime.

A biopsychosocial approach may help clarify both the gender gap and the differences between males and females in particular types of criminal and antisocial acts. A biopsychosocial approach is powerful because it not only focuses attention on social structure and the environment (aspects related to gender) but also brings a physiological element (e.g., sex) into the picture. That there have been stark differences between males and females in antisocial and aggressive acts across time and place (not to mention across most nonhuman species) points to the possibility that more than just structure and culture are at play. The next part of the chapter describes how a biopsychosocial perspective can help answer one of the fundamental facts a theory must fit: the gender gap in offending.

Biopsychosocial Contributions

While the sociological perspective has enabled scholars to incorporate structural theories into the explanation of the gender gap, there are several reasons to question whether this is the whole story. If social structural variables are the only ones at play, why is a gender gap evident across all species of animals—and specifically mammals? For humans, the male/female gap exists in almost all cultures across the globe. It also occurs very early on in life—it is readily apparent that toddler boys and girls are different in the amount of aggression they portray even before much socialization has taken place. Finally, regardless of the time period, as social structures and societies have shifted extensively, the gender gap has remained. Could something broader and more general be at play?

We propose that there is a more universal explanation for the male/female gap in offending that can also explain the existence of current societal institutions and structures. Evolutionary perspectives (biology and psychology) can explain why males commit more crime than females and why masculinity and power structures exist in the first place. Evolutionary perspectives make sense of behavior by linking it to success in mating or survival (or both) throughout long periods of history—what evolutionary psychologists call "fitness." This means that evolution may have played a key role in "selecting" genes that increase the probability of certain types of behavior that are now deemed aggressive/criminal by modern society.

Because evolution explains the survival of genetic information (genes) across successive generations, it also accounts for other biological differences between males and females that contribute to criminal behavior. For example, levels of testosterone are higher in males than females, and testosterone levels have been linked to aggression. Other neurohormones (substances secreted by specialized cells that are then circulated in the body) such as serotonin tend to be higher in females and are linked to reduced aggression (Nishizawa et al., 1997). The structure and function of the brain are also different between the sexes. Brain volume is greater in males, but females have more gray matter (Cosgrove, Mazure, & Staley, 2007). Males have larger grey matter "volume and tissue density" in their amygdala than females, whereas the opposite is true for the prefrontal cortex (Ruigrok et al., 2014, p. 43).[1] Since the prefrontal cortex is implicated in reasoning and judgment while the amygdala governs primitive emotional reactions, the link to criminal behavior is quite clear. These biological factors likely play a role in sex differences in criminal behavior. But they do not act alone. Together with social constraints and cultural factors, they may help fully explain the gender gap in crime.

Evolution

It will become evident as we progress through the book that biopsychosocial criminology makes a lot of sense when viewed through the lens of human evolution. Evolution refers to the slow changes to the human organism (and the human genome) that accrue over time to adapt to environmental conditions (see Campbell, 2009). Specifically, an underlying mechanism in human evolution is "fitness" or "reproductive success." In other words, we, as a human species, have evolved over time to ensure we pass on traits to as many offspring as possible, who will then pass along those traits to the next generation, and so on. Traits and behaviors that promote reproduction of the greatest number of viable offspring and secure their survival will persist and

---

1. These are *average* differences. For example, some females have more circulating testosterone than some males, and some males have more circulating serotonin than some females. But the *average* level of circulating testosterone among males is higher than the *average* for females.

thrive over time. In the human species, reproductive success entails an evolutionary development of two sexes—males and females—with different traits and behaviors (see Konner, 2015). The evolutionary mechanisms that increase reproductive success also influence behaviors that are antisocial as well as prosocial.

On the one hand, theorists have posited that differences between the sexes (in our discussion, we always refer to the sexes as distinctly male and female unless otherwise noted) are due to socialization. Males and females are "different" only to the extent that society has socialized them. Boys are dressed in jeans and a T-shirt, have their rooms colored in blue, and play with GI Joes while girls are dressed in skirts, have their rooms painted in pink, and play with Barbies. Further, society reinforces the notion that girls should be caring, giving, nurturing, and submissive while boys are tough, outgoing, self-centered, and domineering (Fagot, Rodgers, & Leinbach, 2000).

Certainly socialization has a role in the way boys and girls develop, and the sociological literature is replete with examples of the relevance of socialization on traits and behaviors. However, human traits such as empathy, altruism, and caregiving and behaviors such as aggression and permissiveness can be traced to evolutionary adaptation that has occurred over thousands of years with only slight differences between cultures (Schmitt et al., 2008). On average, males are more violent, aggressive, and domineering while females are (again, on average) more nurturing, permissive, and empathetic. Some males are more nurturing and caring than some females, and some females are more aggressive and violent than some males—but, overwhelmingly, males and females are easily identified by the traits and behaviors they exhibit, and these differences are not totally the result of socialization. These differences are present at birth and persist over the life course. Biopsychosocial criminology, using evolutionary biology/psychology as a foundation, can make sense of these sex differences as they pertain to violent and criminal behaviors.

Selection

When social scientists who have not been trained in evolutionary principles hear the term "selection," they often think only of "natural selection." Natural selection refers to the differential success of genes that survive and are passed down through generations because they promote survival within a specific context. Giraffes with long necks could reach a food source their shorter-necked competitors could not. The giraffes who could not reach food died out (as did their short neck genes) while their long-necked counterparts survived and bred with others with similarly long necks. Often the phrase "survival of the fittest" is linked to the concept of natural selection, though it is actually attributed to a sociologist, Herbert Spencer (Applebaum, 2017), not Darwin. Those individuals who have the "fittest" genes will survive while those who are unfit will die off (maybe it is really "death of the unfittest," then).

It certainly is true that some genes that assist in fitness will, in turn, increase longevity and health. These genes will likely be beneficial to the human species and will be passed along to successive generations. But there is also another reason, beside mere survival, that genes can be passed through generations: because they assist in attracting sexual partners, keeping those partners, and reproducing with those partners. This is referred to as sexual selection. Sexual selection plays the biggest part in the survival of genes.

Over a large number of generations, sexual selection filters out genes that correspond to traits that are not attractive to sexual partners. By choosing who we mate with, we are, in essence, choosing which genes to replicate and which ones to lay by the wayside. Genes that correspond to disease, illness, and weakness may be selected out of a population because of the risk to life they incur. Genes corresponding to health, longevity, vitality, and strength are likely to be "chosen," or selected for by mates, because they increase the chance the organism will live and produce offspring.

But animals, including us, do not (generally) give our partners DNA tests to identify their gene stock. Instead, we use other tools. One of these tools is called epigamic display (we will use the terms "display" or "signaling"; although these terms can be more specific, that is out of the purview of this chapter and our purposes). Through various displays of power, strength, and health, animals (and, of course, that includes us humans) can signal to one another the positive qualities that make us a worthy mate. If the three of us want to show our wives that we are quality partners, we might engage in a three-on-three basketball game to display our athletic skills. If we emerge winners, it would surely prove that our genes make us good athletes and deserving of their partnership. While the traits and qualities that are attractive to females are fairly universal, some are strongly related to the social context in which animals exist (see Arnocky et al., 2014).

Evolutionary mechanisms, such as natural selection and sexual selection, have helped shape behavior. It is important to note, and keep in mind throughout this book, that human beings are animals (mammals, to be a bit more specific) and are influenced by many of the same processes as other animals. Humans are not the epitome of evolution and are not the "most evolved" species. This is often how we think of ourselves, but, even though it might be nice, it does not reflect reality. Other species top our strength, agility, reproductive success, and longevity. This helps us understand that evolution has no goal, which is to say there is no objective benchmark in mind. Evolution has no endgame; it just continues as time passes. Perhaps we are the most "intelligent" of species, but this, again, is the result of evolutionary processes that shaped our intelligence because it conferred benefits for us as a species. In any case, evolution shapes not only our physical bodies and features but our behaviors as well. And given that males and females have evolved along different lines (what is adaptive for males may not always be adaptive for females and vice versa), there are some stark behavioral differences between the sexes (see Ridley, 1993). These differences, we argue, can be partially explained through an evolutionary biology perspective.

Let us begin with males. In all cultures, across all time (and for almost all species of animals), males are more aggressive than females. To be sure, this is a *generalization*. But that is exactly what evolutionary perspectives attempt to explain: human general universals. Evolutionary perspectives are not the best at explaining why one person committed one specific crime, but they are very good at, say, explaining why men are more likely to commit homicide than women. As our society grapples with understanding the devastating violence reflected in mass shootings, serial killing, and the like, we often overlook how evolutionary principles can help guide us to the answer.

To begin, one concept from evolutionary biology can set the foundation for explaining differences in violence between the sexes. Epigamic display is the signaling of specific traits and characteristics that are attractive to the opposite sex. The manakin, a bird that moonwalks across a tree branch and clicks its wings to show females that it is agile and fit, is quite literally showing off for potential sexual partners. He is also warning other males, "Stay away, this one is mine." The antlers of a 12-point buck signal strength and health to a doe looking to mate and may even be used as a weapon against other males looking to mate with the same female. In epigamic display, the sex with the least investment in children is responsible for appealing to the "selecting" sex—it is almost always males appealing for selection by females (Campbell, 2009).

Given the epigamic display phenomenon, it should come as little surprise that males are the most likely to engage in specific behaviors to attract mates (although females do much the same thing). One of the most direct forms of this can be seen in status striving. Males with a good reputation and respectability among their peers are more "attractive" than males who are not seen positively among their peers. A large number of studies have confirmed that most mammals have a hierarchical social structure, and males who are dominant—that is, have high social status—have greater access to females and reproduce more (see Clutton-Brock, 1988). Similarly, in humans, males who achieve success in the form of resources, power, and respect are also more likely than their counterparts to be successful at reproduction (Fieder et al., 2005). Therefore, to increase one's chances of obtaining a sexual partner and passing on one's genetic material to successive generations, a main technique is to strive to increase status.

Status driving often requires the necessary genetic makeup for being physically dominant and aggressive. Often, acquiring status entails engaging physically with other males and using manipulation and deception. In humans, this includes involvement in antisocial and delinquent activities ranging from fraud to assault and homicide. In some situations and in certain circumstances, it may "pay off" to increase one's status through deviant means if it can increase one's chance of attracting and keeping mates. In inner-city neighborhoods where resources are stretched, it may pay off to display toughness through joining gangs and engaging in violence—especially in the face of any affront (see Palmer & Tilley, 1995). This type of violence is not likely to be advantageous (or attractive) in middle-class neighborhoods, where it might damage job opportunities. This is an example of social context driving certain evolutionary processes.

Evolutionary perspectives are also capable of explaining cultural differences across time and place. The field of cultural evolution submits that just as human beings have been shaped by evolution, cultures (or groups of people) have been shaped by the same Darwinian processes of competition and adaptation (Mesoudi, 2011). Different geographic locations present different selection pressures that must be overcome for people to survive and thrive. The conditions that people in the Arctic must meet are going to be much different than in sub-Saharan Africa, and both are much different than the mountains of Mongolia. It is no wonder that the diversity of conditions that people must overcome leads to different attitudes, values, and goals (that is—different cultures) across the globe.

From an evolutionary standpoint, the propagation of one's genes is often thought to be a driving (if unconscious) force for human behavior. The ways males and females ensure their genes are passed down successfully differ. For males, a "gnarly dilemma" presents itself (Durrant & Ward, 2015, p. 143). Should they settle down with a female and help protect and raise their young to ensure their children live long enough to reproduce themselves? This seems like a good strategy until one considers that males (in our evolutionary pasts) could not be sure the offspring were theirs. Another strategy would be to have as many sexual mates as possible to increase the odds of genetic reproduction. These two sexual strategies are referred to as r/K selection. In the r strategy, males attempt to "spread their seed" to give themselves the best shot at reproductive success. The K strategy is the opposite and involves pouring time, energy, and resources into a smaller number of offspring. Ellis (1988, p. 699) argued that criminal behaviors "are manifestations of r-selection." Preoccupation with reproductive success may also help evolutionary psychologists explain patterns of homicide and why people are more likely to be killed by a nonfamily member (Daly & Wilson, 1988) and within certain neighborhoods (Wilson & Daly, 1997). Daly and Wilson (1988, p. 71) argue that "sex-differential violence against same-sex antagonists appears to be one of many manifestations of the fact that the human male psyche has evolved to be more risk-accepting in competitive situations than the female psyche."

A micro-level evolutionary concept, called conditional adaptation theory, has been put forth by Jay Belsky. Conditional adaptation theory argues that even in certain neighborhoods, resource inequality can lead to adaptive responses of citizens. In hostile environments where resources are scarce and disorganization is rampant, antisocial behavior is an adaptive strategy one can employ to obtain or secure limited resources, including access to sexual partners. In neighborhoods marked by single-family households, poverty, and disadvantage, girls reach puberty more quickly than their peers in more resource-rich areas (Belsky, 1980; Steinberg, 2014). Early sexual behavior and teenage pregnancy are common in disadvantaged areas, which is a logical choice if one is not expecting to live a long and healthy life but instead is expecting to be incarcerated or killed at a young age. And the prospects for becoming a victim of violence or a ward of the state are likely if resources are gained through illegal means (e.g., drug selling, theft, robbery) and status is gained and maintained through violence and threat of violence.

We have spent some time now discussing why men are more likely than females to engage in aggressive and antisocial behavior from an evolutionary standpoint. To turn this around a bit, it is also necessary to discuss why females are less likely than males to engage in aggressive and antisocial behavior. Perhaps the most comprehensive account of the tendency for females to not engage in crime is the "staying alive" hypothesis from psychologist Anne Campbell. Since women are saddled with the responsibility of carrying a child during pregnancy, caring for the infant in the postnatal period, and taking the primary role in the toddler's development, there is much more at risk if a mother dies during child development (sorry, guys). Therefore, evolution has led females to be risk averse and less aggressive. Females are more likely than males to avoid dangerous situations and rarely pursue status and dominance through violence or threats of violence. When females do commit crime, it is more likely to be in reaction to a threat against their families (e.g., killing an abusive husband) or to secure resources for their family (e.g., shoplifting clothes or food). These behaviors are antisocial but are not as risky or dangerous as the violence often committed by males (Campbell, 1999).

Hormones and Neurotransmitters

So, females and males were sculpted a bit differently through evolutionary processes. Once again, we note that this does not mean either sex is more evolved, better, or superior to the other—just, plainly, different. What exactly is different? While much of our biology is similar, there are documented and replicated differences between males and females regarding physiology and brain structure and function. In this section, we review these differences and link them to behavior.

One of the major differences between males and females is the level of various hormones circulating in the body. Hormones are chemical messengers present in the body that are important drivers of behavior. They are released by the endocrine system, which includes the pituitary gland, thyroid gland, and sex organs (in other words, mainly the brain and sex organs). Emerging evidence suggests that the gut (stomach and intestines) is also a key source of hormone production. Some of the major hormones that differ between the sexes and are relevant to behavior are cortisol and testosterone, among others.

Picture a muscular and athletic man who is aggressive and active and who everyone says is "full of testosterone." This is a drastic example of a male who may have a high level of testosterone in his body (but perhaps not—there are several reasons someone may be a good athlete). Testosterone is largely a male hormone, or androgen, and it is produced mainly in the testes; however, females do have low amounts of testosterone, which is produced by the ovaries. Testosterone has been linked to impulsivity (Bjork et al., 2001), poor decision-making (Carney & Mason, 2010), sensation seeking (Campbell et al., 2010), reduced empathy (Hermans, Putman, & van Honk, 2006), and aggressive behavior (Book, Starzyk, & Quinsey, 2001) in both men and women. Due to the fact that men have many times the amount of testosterone, on average, than women, it is little wonder that men have elevated levels of poor behavior in a variety of domains. Emory anthropologist Melvin Konner goes as far as likening "maleness" to a syndrome—one marked by "androgen poisoning" leading to an array of maladies, such as high mortality, hairlessness, attention deficit disorder, conduct disorder, hypersexuality, and aggression (Konner, 2015). While somewhat tongue in cheek, perhaps Konner has a point.

Criminologist Lee Ellis has proposed a theory to link hormones to antisocial behavior that he calls evolutionary neuroandrogenic (ENA) theory. ENA theory states that evolutionary processes have driven male sex hormones (androgens) to alter brain functioning in a way that increases the likelihood of antisocial behavior. ENA predicts that this is especially true for violent behavior. Ellis, along with Shyamal Das and Hasan Buker, tested key theoretical insights from ENA in 2008. If ENA is accurate, high androgen exposure should be more likely in males than in females, and intrasex differences in criminality (within males themselves) should positively covary with characteristics common of high androgen exposure, such as a deep voice, physical strength, and body hair. Indeed, the study's authors found that criminality is higher in males than females and that, within the sexes, criminality is positively correlated with masculine characteristics. Importantly, the authors also found that accounting for androgen exposure completely accounted for sex differences in violent behavior but not nonviolent antisocial behavior (Ellis, Das, & Buker, 2008).

Another hormone that is critical in studies of behavioral differences between the sexes is cortisol. Cortisol is a steroid released by the adrenal gland in response to stress. Cortisol is the end product of a complex process carried out by the hypothalamus-pituitary-adrenal (HPA) axis. The HPA axis connects the central nervous system to the hormonal system (which is why cortisol is also considered a "neurohormone"). When a person experiences stress, the hypothalamus secretes corticotropin-releasing hormone (CRH), which then activates the pituitary gland to release adrenocorticotropic hormone (ACTH). Finally, the ACTH facilitates the release of glucocorticoids—predominately cortisol (Kudielka & Kirschbaum, 2005). A properly functioning HPA axis is integral to an appropriate stress response.

Several studies indicate that HPA axis activation is different between males and females. Interestingly, ACTH responses tend to be elevated in men compared to women (Kirschbaum et al., 1999), and some of these differences exist from birth (Davis & Emory, 1995). However, androgens tend to dampen HPA activation, meaning that the HPA is activated quicker and stronger in females, suppressing a "fight" response, while testosterone usurps the HPA to some extent, increasing a "fight" response, in males (Goel et al., 2014). The interaction between the gonadal (e.g., the reproductive components such as testes and ovaries) and adrenal systems suggests that behavior is likely influenced by a convoluted web of interplay between endocrine systems in the body.

Aside from hormones like testosterone and cortisol, neurotransmitters have also been found to exist to a greater or lesser extent between the sexes, and they can account for some of the observable behavior differences. Neurotransmitters are chemical messengers in the brain that allow for communication between neurons. Neurons do not touch, so neurotransmitters are released from one neuron and received by another. Two major neurotransmitters implicated in antisocial behavior are dopamine and serotonin.

Dopamine is an excitatory hormone which acts as a "gas pedal" for behavior. Dopamine leads to risk-taking and thrill-seeking behavior. This is good most of the time, as it motivates humans to eat, work, and have sex. But too much dopamine can lead to problems, including aggressive behavior.

Studies on sex differences in neurotransmission have considered the release of dopamine following a particular stimulus. One study observed that males had a substantially greater release of dopamine compared to women following amphetamine ingestion and also rated the feeling as more positive than females (Munro et al., 2006). Similarly, drinking alcohol induced dopamine in both women and men, but the magnitude of the effect was much greater in males (Urban et al., 2010). Dopamine release appears to be greater in men (and enjoyed more by men) than women, lending support to the idea that dopamine may lead men to be thrill seekers more than women.

Serotonin is an inhibitory neurotransmitter that puts the brakes on behavior. It is almost like the counterpart to dopamine. Serotonin is derived from tryptophan and is associated with feelings of happiness. Release of serotonin is also related to a reduction in anxiety, depression, and aggression. Men and women have different levels of serotonin, accounting for some differences in behavior (Gorman, 2006).

In a recent study, women were found to have lower 5-HTT densities (a density of protein networks that transport serotonin) than men, indicating differences in serotonin transmission between the sexes, and the study concluded that these differences may increase understanding of higher rates of depression and anxiety in women and more externalized aggression in males (Jovanovic et al., 2008). In another study, individuals who had a variant of the serotonin transporter gene, 5-HTTLPR, were found to be at greater risk for psychopathic traits than those without the specific variant.[2] This ef-

---

2. Variants of genes are often referred to as "polymorphisms" or "alleles."

fect was only found in males; females scored higher on psychopathy when the short allele was present (Herman et al., 2011). Biological sex differences not only exist, but biology might differentially influence behavior in males and females.

It is also worth noting that females go through specific biological changes during and after pregnancy that reduce the likelihood they will engage in dangerous activity that might diminish their well-being in critical developmental periods of their children. Prolactin, a hormone produced during breastfeeding, reduces the chances of a quick subsequent pregnancy, simultaneously reducing sexual activity. Oxytocin (a neurotransmitter) levels spike after pregnancy, facilitating a calming bond between the mother and her child (Campbell, 2008). In fact, there is evidence that married men and men with children have reduced testosterone levels, facilitating parenting and reducing competitive behavior (Gray et al., 2002). Once again, these findings illustrate the interplay among various biological systems that have an impact on aggressive and antisocial behavior.

Neurology—Brain Structure and Function

Evolution has also shaped the structure and function of the brain. This, in turn, has had an impact on physiology. Brain structure refers to the size of parts of the brain and the density of gray and white matter. Function refers to the processes carried out by the brain and the activation of different parts of the brain when responding to a stimulus. A substantial literature shows that there are significant sex differences in the size of various parts of the brain and in the primary functions the brain carries out that impact behavior.

The human brain consists of two sides that we generally refer to as the right and left hemispheres. The hemispheres are separated by the medial longitudinal fissure and connected by the corpus callosum. Some functions and processes tend to occur in one hemisphere over the other. This is referred to as brain lateralization. While behavior writ large is affected by activity from both sides of the brain and their interconnection via the corpus callosum, neuronal activity related to some physiological process is more dominant in one side of the brain than the other. And we now know that there are sex differences in brain lateralization (Tomasi & Volkow, 2012).

There are a few myths to dispense with before any further discussion on brain lateralization and sex. First, there is no "female side" or "male side" of the brain. The second point is related: behaviors that characterize femininity or masculinity cannot be reduced to one side of the brain. Third, readers should be aware that there are common misperceptions that someone can be "right brained" or "left brained." Often the general public and pop psychology make too much of lateralization, suggesting that the sides of the brain act almost independently and that behaviors are the result of which side of the brain is being used most (or least). This is far too simplistic (see Reber & Tranel, 2017).

Given these caveats, empirical research *does* conclude that there is brain lateralization and that there are general sex differences to be found in the brain (Ritchie et al., 2018). Females tend to have greater neuronal connectivity in the left hemisphere whereas males have greater connectivity in the right hemisphere (Tomasi & Volkow, 2012). These differences are linked to brain disorders such as schizophrenia and schizoid personality, which are directly linked to offending (Raine, 2013).

Another difference in the brain between the sexes is found in the amount of gray matter in key regions that influence behavior. Gray matter consists of "clumps" of neuronal cells that appear to be gray on brain scans. Males tend to have a smaller amount of gray matter in the orbitofrontal and middle-frontal brain regions when compared to females. Once accounting for these brain differences, Adrian Raine and his coauthors found that the gap in sex offending was decreased by 77.3 percent (Raine et al., 2011). This is not a trivial amount. While it is unlikely that brain differences are the *only* factors responsible for the gap in offending, they could be among the most substantial.

The brain also controls physical arousal, such as skin conductance and heart rate. The brain governs both the sympathetic and parasympathetic nervous systems in males and females. The sympathetic nervous system controls the fight-or-flight response while the parasympathetic nervous system controls mostly involuntary processes such as heart rate and gland activity (Barnes, 2013). These systems are affected by both genes and the environment and have a significant impact on behavior.

Resting heart rate is one of the strongest correlates of antisocial behavior. Both males and females with low resting heart rates are at risk of antisocial behavior (Portnoy & Farrington, 2015). Low resting heart rate is uncomfortable physiologically as it is related to sluggishness and underarousal. Those with low resting heart rates often engage in behaviors that raise their heart rate to normal levels to feel better. Sometimes this is extreme sports (e.g., skydiving) while at other times it may be antisocial behavior such as fighting and breaking into homes. Understimulated individuals can also more easily engage in behaviors that make others nervous and uncomfortable given their low baseline heart rates.

Across the life course, females have higher resting heart rates than males (Ostchega et al., 2011). Sex differences in heart rate appear early, even at birth, and persist across biological development into adulthood. The same can be said for antisocial behavior (see, for example, Tremblay et al., 1999). Given this correlation, it is not out of the realm of possibility for heart rate to account for a portion of the sex gap in offending. There is recent support for this position. Criminologist Olivia Choy and colleagues (2017) assessed the association between heart rate and criminality of 894 individuals at age 11 and age 23. They found that heart rate was linked to criminality for both males and females, and between 5.4 percent and 17.1 percent of the gap in offending (depending on the measure of offending) was accounted for by resting heart rate. While replication is certainly needed, the results are promising for establishing a major reason why crime is much more prevalent among males than females.

Considering Gender in Crime Prevention and Intervention

One of the most common misperceptions of biopsychosocial criminology, from our point of view, is that evolutionary and biological perspectives are not useful in directing policies and programs intended to reduce or intervene in crime (or may, in fact, be dangerous). This is very unfortunate, as it cannot be further from the truth. In fact, any approach that does not take seriously the nature of human beings and their evolved behavior is doomed to failure (see also Vaughn, 2016). Also, many scholars and the general public alike fall for the naturalistic fallacy—that what *is* represents how things ought to be. In other words, because aggression and violence are found in nature, they are inherently good and ought to exist in society. This is a fallacy. Whether or not something occurs naturally has no bearing on whether or not it should exist or be promoted by people. That differences may exist in nature does not justify treating people differently. Moral and ethical principles must dictate those activities (Pinker, 2002).

We think there are some moral implications for *not* using important information about people to make good decisions about treatment. If we can use nonintrusive methods to obtain biological information, which can then be stored safely and securely to increase the potential to improve health and wellness, is there not an obligation for us to do so? This is an important question, particularly as research is beginning to uncover how treatment might be effective for some people and not others depending on their biological makeup.

Heart rate might not only help establish a potent cause of crime and account for a good portion of the sex gap in offending, but it also can inform crime prevention programs. One recent study concluded that physiological arousal predicted the responsiveness of participants to an intervention for conduct problems. Participants who had low parasympathetic functioning were higher in conduct disorder preintervention and benefited more than those with high parasympathetic functioning. Additionally, those with low functioning were more receptive to an individualized intervention strategy than a group intervention strategy (Glenn et al., 2018a). This suggests that biological information can inform social crime prevention programing, and it may be beneficial to look at how physiological functioning plays a role in receptiveness to programming by sex.

Importantly, crime prevention and offender rehabilitation programs should not rely on solely social or biological factors since both are implicated in criminal behavior. In one study, researchers sought to examine neuropsychological deficits (risk factors) as a cause of early onset criminal behavior. They found that those with such deficits who lived in relatively underresourced areas were at heightened risk for an early onset of crime. Yet, interestingly, this was only found for males, not females (Tibbetts & Piquero, 1999). The ways biological and social/environmental factors operate differently for males and females is important information to guide policy.

In addition, if there are certain biological "deficits" that apply to males, increasing their odds of offending, those risk factors should be targeted by policy. For example, as noted, males differ from females in terms of empathy. Social programs may take advantage of this information and help improve empathy for males as a way to reduce offending. Research in business and medicine has examined the ability of certain programs to improve empathy, finding some efficacy (Lee et al., 2018; Young, Haffejee, & Corsun, 2017). One area in which biological and social information could be put to good use is in treatment programs for domestic violence, which have not shown strong results (Babcock, Green, & Robie, 2004; Day et al., 2009).

One criticism of biopsychosocial criminology is that it may imply that certain crime is "natural" and therefore there is nothing we can do about it. That sort of critique may be levied at evolutionary explanations, which suggest that due to factors long in our species' past, males are more likely to behave in antisocial ways. Yet this simply suggests that being male may be one (of many) risk factors for crime. Crime prevention programs are designed in two ways: to apply to entire populations ("universal programs") or only select groups ("targeted programs") (Sherman, 1997). Targeted programs often seek to recruit at-risk families, where being at risk is defined as single motherhood and poverty. Considering sex to be a risk factor seems no more inappropriate, in our view. Sex, along with social disadvantage, may provide a clearer picture of "risk" than social factors alone.

Fitting the Facts and Missing Puzzle Pieces

We know a lot about sex differences in antisocial behavior. First, we know that as a society, we "construct" what we define as crime. We call forcefully stealing from someone else robbery and taking another person's life without cause murder. Males are more likely to commit these crimes. Women are more likely to engage in prostitution—what we have defined as getting paid to have sex with someone who is not also getting paid. If we redefined these laws or decriminalized these activities, we would see changes in sex differences in crime.

However, that appears to be somewhat arbitrary, as all forms of aggressive and antisocial behavior (whether defined as criminal or not) are more likely to be committed by males—even in societies and species that do not have any formal definitions of crime. Along with Braithwaite, we believe this must be explained. Further, while social conditions such as masculinity and patriarchy and social con-trol are likely to play a part in criminal behavior, together they are inadequate to account for much variation in behavior. Most societies and animals with hierarchical social structures have a system that re-sembles patriarchy and masculinity, and this is pervasive across time, place, and species. Why, then, is there so much variation between and within groups and individuals? We submit this can be accomplished through integration between biological and sociological perspectives.

Needless to say, there is a lot we still do not know. For example, read-ers will notice that, for the most part, social and biological explana-tions of male and female criminality are separate. That is, there are few integrated, truly "biopsychosocial" theoretical accounts of crime. Males and females are differentially socialized (Gottfredson & Hirschi, 1990) in ways that likely influence differences in behavior. Males dif-fer from females biologically in ways that bear on crime. Yet *most* males are not criminal, even if they carry the hormonal differences that may set them at risk for violence. Why? It is likely that biopsychosocial ex-planations can help fill the gaps in both social and biological work. One example concerns the role of hormones, particularly testoster-one, on violence. While, as noted, research has found a link between testosterone and crime, the direction of this effect is not well under-stood (Duke, Balzer, & Steinbeck 2014). Further, some research has found that testosterone influences crime for females, as well (Dabbs & Hargrove, 1997).

What is needed is a true biopsychosocial integration to account for the sex differences in criminal behavior. How does a biological difference in brain function operate in concert with differential so-cialization practices to increase the odds of offending? Clearly, biolog-ical factors on their own are not sufficient to explain male offending since most males are not criminals. What is needed is an account that explores both the social and the biological *together*.

Strain theory may be a useful framework to understand how bio-logical forces combined with environmental triggers may push males and females into different types of behaviors. As noted prior, in Broi-dy and Agnew's (1997) theoretical overview, they argued that males and females experience similar levels of stress, yet males often react with anger and outward aggression while females react with other emotions (such as depression) and often with inner-directed behaviors (e.g., self-cutting) (see Posick, Farrell, & Swatt, 2013). Biological factors as moderators of the strain-crime relationship will go far in helping us better understand the gender gap in offending.

Along with sex differences in offending, one of the other stable and powerful predictors of crime is age. Violent crime begins in the early teen years, increases to its peak in the late teen years, and then decreases precipitously in early adulthood. There are social reasons that explain this age-crime curve, but they do an incomplete job. By combining insight on biological maturation and social development during different life stages, researchers can better understand the age-crime curve and can develop strategies for early prevention and intervention during critical crime periods. This is the focus of the next chapter.

3

Age Differences in Criminal Behavior

In the summer of 2003, Evan Miller and his friend Colby Smith bought drugs from an acquaintance named Cole Cannon. Miller and Smith had gone over to Cannon's trailer to buy the drugs and hang out. At one point when the three were together, Cannon fell asleep. Miller thought this would be a good time to steal Cannon's wallet and make a run for it. However, after his wallet was stollen, Cannon woke up and grabbed a bat to confront the thief. Miller ended up taking the bat from Cannon and brutally beating him unconscious. Miller and Smith then fled the scene.

Miller and Smith, fearing evidence would be discovered implicating them in the crime, returned to Cannon's trailer and found him still alive. Miller set the trailer on fire to destroy the evidence of the crime. Cannon, still injured and in the trailer, died of smoke inhalation. The two perpetrators were caught and prosecuted. Smith received life with parole. Miller received life without parole. He was 14 years old.

In *Miller v. Alabama* (567 U.S. 460, 132 S. Ct. 2455 [2012]), a jury found Miller guilty of murder, and the judge sentenced him to life without the opportunity for parole. In essence, this would mean Miller would be incarcerated for his entire life. His lawyers filed a petition to the Supreme Court arguing that a mandatory life sentence for a juvenile was cruel and unusual punishment. The Supreme Court decided to hear the defense out.

Along with a companion case (in which 14-year-old Kuntrell Jackson; the shooter, Derrick Shields; and Travis Booker robbed and shot a store clerk in Arkansas), Miller's case was under review from the nine U.S. Supreme Court justices. Jackson, like Miller, had received life without parole. In a 5–4 decision, the court determined that life without parole *is* unconstitutional for minors, reversing the Alabama and Arkansas court decisions. This was a case where justice fundamentally disagreed on the interpretation and application of the law. This case also illustrates how science can be brought into the courtroom to inform justices of the theoretical reasons why people commit crime—and why they do so differently across ages.

One piece of evidence brought to trial by the petitioner (Miller and his lawyers) was related to research in neuroscience. The reason that sentencing juveniles to life without parole is unjust is that juveniles are unable to adequately establish the mindset to appreciate the consequences of their decisions. The prefrontal cortex, the decision-making part of the brain, is not fully developed until the mid-20s. A 14-year-old's prefrontal cortex is quite underdeveloped at the same time that other changes are taking place in the body, including the increase of sensation-seeking hormones like dopamine. An underdeveloped prefrontal cortex, coupled with increases in excitatory hormones, is a pot ready to boil over in aggression (see Steinberg, 2005).

This story exemplifies a common rule (what some have referred to as the "brute fact" of crime) in criminological research—criminal behavior increases in the early teen years, reaches a peak in the late teen years, and then decreases into the early 20s (Hirschi & Gottfredson, 1983). By the late 20s and early 30s, almost everyone has stopped their offending behavior. Figure 3.1 uses data from the Uniform Crime Report Program on arrests in the United States in 2018 to illustrate this curve. As can be seen, the data are in age groups, with a peak in the early 20s.

Age is so strongly associated with criminal behavior that Braithwaite included this fact second only to sex/gender differences in crime. His second fact states that "crime is perpetrated disproportionately by 15–25 year olds" (Braithwaite, 1989, p. 45). Like sex differences in the commission of crime, this age-crime relationship is invariant across

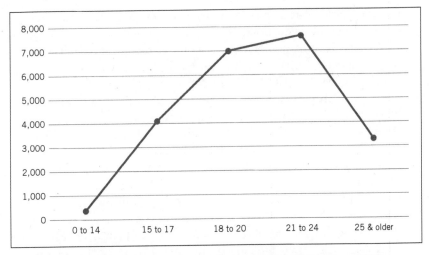

Figure 3.1. Arrest Rate in the United States per 100,000 by Age, 2018 (*Source*: U.S. Department of Justice, Office of Juvenile Justice and Delinquency Prevention Statistical Briefing Book, "Estimated Number of Arrests by Offense and Age Group, 2019," https://www.ojjdp.gov/ojstatbb/crime/ucr.asp?table_in=1.)

cultures and historical time periods. However, Braithwaite does acknowledge that opportunity plays a role here. White-collar crime is committed later in life, given that 15-to-25-year-olds have little access to the types of occupations and situations that enable this category of crime. Still, for the majority of property and violent crime, the age-crime curve holds up, and biopsychosocial theories can explain this curve as well as other crimes, like white-collar crime, that may fall outside this "fact."

This noted age-crime curve is a fact found in nearly all cultures across history. Because this finding has been established for so long, there has been a great deal of research on the causes of this phenomenon, including both biological and sociological perspectives. Yet there is still room to develop and expand explanations of age and crime using a biopsychosocial model. This is the focus of this chapter. We begin with traditional, mostly sociological, approaches to understand the age-crime curve before moving into biopsychosocial perspectives that include the role of puberty, changes in hormone and neurotransmission, and brain development before moving into how this information can direct tailored crime prevention and intervention strategies. Finally, we discuss remaining questions, such as the impact of recent period and cohort effects that might change the way we understand the role of age as a cause of crime.

Traditional Theoretical Approaches

Age has long been known as one of the most impactful variables in the commission of violence. In 1831, French astronomer and mathematician Adolphe Quetelet wrote extensively on the relationship between age and crime. Using the rudimentary crime statistics of the time, he noted that children are rarely involved in criminal activity. Neither were the elderly. In fact, crime started to increase around the age of puberty and declined precipitously around age 25. This led Quetelet ([1831] 1984, p. 55) to state, "It is, in fact, with age that man's physical strength and passions develop and that their energy afterwards diminishes. . . . This propensity must be practically nil at both extremes of life." With this work, research on the age-crime curve had begun.

Using statistics at the turn of the twentieth century, American psychologist G. Stanley Hall noted the same trends that Quetelet wrote about over half a century earlier. In his 1904 book, *Adolescence*, he concluded, "In all civilized lands, criminal statistics show two sad and significant facts: First that there is a marked increase in crime at the age of twelve to fourteen, not in crimes of one, but of all kinds, and that this increase continues for a number of years" (Hall, 1904, p. 325). Clearly, evidence was building for an age-crime relationship from the 1800s (at least) into the 1900s. It was not until the mid-1900s that criminologists latched on to the finding of earlier mathematicians and psychologists and sought to explain this relationship within a criminological context.

One particularly noteworthy work recognizing the age-crime curve was David Matza's *Delinquency and Drift*, written in 1964. Matza took existing theories to task for overpredicting crime. He argued that most theories—such as strain, control, and learning—predict that youth continually accrue criminal risk factors and then, just at the point they should be at their most deviant, begin to reform! He called this an "embarrassment of riches" (Matza, 1964, p. 21). He argued that delinquents are not really committed to antisocial behavior but rather drift in and out; thus, when they mature, they are able to simply walk away from it.

For criminologists, it was the 1983 article written by Travis Hirschi and Michael Gottfredson that finally directed proper attention to the age-crime curve within the field. The authors noted that the age-crime curve was invariant across time and place and that the relationship was a "brute fact of criminology" (Hirschi & Gottfredson, 1983, p. 552). They argued that because the age-crime curve was the same for different groups and different crimes, it had to be driven by something other than the sociological. They were not clear what this was, but they felt that sociological "variables" could not explain the age-crime curve. Many took this to mean that biology—or aging itself—is responsible for the decline in crime in adulthood. Gottfredson and Hirschi seemed to take just such a "burnout" stance in later publications, suggesting that the decline in crime with age is akin to a baseball player not having the same level of output at later ages as he did when he was younger (Gottfredson & Hirschi, 1986).

Not many dispute the age-and-crime "fact"—which is also why Braithwaite (1989) includes it among his "facts of crime"—but some have criticized Hirschi and Gottfredson's view that the relationship between age and crime cannot be explained by sociological variables, that they are invariant, and that they are a waste of resources to study (since they are always the same). In fact, the debate around the meaning of the age-and-crime relationship was so heated that it began what is now known as the "great debate" in criminology (see Posick & Rocque, 2018).

While Hirschi and Gottfredson occupied one side of the age-crime debate, on the other side stood researchers such as Alfred Blumstein, Jacqueline Cohen, and David Farrington. They conceded that the age-crime curve exists—in the aggregate and over time—yet contended that there are social factors that can explain why certain people, and certain groups of people, might vary a bit from the average trend (Farrington, 1986). Of interest, these researchers note, is whether the decrease in crime after the age of about 25 is due to the *same people* reducing their offending or whether *many different people* are just dropping out of offending. This point cannot be overemphasized. Most age-crime curves are "aggregate" and cross-sectional. In other words, as shown in Figure 3.1, they take a snapshot at one point in time and plot the rate or percentage of crimes across age ranges. Showing that the line moves downward after about age 20 or so *could* mean that people slow down and stop offending with age. Or it could mean that there are simply *fewer* offenders at older ages. Those who are still active continue to offend at similar rates as they did in earlier ages. So, do offenders just drop out of the criminal ranks at later ages, or do they slow down and slowly get themselves out of the life? That is an important question for understanding age and crime. Later in this chapter, we address whether this question has been answered.

Further, certain crimes do not follow the age-crime curve. In 1989, Darrell Steffensmeier and colleagues showed that offenders involved in crimes such as gambling, drunk driving, and domestic violence were much older than those engaged in other types of offenses. There is something about these crimes that require certain events to take place (e.g., get married, reach the age of driving or gambling), and these events must be explained by theoretical orientations related to the age-and-crime relationship (Steffensmeier et al., 1989). Given advances in both theory and statistical analysis, more nuanced approaches to examining the age-crime curve are molding our understanding of the relationship (see Nagin & Land, 1993).

The leading theoretical explanation for why crime increases from the teen years into the early 20s and then declines thereafter was offered by two sociological criminologists, Robert Sampson and John Laub. In their highly influential book *Crime in the Making: Pathways and Turning Points through Life*, they present their age-graded theory of informal social control. For Sampson and Laub, the reason children do not commit much deviance is that they are bonded to prosocial people in their lives, including parents, teachers, coaches, and the like. When individuals reach their teen years, the need to become autonomous, create a new self-identity, and establish peer (over familial) relationships becomes strong. Bonds are reduced with prosocial forces and created with those that exert less social control on the individual (Sampson & Laub, 1993).

The age-graded theory of informal social control continues to explain why crime declines as well. As individuals age and move into their early 20s, new informal social control mechanisms enter a person's life. Most significantly, perhaps, is marriage and children. Once again, the family unit comes together and exerts control on one another, and peers begin to lose their importance in an individual's life. Other commitments, such as military service and a career, will do the same. Individuals are unlikely to jeopardize their loved ones or their prospects for a good future by committing crime. Of course, not everyone is presented with these opportunities—what Giordano and colleagues refer to as "hooks for change" (Giordano, Cernkovich, &, Rudolph, 2002). Further, even if these hooks are present, people still need to take hold of them. The many hooks for change and the reasons people take hold of those hooks are still not fully understood, revealing pathways for integrative criminological theory and research.

Other sociological work has suggested that leaving crime is part of the transition to adulthood. Uggen and Massoglia (2003) reviewed recent literature on traditional transitions to adulthood, such as graduating, getting a job, leaving parents' homes, and getting married. These life events seem to align with when crime is left behind, and so maybe desistance is simply part of "growing up."

The work of criminologists over the past half century has elucidated the age-crime curve and highlighted the explanations for overall consistency in the curve as well as contingencies that vary from the average function and form. Yet much remains unknown. The biopsychosocial approach aids in understanding the link between age and behavior because it acknowledges both social and biological changes that occur during child development, transition into adulthood, and the regular aging of the individual. This is a comprehensive view in which age represents both a social construct marking key environmental transitions and the biological changes that occur over the life course.

Biopsychosocial Contributions

Before we review specific biosocial factors related to age and crime, we point out here that there is a relatively early example of a theoretical statement taking psychological, physiological, and social factors into account. Walter Gove (1985) argued that sociological theories were not up to the task of explaining why crime peaks in adolescence. Interestingly, Gove did think that social factors mattered; for example, the social expectations that arise with age create stress and anomie;

there is a lack of tethering to society that is present at other ages. From a psychological perspective, Gove reviewed research showing that things like concern for others and self-concept changed with age in ways that should predict less antisocial behavior in adulthood. In terms of biological variables, he discussed decreasing drive from things such as a decrease in testosterone and a slowing of physical strength. Importantly, Gove argued that all these factors interacted to explain the age-crime relationship. Since the time of Gove's piece, much has been learned about how the body changes in ways that should influence behavior.

Hormone and Neurotransmitter Changes during Puberty that Affect Behavior

There is little doubt that during puberty, a person's biology and social environment are changing. As most individuals reading this book have very likely gone through this tumultuous time in their lives, it is probably easy to think back on this critical period and remember all the physical, mental, and social changes and how those changes led to some new, perhaps deviant, behaviors. To begin, one of the more well-known—and well-studied—changes will be discussed: the hormonal changes during puberty.

To say that adolescents are "hormonal" is a bit crude but not entirely incorrect. At the onset of puberty, around ages 9–10 for females and 10–12 for males (Euling et al., 2008), sex hormones increase for both males and females. For males, increases in gonadal testosterone are the most noticeable hormonal change during puberty; for females, estradiol, produced by the ovaries, increases during puberty. Both males and females have testosterone and estradiol hormones, but, on average, greater levels of testosterone are found in males while females have higher levels of estradiol (Peper & Dahl, 2013). Certainly, males and females vary within each sex in their hormone levels. Some males have more testosterone or estradiol than their counterparts, and the same goes for females. Some of the reasons that males commit more crime than females were discussed in Chapter 2, but similar reasons exist for why males, especially during adolescence, commit more crime than females—even during adolescence, when antisocial behavior increases for both males and females.

Testosterone is functional for both males and females but has a specific importance in males. Evolutionarily, males are responsible for hunting, foraging, and protecting family. To assist in these activities, increases in testosterone promote sensation-seeking behavior. The surges in testosterone during puberty activate the ventral striatum especially in males after they seek rewards (Op de Macks et al., 2011). As testosterone rises, so does seeking out rewards and opportunities for success. Adolescent males with more gonadal testosterone engage in more reward-seeking behavior than others with lower levels of testosterone (Harden et al., 2018). While not all adolescent males focus their award-seeking behavior on criminal activities, aggressive and antisocial behaviors are often ways to obtain rewards quickly and easily, and the association between testosterone and criminal activity is well established (Bernhardt, 1997). However, recent research suggests that testosterone, on its own, is only weakly associated with aggression (Book, Starzyk, & Quinsey, 2001; Pratt, Turanovic, & Cullen, 2016).

An interesting divergence happens with females at the time of puberty. While testosterone is spiking in males, estradiol is spiking in females. Estradiol is associated with *lower* reward-seeking behavior (Harden et al., 2018). Hormones that reduce sensation-seeking behavior—which is often risky—is in line with the "staying alive" hypothesis (Campbell, 1999). As females enter puberty and are at their most viable for reproduction, their drive for risky behavior that would place them—and their potential children—in harm's way is stifled by inhibitory hormones. However, this reduction in reward-seeking behavior appears to be inconsistent with the fact that female antisocial behavior also increases during adolescence (albeit less so than males). Social pushes toward antisocial behavior may partially explain this, pointing again to the complex way that biological and social forces shape behavior.

Along with hormones, neurotransmitters—chemical messengers in the brain that allow neurons to communicate with one another—are changing in the adolescent brain. Two of the most important neurotransmitters for behavior—the monoamine neurotransmitters dopamine and serotonin—are in flux during puberty. Dopamine (an excitatory neurotransmitter) is increasing during puberty. Like testosterone, dopamine increases behaviors that return rewards for sexual and social success. During puberty, boys and girls are both moving from a reliance on parents to establishing peer relationships and setting the stage for their independence. Adolescence is also a time where people are establishing their social hierarchies. It turns out that individuals who have greater dopamine binding in the striatum are more likely to have higher social status and greater social support (Martinez et al., 2010). Social environment also matters here. Josephs and colleagues find that testosterone levels impact aggression only when social status is threatened (Josephs, Mehta, & Carré, 2011; Josephs, Sellers, Newman, & Mehta, 2006). Combining knowledge about the social environment and how biological changes interact with those environments allows us to better answer the questions of why people commit crime and what to do about it.

Neurological Changes during Puberty that Affect Behavior

Along with the endocrine system, brain structure and function are changing during puberty. The hormonal and neurotransmission changes in puberty—in order to have an impact on behavior—must impact the brain. What research has continually confirmed is that the development of the limbic system (the "primitive" part of the brain that is responsible for visceral functioning) outpaces the development of the prefrontal cortex (PFC), the reasoning and regulating structure of the brain (Casey, Jones, & Somerville, 2011). When exposed to a particular pressing situation in adolescence, especially a threat, the limbic system wins. This is what the courts began to understand in the mid-2000s when rulings came down on sentencing juveniles in line with their brain development.

As the limbic system finishes developing and the PFC continues to develop, another important process is taking place in the adolescent brain. The connections of neurons so important for learning, communicating, and responding to critical situations are strengthening, and connections that are superfluous or unnecessary are being eliminated. This process, known as synaptic pruning, increases efficiency in the brain and can impact behavior.

Relatedly, white and gray matter are increasing in the brain during puberty for both boys and girls. White matter includes the myelination of neurons, which improves information processing. Gray matter is the density of cells that make up critical regions of the brain. The names for both come from the color they appear on scans of the brain. The whiter and darker gray the regions of the brain, the more white and gray matter exists in those regions. Because this matter is increasing during puberty, communication in the brain begins to improve (with increases in white matter), and the density of brain cells (gray matter) improves overall brain functioning. Girls tend to develop gray and white matter at earlier ages than boys (Giedd et al., 2006). This may be one of the reasons adolescent boys commit more delinquency than adolescent girls, as mentioned in the previous chapter. Lack of gray and white matter is linked to increases in delinquency and antisocial personalities (Raine et al., 2000; Sundram, 2012; see also Raine, 2013).

Importantly, gray matter peaks in the mid-20s while white matter continues to develop throughout life (Sowell et al., 2003). This means that the connections between neurons in the brain that process information can continue to develop regardless of age. When we learn and experience new things, our brains change. This process may be useful for criminologists because it means that exposure to maladies can disrupt this development while exposure to learning opportunities can assist in the development of white matter, leading to opportunities to intervene in problem behavior using brain-based strategies such as cognitive behavioral therapy (Vaske, Galyean, & Cullen, 2011).

Adolescence-Limited and Life-Course-Persistent Offending

In 1985, criminologist David Greenberg suggested that adolescents begin to engage in crime because the pocket money they receive from their parents becomes insufficient as they look toward their future as husbands, fathers, workers, and the like. The individual is no longer a child but also not yet an adult, creating a social status strain that leads to antisocial behavior (Greenberg, 1985). In 1993, psychologist Terrie Moffitt expanded on the work of individuals like Greenberg to propose her dual taxonomy of offending. She agreed with Greenberg that a gap between being a child but wanting to act and be treated as an adult creates an environment that promotes antisocial behavior. However, she says that this "maturity gap" is a common reason someone will start offending but then stop when they become an adult. She called these individuals adolescence-limited offenders.

For Moffitt, persistent offenders are different. She states, "Fewer than 10 percent of males should show extreme antisocial behavior that begins during early childhood and is thereafter sustained at a high level across time and circumstances" (Moffitt, 2018, p. 179). Although a small portion of the entire population, life-course-persistent offenders will begin their offending early and escalate their violence quickly. Why? Moffitt suggests, drawing on her 1993 article "that the strongest prospective predictors of persistent antisocial behavior are individual characteristics (e.g., difficult temperament, neuropsychological deficits, hyperactivity) and family characteristics (e.g., socioeconomic deprivation, poor parenting), but not age" (Moffitt, 2018, p. 185). In other words, age is only related to criminal behavior to the extent that it is related to these other factors implicated in the etiology of crime.

In 1993, Moffitt's theory was more theoretical than empirical. It was not until later that researchers began to test her ideas. Is it true that trajectories can be explained by environmental exposure and genetics? One of us explored this directly. In Barnes, Beaver, and Boutwell (2011), it was found that genetic factors could account for about 56 to 70 percent of the variance in being classified as a life-course persistent offender, 35 percent of the variance in being classified as an adolescence-limited offender, and 56 percent of the variance in being classified as an abstainer. Overall, this study provided support for the genetic underpinnings of offending trajectories (and nonoffending trajectories), a finding that was later supported with measured genomic markers (Wertz et al., 2018). Of course, in no trajectory is the classification determined purely by genetics, once again supporting a biopsychosocial approach to the study of antisocial behavior.

The strength of Moffitt's theory is that it does a good job empirically identifying these two groups of individuals and explaining why the groups exist in the first place. Most of us do commit some crimes or antisocial acts during our adolescence before quickly stopping our bad behavior. Some of us, a smaller minority, start antisocial behavior early because of psychosocial deficits and become ostracized from other people and institutions that could constrain our behavior (who wants to hang around with a wild, aggressive person except other wild and aggressive people?). These individuals remain antisocial even though they may decrease their involvement in poor behavior later in life.

A similar set of studies indicates that stable offending trajectories might even start sooner than previously thought. For example, psychologist Sylvana Coté and her collaborators show that most children display some level of physical aggression in the first few years of life. After that, some will slowly desist (about one-third) and become prosocial while the majority (over half) will moderately desist over time. About 16 percent of children showed a high stable trajectory of physical aggression that lasted up to adolescence; this group contained mostly children from low-income homes who were exposed to hostile and/or ineffective parenting strategies (Coté et al., 2006). This confirms but also adds to the work of Moffitt and others on identifying trajectories of children and adolescents across their life course.

Robert Agnew, known for his general strain theory, provided an explanation for why offending peaks in adolescence that is similar in some ways to Greenberg's and Moffitt's approaches. Agnew argued that in modern times, adolescence is a unique period. In fact, it was not until the late nineteenth century that adolescence came to be recognized as a distinct life stage. In today's world, adolescence is an interesting time characterized by more responsibility but at the same time a limit on freedom. Agnew states that this provision of *"some but not all* of the privileges and responsibilities of adults" represents the key factor "responsible for the adolescent peak in offending in modern, industrial societies" (2003, pp. 272–273). Because of this extension of some privileges and responsibilities, adolescents are less closely monitored than children, have more expectations (social, education, etc.), have more opportunity for peer socialization, experience a strong pull for all adult privileges, and do not know how to cope with stress and strain as well as adults. This leads to a toxic brew ripe for antisocial behavior.

The Integrated Maturation Theory

While criminologists have long known about the age-crime curve, explanations for why crime peaks in adolescence/early adulthood and then declines were relatively slow to take root. This is particularly true for the decline in crime observed in adulthood. It was really not until the 1980s that the "criminal career" became a focus of study for criminologists. This meant that attention was paid to all stages of the life course, including what became known as desistance from crime (the decline in adulthood).

From that point, scholars began to theorize in earnest, trying to explain why people enmeshed in a life of crime eventually seem to stop. A number of perspectives emerged, including those focused on social relationships (Sampson & Laub, 1993), cognitive factors (Giordano, Cernkovich, & Rudolph, 2002; Maruna, 2001), identity (Paternoster & Bushway, 2009), and neurocognitive development (Collins, 2004), among others. However, each new desistance theory seemed to focus on elements of development, but in isolation.

The integrated maturation theory (IMT) of desistance was developed in recognition of the need to offer a comprehensive account of development that can make sense of the nearly universal decline in crime in adulthood. To do so, one of us (Rocque, 2015, 2017) drew on existing theories of desistance along with a lost concept in criminology: maturation. Maturation had been used by criminologists in the early twentieth century to explain what can essentially be viewed as "growing out of" crime. The husband-and-wife research team Sheldon and Eleanor Glueck conducted some of the earliest longitudinal crime studies and noticed that many offenders tended to reform after a period of time. They called this maturational reform and called on future researchers to utilize information from multiple disciplines to fully explain what maturation is and how to measure it (Glueck & Glueck, 1940).

IMT is, in some ways, an answer to this call. The theory argues that maturation consists of several interrelated domains. In other words, we do not just mature physiologically, though that is certainly part of development. We also mature socially, psychologically, and cognitively. The first domain, adult social role maturation, consists of social roles and relationships, such as education, marriage, children, and employment. These are often considered markers of adulthood (Uggen & Massoglia, 2003). The second domain is called civic maturation and represents the tendency to want to give back or work for something greater than oneself in adulthood. This domain refers to volunteering, voting, and being a "good citizen." Third, psychosocial matura-

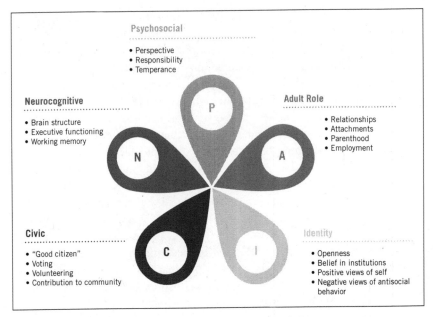

Figure 3.2. Domains of Maturation in the Integrated Maturation Theory (*Source*: Redrawn after an image created by Evan McCuish. Image used with permission.)

tion, is related to psychological development, from personality traits to factors such as self-control and future orientation. Much occurs from adolescence to adulthood in these traits, all of which make for a more mature, less antisocial individual.

Fourth is identity, or cognitive transformation identity. This domain refers to the ways in which one's view of oneself as well as one's view of particular behaviors changes throughout time. For example, people tend to begin to see criminal behavior as less favorable and also tend to see themselves more as a "good person" than when they were younger. Finally, neurocognitive maturation refers to the relatively recent work showing that brains continue to mature beyond childhood and adolescence and into adulthood. This work supports the notion that as brains mature, people are better able to control their impulses and make reasoned decisions. Figure 3.2 illustrates the domains of maturation in IMT.

Even though IMT is a newer theoretical perspective, there has been some empirical examination of the theory. Work has tended to show that certain domains (e.g., psychosocial and identity) are consistently related to desistance while also pointing out possible revisions for the theory (McCuish, Lussier, & Rocque, 2020; Rocque, Beckley, & Piquero, 2019; Rocque, Posick, & White, 2015; Stone & Rydberg, 2019). Importantly, the domains, which Rocque argued can be thought of as parts of a larger whole, do appear to be interrelated (McCuish et al., 2020). Stone and Rydberg (2019) found that parenthood does not influence offending through maturation. This may indicate that becoming a parent does not instigate maturation, which then sparks desistance from crime, or it could indicate that parenthood is a form of maturation itself that is not related to other aspects of maturation.

While IMT was designed to explain desistance, there is no reason the maturation domains cannot be adapted for childhood or adolescence. Indeed, to the extent that maturation describes life-course development at all stages, childhood behavior may also be a function of growth in particular domains. For example, social role maturation could account for relationships with teachers and parents that social control theory has long argued restrain youth from engaging in antisocial behavior.

A Critique of the Age-Crime Curve

While it is empirically true that violent crime increases and decreases in the ways described in this chapter, some have taken issue with the idea that antisocial behavior in general peaks in early adolescence and decreases through early adulthood. Psychologist Richard Tremblay, along with his team, argues that it really is early childhood where people (especially young boys) are most violent. They hit each other with abandon, steal toys from each other, and have little if any empathy for their behavior! In one study, researchers found that physical aggression is common, even normal, at one and a half years old. However, only a small percentage of children maintain or increase their aggressive physical behavior past 42 months (Trembley et al., 2004). Further, at 19 months, children are highly aggressive, and this aggression is highly heritable, suggesting a genetic link between early childhood and aggression (Dionne et al., 2003).

The number of trajectories into and out of delinquent behavior are variable depending on the study. Moffitt's "dual taxonomy" might, in fact, be multiple taxonomies. In a meta-analysis of 105 studies, Jennings and Reingle (2012) determined that the number of offending trajectories varied from two to seven, with most studies finding three or four offending trajectories. While the number of trajectories appears to be in question, so too is the explanation of these trajectories. It is likely, as the Barnes, Beaver, and Boutwell (2011) study described early highlighted, that these trajectories are the result of both social and genetic factors and that each trajectory might be differentially influenced by these factors. In other words, some trajectories may be influenced more greatly by genetic factors—particularly trajectories that are "abnormal," such as total abstinence from offending or frequent violent offending. Trajectories that follow more normative offending levels may be less genetic and more driven by social psychological factors like peer and family bonding.

Another important issue is whether the age-crime curve is a function of, well, age, or something else. Some have argued that simply calling something an "age effect" is meaningless because it simply describes a trend and we have to understand how age affects behavior (Sampson & Laub, 1992). However, efforts to explain away age's effects on crime have not been entirely successful. One of the most comprehensive efforts took place just a few years ago. Sweeten and colleagues (2013) used data from a study on serious offenders that included a wealth of variables. They were able to explain quite a bit about the age-crime relationship (69 percent), but not all. Gottfredson and Hirschi (1990), among others (e.g., Wilson & Herrnstein, 1985), argued that age has an independent effect on crime, not through other variables. It is not explainable, it just is. Whether that is the case remains to be seen.

Considering Age in Crime Prevention and Intervention

The work of Hirschi and Gottfredson was closely linked to social crime policy. One of the major implications of their work, which they discussed at length, was that by the time violent, frequent offenders were identified, they were already aging out of crime (i.e., desisting). By the time people commit enough crime to catch the attention of authorities, they are already older and on the downward trajectory of offending. Therefore, selective incapacitation—that is, identifying high frequent offenders and locking them up in prison—is counter-productive because these individuals will not commit much crime in the future (Gottfredson & Hirschi, 1986).

The work of researchers who study criminal careers and development of criminal behavior suggests something very different. Since different offenders have different trajectories, violent offenders can be identified and focused on for optimal intervention. Further, some violent offenders do not fully desist and remain a threat to public safety. Surely these individuals must be taken out of communities and supervised by the criminal justice system. Many scholars of this view do not see incarceration as the only option for dealing with frequent offenders. Community and medical interventions can go a long way in reducing offending and improving community safety.

Most scholars of age and crime recognize that the risk of reoffending decreases with age. To that end, it is not sensible to treat older offenders the same as younger offenders. What is the cost, for example, of life imprisonment for those who are beyond their peak offending years? Some scholars have shown that the imprisoned population is getting older, which is driving up the costs of incarceration overall due to greater medical care needs (The Osborne Association, 2018). One way to reduce incarceration in the United States would be to focus on low-risk, elderly offenders. Age should be a factor in determining risk of recidivism, yet it is not included in certain well-known risk-assessment tools, such as the Level of Service Inventory (LSI) and Correctional Offender Management Profiling for Alternative Sanctions (COMPAS). We recommend that age be factored into decisions regarding treatment and supervision of offenders.

Sociological intervention mechanisms hinge on social relationships, such as romantic, familial, and in the context of employment. It would be ideal for correctional programs to not only increase access to these hooks for change and desistance (e.g., liberal visitation programs, educational and vocational programs) but also encourage individuals to take advantage of those hooks (Giordano, Cernkovich, & Rudolph, 2002). For many, these hooks are unavailable or scarcely available. Some people will not grasp hooks even if they are present. This allows for multiple points of intervention.

A public health prevention/intervention approach to juvenile justice has been introduced by Michael Baglivio focusing on exposure to adverse childhood events. This model has four tiers: (1) ACE prevention; (2) ACE screening, staff training, and service referrals; (3) targeted mental health and trauma-informed intervention service provision; and (4) systems alignment. This approach acknowledges that children are often exposed to multiple forms of harm early on in life that decrease their well-being and increase their chances of offending in adolescence, leading to involvement with the juvenile justice system. By focusing first on prevention (tier 1), such as parent training, home visitation by health professionals, and prenatal/early childhood care, a person might not need intervention in the first place. However, if a child does go on to become involved in antisocial behavior, intervention personnel (e.g., teachers, police officers, and victim service providers) must be trained to identify ACEs (tier 2) and target personalized intervention for adolescents involved in problem behavior (tier 3). Finally, in the case that a youth does move on to the juvenile justice system (tier 4), it is important for multiple systems—such as foster care, victim services, and the juvenile justice system—to work together, as it is very likely that youth will spend time in several systems across their early life (Baglivio, 2020).

Fitting the Facts and Missing Puzzle Pieces

While age is among the most studied and understood correlates of crime, there are aspects of the relationship that remain unknown or little understood. First, while the age-crime curve remains fairly stable across time and place (but see Steffensmeier, Zhong, & Lu, 2017), there are contingencies dependent on certain people and for certain crimes—particularly financial and white-collar crimes (Steffensmeier et al., 1989). What is it about certain individuals' psychobiological dispositions and the time period in their life that contributes to the commission of certain types of crimes? What are mechanisms that might drive someone to commit crime later in life? Certainly, social factors such as the loss of a job, divorce, or death in the family may lead to criminal behavior in an individual who otherwise would never have committed crime. While military service may temporary halt criminal behavior, could it also be that exposure to war may lead to long-term negative health outcomes such as post-traumatic stress disorder? Other physical changes, such as head trauma (see McCormick, Connolly, & Nelson, 2020), might also lead to a change in behavior. All these factors may be age graded and contribute to behavioral outcomes.

We also do not know how legal changes related to age will impact criminal behavior for juveniles and for crime rate writ large. Laws limiting the punishment of juveniles (prohibiting life without parole and the death penalty) are still relatively new, and it will take decades to collect data to fully evaluate these policies. Preliminary evidence shows that these reductions in punishment for juveniles may be promising. Another promising development is the formation of "young adult offender programs," recognizing that even those over the age of 18 are still maturing and that placing them in prisons with more hardened criminals is not likely to be helpful. Farrington, Loeber, and Howell (2012) argued that 18 is not a magic number that delineates adulthood and that our justice system should recognize that. If the U.S. Supreme Court has taken brain maturation into account to justify treating juveniles differently than adults, then the entire body of literature should be utilized—and this body of literature suggests brain maturation continues well beyond age 18. Some states are taking this idea seriously, implementing programs designed for young adults that are more treatment oriented (Rocque, Serwick, & Plummer-Beale, 2017). The jury is out, however, on whether these approaches work.

Recent decades have also seen a drastic shift in critical periods in the life course. Biologically, the onset of puberty has changed—albeit not drastically. Social events, such as home ownership, beginning a long-standing career, getting married, and having children, have changed rather sharply. For example, in 1950, females got married at 20.3 years of age while men married at 22.8 years of age, on average. By 2020, this changed to an average of almost 28.1 years for women and 30.5 years for men (U.S. Census, 2020). For age at first child, women were an average of 21.4 in 1970 and 26.3 in 2014 (Mathews & Hamilton, 2016). How these changes correspond to criminal behavior—on both the individual level as well as on the macro level is not well understood.

Along with changes in major life transitions and turning points, certain cohort effects (e.g., influences that affect people with similar experiences, such as birth year) may also have biopsychosocial changes that influence offending. In the past 20 years, the United States has gone through 9/11 in 2001, the 2008 economic crash, and the COVID-19 pandemic that affected the world in 2020. The age someone was when these events occurred could certainly impact their health and well-being, as we already are beginning to see.

A particular impact that a traumatic event has on a certain group of people is a cohort effect. One cohort that has been of recent interest is women who were pregnant on September 11, 2001, and at or near the location of the New York attacks. Rachel Yehuda, a professor of psychiatry and neuroscience at Mount Sinai Medical Center, found that pregnant women traumatized by the events of 9/11 had reduced cortisol levels and that their children also had elevated cortisol levels compared to others. Epigenetic analysis revealed that two specific genes that regulate cortisol were altered by exposure to trauma—the FKBP5 and STAT5B genes (Yehuda et al., 2005; 2009).

In sum, age is an important consideration for both understanding antisocial behavior and reducing it. Because of the social and biological aspects of aging, it is one of the most important topics to which biosocial criminological work can be applied. Aging has societal and relational components as well as physiological ones. The role of age cohorts and how events that impact a whole generation of children and adolescents either positively or negatively must be integrated into age-related explanations of behavior. If we are to truly understand why age is so strongly related to crime and deviance, we must take seriously both the social and biological mechanisms underlying the relationship.

4

Class Differences in Criminal Behavior

Eddie Bocanegra just heard that his friend Ricardo, a fellow gang member, had been shot by a rival gang. He quickly made his way to the hospital. Ricardo lay in the bed, paralyzed by a gunshot directly to his spine. Eddie vowed revenge. He would find the shooter and return the violence. Months later, he got his wish.

Eddie was informed that the shooter who had injured his friend was down the street. He quickly drove there, armed with a gun. When he saw his friend's assailant, along with his crew, he shot twice at him and once at his group. He then made a getaway. In *Bleeding Out* by Thomas Abt (2019), Eddie recounts these events in Chicago's most violent areas—and this encounter, in particular. He initially felt redeemed. He recalled intentionally aiming for the man's spine to injure the shooter like the shooter had injured his friend. In fact, he did not injure the man—he killed him. The shooter's name was Michael, and he was 18. Eddie no longer felt redeemed; he felt devastated.

Today, Eddie Bocanegra is an outspoken leader of anti-violence strategies in Chicago, and he has experience in several community-focused programs (Upswell.org, n.d.).[1] He works tirelessly to stop the

---

1. See https://upswellarchive.org/speaker/eddie-bocanegra/.

violence he had endured early in life and enacted later in life. This cycle of violence is all too common in disadvantaged urban neighborhoods. But why? And what would make an otherwise nonviolent individual capable of wanting to hurt—and even kill—someone with a gun? It is our claim that there is not one answer. However, a better understanding of violence in disadvantaged areas among individuals in disadvantaged classes is best understood by a confluence of biological and sociological factors. The cycle of violence is a cycle of trauma and revictimization. This trauma penetrates people (often children) to the core and has drastic consequences for the rest of their lives.

Braithwaite, in his twelfth fact of crime, wrote: "For both women and men, being at the bottom of the class structure, whether measured by socio-economic status, socio-economic status of the area in which the person lives, being unemployed, being a member of an oppressed racial minority (e.g., being black in the US), increases the rates of offending for all types of crime apart from those for which opportunities are systematically less available to the poor (i.e., white-collar crime)" (Braithwaite, 1989, p. 48). This is not to suggest that only "poor people" commit crime or that crime is something that only happens in the "inner city." What it does mean is that the systematic disadvantages that are predominantly experienced by those who live in poverty, especially in larger cities and among racial minorities, are a risk factor for antisocial behavior.

An additional caveat is that biopsychosocial criminology does not suggest that people who live in disadvantaged areas are somehow biologically "different" than those who live in more affluent areas. Actually, the opposite is often true. *Anyone* would exhibit different behaviors if exposed to harsh external pressures. It is generally the case that adverse environments can shape physiological responses that are completely *normal* and even to be expected within a specific environment. This will become clearer throughout the chapter.

In this chapter, we discuss how people in disadvantaged areas are exposed to both sociological and biological factors that are important in understanding criminal behavior (Apel & Kaukinen, 2008). Because Braithwaite also included race in his twelfth fact, we touch on it briefly here, noting that there is much overlap in the factors leading to disproportionate crime in disadvantaged areas and in disadvantaged groups. These factors are extremely important to acknowledge because they highlight that street violence—which is disproportionately committed by and harms individuals in disadvantaged classes—is not the result of inherent forces but is shaped by structural issues that have wide-ranging social and biological effects.

Traditional Theoretical Approaches

To borrow another passage from Abt's (2019, p. 198) book on urban violence, he states:

> Urban violence acts as a lynchpin for urban poverty, locking the conditions of concentrated poverty into place and undermining efforts to achieve broader social and economic progress. Teachers cannot teach and schools cannot educate when surrounded by violence. Doctors and hospitals cannot treat whole neighborhoods suffering from trauma induced anxiety and depression. Businesses will not stay or hire in areas where murder is commonplace.

This passage reflects a theme of this chapter. Places that are often very small in size account for a very large portion of a community's violence. These places suffer from various social ills and are stuck in a perpetual cycle of poverty, inequality, and violence. The reasons for this cycle are myriad and include sociohistorical, psychological, and biological factors. To craft prevention and intervention mechanisms, we need a holistic perspective.

Sociological Theories

A well-known sociological perspective on violence was published in the early 1980s by Judith and Peter Blau. Their study sought to examine the reasons some cities are more or less violent than others. The authors suggested that inequality overall and inequality across race would drive violence. Interestingly, their analyses found that inequality accounted for much of the relationship between race and violence as well as between poverty and violence. Their conclusion is telling: "Thus, aggressive acts of violence seem to result not so much from lack of advantages as from being taken advantage of, not from absolute but from relative deprivation" (Blau & Blau, 1982, p. 126). Prevention efforts must not address just individual risk factors for disadvantage but also the systems that perpetuate disadvantage.

In the mid-1990s, Robert Sampson and William Julius Wilson (1995) offered an explanation for why violence concentrates in certain areas of the city. People, mostly young adolescents, who live in urban areas within large and mid-sized cities are blocked off and isolated from mainstream society. Without much knowledge beyond their neighborhoods or their small block, their ways to make a living, raise a family, and respond to violence are very limited. This restricted "toolbox" of solutions to problems—or what the authors consider a restricted "cognitive landscape"—results in only a few strategies being employed to overcome normal life barriers. These strategies are often violent, as nonviolent solutions are less available and relying on third parties (e.g., the police) is frowned upon given widespread distrust of authorities. As the authors state, crime is a choice—not a value.

In 2000, just a few years after Sampson and Wilson brought the idea of cognitive landscapes to criminology, sociologist Elijah Anderson released his now-classic book on urban violence, *Code of the Street*. Focusing on Philadelphia, Anderson explores the reasons behind the violence that appears to plague generation after generation of people in disadvantaged areas. He put the majority of the blame for violence on a street code that dictated retaliation for any slight or sign of disrespect. For Anderson, respect and violence are the currency in neighborhoods where money is in short supply. Losing respect is just like losing money because it makes it harder to survive. To make it, one must use the tool of threat and back up those threats with violence.

Disadvantaged areas are characterized by many interrelated social problems, including lack of jobs, drug use and trafficking, the stigma of race, and an overall lack of hope for the future (see Ousey, 2017). This harsh reality results in alienation from mainstream society, which tends to be conforming and prosocial. Mainstream values are replaced by a value of respect that must be won through violence. Even if a person does not adhere to the code of the street—and many do not, or not as fully as they let on—to abandon the code is a recipe for disaster. Even the "good kids" must know and present as tough in front of their peers or risk retaliation (Anderson, 2000).

Similar to Anderson, sociological criminologists Robert Sampson and William Julius Wilson remind us that hurting people is not an explicit value of people, even teens, who live in disadvantaged areas. Rather, it is a persistent choice one makes to solve problems. Because individuals who reside in inner-city environments tend to be poor and isolated, their everyday "landscape" is devoid of examples of pro-social behavior that can achieve goals. Instead, violence is a way of life—a choice of behavior passed down throughout generations.

Wilson has expanded on these ideas in his sole work. In *The Truly Disadvantaged*, Wilson states that "a person's patterns and norms of behavior tend to be shaped by those with which he or she has had the most frequent and sustained contact and interaction" (Wilson, 1987, p. 61). Wilson argues that the inner city has gone through change and dislocation—losing jobs, increasing poverty, and socially isolating its residents. In a more recent book *More Than Just Race: Being Black and Poor in the Inner City*, Wilson (2009) brings together and makes sense of complex arguments regarding social and cultural forces on the behavior of lower-income black families. In particular, he thoughtfully suggests that there is a "symbiosis" in which harsh social forces (e.g., poverty and the loss of jobs) shape cultural attitudes (e.g., street codes and attitudes toward violence) in violent areas and that these, in turn, result in harshening social conditions (mass incarceration)—and the cycle continues.

Armed with the knowledge that crime is concentrated in a small number of places, criminologists have begun to promote a "place-based criminology" (Weisburd et al., 2016). Place-based criminology emphasizes the finding that neighborhoods that are often marked by poverty also carry the burden of high violence rates. By focusing on these few neighborhoods or even street segments, crime can be reduced through prevention, social services, and suppression activities.

Place-based criminology often relies on new technology and geospatial mapping techniques. By mapping crime, researchers can see which *places* are the most criminogenic and, through use of statistical techniques like risk-terrain modeling, can identify which factors attract crime to those locations. In Minneapolis, Minnesota, it was found that 3 percent of addresses in the city produced over 50 percent of all calls to the police (Sherman, Gartin, & Buerger, 1989). In Seattle,

Washington, 5 percent of street segments produced 50 percent of all crime in the city (Weisburd et al., 2004). Studies such as these highlight that a small number of places can generate the majority of crime. This is important for understanding the causes of crime as well as pointing toward effective crime prevention and intervention strategies.

Social Class

We would be remiss if we did not briefly note here that being in a disadvantaged environment is correlated with, but not synonymous with, social class. In other words, an individual or family can be in a lower socioeconomic status but live in an advantaged area; they would not be expected to be exposed to the same degree of criminogenic factors as those in disadvantaged areas. In fact, individual-level social class has long been a subject of some controversy in criminology. Early in the field's history, there seemed to be a clear link between social class and criminal behavior, drawing mostly on official records, which may have been biased. When self-report surveys were developed as a method, criminologists began to realize that delinquency was widespread throughout the population, not just in the lower classes (Mosher, Miethe, & Phillips, 2002). This led some to argue that social class was, in fact, *not* related to crime (Tittle, Villemez, & Smith, 1978). However, by and large, scholars have found that social class is related to crime and delinquency in the theoretically expected directions (Braithwaite, 1981).

Race

While the focus of this chapter is on class and socioeconomic disadvantage, one related finding—and one that Braithwaite includes in his twelfth fact—is that race is related to criminal behavior. Particularly with respect to street crimes (to which Braithwaite was referring), oppressed racial groups tend to be overrepresented, and this is true whether data are from self-reports or official records. As an example, the FBI's Uniform Crime Reporting Program collects data on known offenders for various crimes, such as murder. In 2018, while black or African Americans represented around 14 percent of the population, this group accounted for 38.7 percent of all murders.

There are several sociological explanations for these race-based differences in crime, including inequality between races (Blau & Blau, 1982), subculture of violence theories (Wolfgang & Ferracutti, 1967), and more recent work on a theory of African American offending (Unnever & Gabbidon, 2011). This theory argues that prejudice and racism, and the strain that instills on African Americans, help explain black crime rates. It should be noted that there is a nontrivial overlap between class and race in the United States, with African Americans much more likely to experience poverty and disadvantage than whites (Sampson & Wilson, 1995).[2] For example, data indicate that white juveniles are about half as likely to be in poverty as black or Latinx youth (APA.org, 2017). Thus, any explanation of one factor (e.g., class) must necessarily grapple with the other. This also means that explanations of social class differences in antisocial behavior may be largely applicable to race-based differences.

One of the mechanisms linking the environment to the body that is overlooked in purely sociological theory is how environmental and sociological conditions are able to impact the one thing that makes us do anything—the brain. Trauma—like that experienced by Eddie Bocanegra as narrated at the beginning of this chapter—is a condition that has massive impacts on the biological individual. Exposure to indirect community violence (e.g., shootings, beatings, or robberies) and direct community violence (e.g., being mugged, beaten, or robbed) has lasting effects on the brain. These impacts increase reactive and violent behavior—not because the individuals are inherently bad people but because they have been conditioned through their exposure to the environment. This is greatly expanded upon in Chapter 7. In this chapter, we review the evolutionary perspective of living with scarce resources before addressing the role of exposure to environmental toxins in human behavior. We then discuss how many aspects of health—including sleep and diet—contribute to antisocial behavior. All these areas can help inform policy and practice on crime prevention in low-income areas.

The theories put forward by Anderson, Sampson and Wilson, and others are sociological approaches that offer what we believe is a strong foundation for a more comprehensive theory of urban violence.

---

2. See also https://www.apa.org/pi/ses/resources/publications/minorities.

The missing link in these approaches is that they fail to adequately explain the connection between structural disadvantage and violence. So, *why* is violence a replacement currency in urban neighborhoods? What is it about poor urban environments that increases the probability of offending? And how are the conditions of poor communities capable of *moving* someone toward offending? We believe this is where biopsychosocial perspectives can contribute the most to theorizing about crime and antisocial behavior.

Biopsychosocial Contributions

Resource Scarcity and Fast Life Histories

In a now-famous experiment in psychology, the "attention in delay of gratification test"—or, as it is better known, the "marshmallow test"—judges a child's ability to delay gratification by placing a marshmallow in front of them and asking them not to eat it. If they could wait and not eat the marshmallow, they would get double the prize (two marshmallows). There have been variations using pretzel sticks and animal cookies. In any case, the hypothesis was that if children could delay gratification, they would be able to exhibit self-control in many other situations, leading to better life outcomes. Indeed, those who could delay gratification did better in academics and other positive life indicators (Mischel, Shoda, & Rodriguez, 1989). It appears that kids who exhibit self-control and are not impulsive are set up for a better life.

But what is the true story here? What might account for the fact that some kids ate the marshmallow and others did not? Sure, some children are just more impulsive. But what would you do if you did not know where your next meal was coming from? Or what if you were hungry because you had not eaten much in a while? Only some of us have the luxury of delayed gratification. If you were uncertain about your future—you might go hungry, lose your job, or get killed—how much would you stake on that future, and would you plan for living long?

We can make sense of behavior when environments have plentiful or sparse resources. One effective tool is evolutionary biology. In their definition of evolutionary biology, Del Giudice, Gangestad, and Kaplan (2016, p. 88) state, "Individuals 'capture' energy from the environment—for example through foraging, hunting, or cultivating—and 'allocate' it to reproduction and survival-enhancing activities. Selection favors individuals who efficiently capture energy and effectively allocate it to enhance fitness within their ecological niche." They continue, "The best allocation strategy for individuals in stable circumstances differs from that of individuals whose future circumstances are unpredictable." When someone has many great options for the future, it makes sense to invest in that future and not jeopardize it by getting arrested, incarcerated, or injured/killed. It makes sense to invest your resources, such as time and money, in the future. If your future is uncertain or predicted to be poor, it makes more sense to invest previous resources on the here and now—who knows if you will have them again in the future . . . or if you will be around to take advantage of them.

Individuals for whom resources are in short supply, who are often described as having low socioeconomic status (low SES), are said to generally have a "fast life history." Del Giudice, Gangestad, and Kaplan (2016, p. 105) state that "people with low SES childhoods respond to mortality threats by expressing a desire for having children earlier, even at the cost of delaying one's education or career development, whereas those with high SES childhoods react with a preference shift in the opposite direction." They further conclude, "Mortality threats prompt participants with low-SES childhoods to choose riskier but more diversified options over safer and less diversified ones." A person's life situation can dictate—at least partially—his or her behavior, and that behavior is related to a long evolutionary history.

Slower life histories are common in resource-rich and affluent areas. Those with resources are able to delay their short-term desires for longer-term rewards. Where a poorer person might forgo a college degree because they need money immediately, a more affluent person will be just fine relying on family while they enroll in expensive college courses. It is not so much that the individual from the more disadvantaged class does not want to go to college, it just does not appear wise given the circumstances (it is not a tool in the cognitive landscape). The same goes for crime. Crime can give you something you need immediately (e.g., stealing a wallet) but at a potential cost. It takes much more patience and greater resources to go to school, get a job, work long hours, and *then* get money.

To be clear, humans as a species have a slow life history. Even families with very fast histories with many children do not compare to a mouse that can give birth every six weeks or so and have a litter of around six pups each time. And the mouse does not compare to many spiders that have up to 1,000 spiderlings at one time. But within species, there is variation (some spiders lay 2 eggs at a time instead of 1,000). And those variations have to do with life circumstances and context. In human contexts where resources are scarce and the future is precarious, it is more likely for a person to adopt a faster life history.

Exposure to Environmental Toxins

The unfortunate truth is that impoverished communities are not only exposed to interpersonal harms but environmental harms as well. Heavy metals and other environmental toxins disproportionately impact disadvantaged communities. Often referred to as "environmental racism," poor communities and communities of color are often neglected when it comes to protection from harmful toxins that are the by-products of urban industrial and rural agricultural production.

The most studied of these toxins is probably lead. Once found in paint and gasoline, lead has been removed from products around the globe owing to its negative impact on the body. Unfortunately, lead is still found in old homes and soil in older, dilapidated urban and rural communities. Exposure to lead reduces neurological function and reduces IQ, which have been associated with crime. Areas with higher levels of lead also have higher levels of crime even after controlling for other confounding factors (Boutwell et al., 2016). Reductions in exposure to lead may be a large contributor to the reduction in crime (both violent and property crime) seen in the late 1990s and also may account for (or mediate) the link between social structure and crime rates (Stretesky & Lynch, 2004). Boys exposed to high levels of lead are rated by their teachers and themselves as being more delinquent than those who have not had high exposure to lead (Needleman et al., 1996). This heavy metal has clearly been linked, at least on the individual level, to changes in behavior and personal health.

Lead is not the only industrial toxin linked to antisocial behavior. Similar findings are revealed for cadmium (Marlowe et al., 1985) and manganese (Bowler, Mergler, Sassine, Larribe, & Hudnell, 1999).

Mercury nitrate, which was commonly used to make hats in the eighteenth and nineteenth centuries, is commonly mentioned in fictional stories, such as in the character of the Mad Hatter in *Alice in Wonderland*. However, the problem is far from fictional. Mercury poisoning was—and is—very real and can cause serious impairment of physiological functioning (Rice et al., 2014). Heavy metals are certainly linked to a host of poor health and behavioral outcomes and must continue to be tested for harmful effects on humans, animals, and the environment.

Toxic environmental chemicals are not only an urban problem; they are a rural problem, too. The most glaring example of exposure to environmental toxins in rural areas was the use of the agricultural pesticide dichlorodiphenyltrichloroethane (DDT). DDT was used as an insecticide until it was banned in the early 1970s, partly due to the harrowing critique by Rachel Carson (1962) in her book *Silent Spring*. The book's title refers to the lack of animal (especially bird) sounds that used to be abundant in the springtime.

DDT was linked to cancer, hypertension, impaired neurological functioning, obesity, and reproductive problems (Kreiss et al., 1981). While DDT use was widespread, factories were constructed in primarily poor minority, and rural communities. The most notorious of these communities is Triana, Alabama. The Calabama Chemical Company located its facility six miles from Triana and emptied their waste into tributaries that led to Indian Creek. Residents of Triana relied on the creek for drinking water and fish. The residents of Triana, 75 percent of whom were black, were plagued by all sorts of the aforementioned health maladies. These residents were told about the contamination—which was known to cause harm to residents—three decades after those discoveries were made (Taylor, 2014).

This is not an isolated incident. Others have occurred and continue to occur, including when the Ward Transformer Company drove along remote rural roads, spraying fluids contaminated with polychlorinated biphenyl (PCB). While hundreds of industrial and agricultural chemicals have been found to be harmful to humans, around 60,000 other chemicals have not even been tested for any negative effects. The areas exposed to these chemicals have been called "sacrifice zones" given the way they are negatively affected and ignored by manufacturers and companies (Taylor, 2014).

This should be of importance to criminologists for many reasons. First, intentionally or negligently exposing communities and individuals who are predominantly poor and of minority status is almost always illegal. Violating laws and policies against pollution and disposing of harmful chemicals are criminal actions in many cases and deserve more attention by the criminal justice system and criminological researchers. Even if some practices are not criminal, they can be harmful and deviant. This is under the purview of criminologists and victimologists. Second, exposure to these chemicals can lead to increases in criminal behavior. It is clear that exposure to chemicals has several negative health and behavioral consequences of interest to criminologists. Third, along with other pertinent issues related to mass incarceration, police-community relations, and unequal treatment in the courts, environmental justice is a piece of the social justice push and should be included in larger societal justice efforts.

Healthy Living and Antisocial Behavior

Living in disadvantaged communities can be traumatic. As discussed at length, living in areas that experience heightened violence increases poor health outcomes. Two concerns—sleep and diet—are particularly biosocial in nature and impact several facets of life. Research shows that living in disadvantaged communities worsens quality of sleep (e.g., Bagley et al., 2018). One study gathered data on subjects using an activity monitor worn on the wrist. African Americans scored worse than whites on sleep quality (e.g., they had a greater incidence of waking after falling asleep), but a large percentage of the difference was attributed to disadvantaged neighborhoods (measured via a number of factors, such as welfare and poverty) (Fuller-Rowell et al., 2016). The association between racial minority status and disadvantaged environment may go a long way toward explaining racial differences in sleep quality (Johnson et al., 2019). Sleep quality, research also shows, is associated with poorer diet (in perhaps multiple ways; for example, poor sleep leads to poor diet and vice versa) (St-Onge, Mikic, & Pietrolungo, 2016). In turn, this results in worse educational outcomes, poorer mental health, and elevated antisocial behavior. Sleep may also be related to crime and delinquency via effects on self-control (Meldrum, Barnes, & Hay, 2015).

Imagine hearing about a shooting in your neighborhood or even hearing the shooting go down outside your bedroom window. How would you feel that night? Would you get a lot of sleep? Imagine that similar incidents happen several times a month. Would you be scared to go outside? Walk to school? This is the reality for many children in the United States.

This is certainly problematic for school-aged children. Children who cannot concentrate in school will often be viewed as problem cases—children who just refuse to try hard and learn. Often this is not true. Likely there are more fundamental problems, such as lack of sleep. Criminologist Patrick Sharkey discusses and contextualizes his research on this topic in his book *Uneasy Peace*. Sharkey (2018) specifically studied how exposure to violence impacts students' ability to take tests and perform well in school. He found that when a shooting occurs close to a student's home, it has appreciable negative effects on the ability of that student to focus in school. Sharkey wondered if exposure to shootings lowered general intelligence or some fairly stable aspect of a student's ability to learn, but the results showed they did not. After an amount of time passes, the student returns to his or her "normal" level of performance. It was as if, shortly after a shooting, a student's cognitive resources are directed toward coping with the stress caused by violence. But after this latency period, a person may recover.

Sharkey (2018, p. 18) explains this situation: "Local violence does not make children less intelligent. Rather, it occupies their minds. The shock of a local homicide means that everyone who drives through the neighborhood is a potential threat, that a killer might be nearby, that more violence might be coming. It means sirens at night and police tape on the walk to school. For young men of color in particular, it means walking through one's own neighborhood as a potential target and a potential suspect." And how does this impact an individual? Sharkey (2018, p. 80) eloquently explains at some length:

We receive information about the threat through our senses and transmit it to certain key areas of the brain, most notably the amygdala (an area associated with emotional processing) and the hippocampus (an area associated with learning and memory formation). Our brain then triggers a set of automatic responses to the threat, or the possibility of a threat, nearby. In response, our body exits the state of rest and regeneration and enters a state of vigilance. Stored energy is mobilized for action. The sympathetic nervous system transmits a message of vigilance from the brain throughout the body. Nerve endings release a surge of epinephrine (adrenaline) and norepinephrine (noradrenaline), giving rise to a set of physiological changes, which may include an elevated heart rate, a rise in blood pressure, sweating, quick breathing, or goosebumps arising from fear. The HPA axis (the hypothalamus, pituitary gland, and adrenal glands) release glucocorticoids, like the hormone cortisol, which act to maintain our heightened state of awareness and vigilance in the face of the continuing stressor.

While some people fully recover after an exposure (or a few exposures) to violence, some neighborhoods are particularly conducive to violence, and those who live in these areas are continually exposed to stressful and violent situations. This chronic exposure to violence has more serious and sustained impacts on the physiological system. One particular system that experiences overload is the HPA axis. Since the HPA axis is impacted by several external/environmental variables, it is discussed at several points in this book. It is relevant to the discussion here as it is very likely that living in dangerous and precarious places will activate the HPA axis and result in changes in behavior.

Linking a few concepts mentioned already, exposure to community violence might disrupt sleep by increasing the chances of a later bedtime. The closer a violent incident occurs to a child's home, the later his or her bedtime. This disrupts cortisol levels the morning after. These disruptions can have drastic negative impacts on learning and functioning over the next few days (Heissel et al., 2018). Once again, research highlights the multiple physiological impacts of exposure to crime that negatively influence behavior and health through altered physiological functioning.

One of the biggest disadvantages of living in impoverished areas is access to healthy food and establishing a healthy diet. Sometimes this is related to lack of access to nutritious food (e.g., "food deserts"). At other times, the challenge is affording the food that may be available. Interesting emerging research links nutrition to behavior. Some experimental work has shown that fish oil (recently touted for its health benefits) may be related to reduced aggression in children (Dean et al., 2014; Itomura et al., 2005). Just how this relationship works is not well understood, but speculation exists that fatty acids in fish oil are beneficial to the operation of the brain (Hamazaki & Hamazaki, 2008).

What we do know with relative confidence is that a healthy diet is important for overall healthy development. Research dating back over 50 years has indicated that malnutrition damages brain growth (Winick, 1969). Combined with the research linking fatty acids to behavior, it seems plausible that nutrition is an important part of the association between disadvantage and misbehavior. A recent line of research on the ways health and crime intersect has considered how nutrition is linked to crime. Health criminologist Dylan Jackson (2016) found that poor nutrition (e.g., not enough fruits and vegetables, too much soda or snacks) was related to delinquency, controlling for environmental and genetic factors. Similarly, some work has shown that food insecurity, defined as not having access to some types of food in the house, is related to self-control in youth. Specifically, Jackson and colleagues (2018) found that those with food insecurity scored higher on measures of low self-control and delinquency.

Considering Differences in Advantage in Crime Prevention and Intervention

When considering prevention and intervention strategies within the context of disadvantage, it is necessary to include both macro-level and micro-level efforts. Macro-level efforts include wide-scale and generalized strategies that are societal in effect. Micro-level efforts focus on specific individuals who often have few resources to access paid services. Both levels affect one another making these efforts complex.

Environmental justice is the large-scale movement to address the harms caused to the environment that disproportionately impact disadvantaged classes. Environmental justice is usually carried out through activist activities that educate the public about salient environmental issues and speaking out against exposing poor and indigenous peoples to environmental harm, deforestation, climate change, biopiracy (placing patents on the use of plants and animals and thereby restricting use), land grabbing, and water justice (Martinez-Alier et al., 2016). The environmental justice movement promotes sustainable living, prevents the destruction of natural resources, and seeks justice for those—particularly of disadvantaged classes—who have been harmed by environmental destruction.

There is also a need to do more testing on agricultural pesticides and fertilizers being used in mainly rural areas. There are hundreds of chemicals humans and other animals come into contact with that have an unknown impact on the body. To harken back to Rachel Carson, "A Who's Who of pesticides is therefore of concern to us all. If we are going to live so intimately with these chemicals eating and drinking them, taking them into the very marrow of our bones—we had better know something about their nature and their power" (Carson, 1962, p. 17).

Improving the living conditions of those in poverty can reduce antisocial behavior, which often occurs disproportionately in disadvantaged communities. Reducing exposure to environmental toxins, increasing access to healthy and nutritious foods, and providing safe communities, we argue, would be significant steps in addressing crime and delinquency in disadvantaged areas. We are particularly enthusiastic about developmental programs aimed at youth, as earlier work has questioned whether, for example, nutritional interventions for those already engaged in crime would be effective (Fishbein & Pease, 1994).

Increasing the potential for healthy living is a worthy point of intervention in disadvantaged communities. Because it is often difficult to find and afford healthy food in isolated communities, efforts must be focused on getting foods such as fruits and vegetables into low-income communities. DeWit and colleagues (2020) identified three major barriers for healthy eating in disadvantaged areas: (1) affordability, (2) accessibility, and (3) desirability. In order to overcome these barriers, they offer a multilevel strategy. First, individuals and groups must engage in advocacy to make healthy food more affordable and tax free. Coupons should also be available for neighborhood residents. Second, healthy food must be provided through mobile food markets and community gardens. Third, community events should be convened to distribute information and provide healthy goods to residents. Fourth, an office of healthy eating can be established to provide education (workshops, counseling sessions) and outreach and connect services directly to families (e.g., fruit baskets). Finally, health-care systems can offer incentives for children to maintain healthy diets, which would hopefully increase their desire to continue eating healthy.

Ensuring that communities have access to adequate nutrition is especially important during stressful times, such as the COVID-19 pandemic. After COVID-19 hit the United States, there were increases in new clients who needed to use food service providers of up to 75 percent in some places. Racial and ethnic minorities, along with those in low income brackets, were most affected, exacerbating vulnerable communities and families even more. Preparing for widespread events like pandemics and natural disasters is essential to ensure that citizens have access to affordable and nutritious food in the face of adversity (Fitzpatrick et al., 2020).

A developing literature is exploring the role of later school start times to improve the sleep patterns of children and adolescents. Semenza and colleagues (2020) suggest that later start times would improve student outcomes and reduce delinquency. Along with improving sleep leading to better self-control, later times would correspond with larger work patterns to increase supervision of youth. The Adolescent Sleep Working Group (2014, p. 642) of the American Academy of Pediatrics supports later start times and has made this clear in their formal statement:

> The American Academy of Pediatrics strongly supports the efforts of school districts to optimize sleep in students and urges high schools and middle schools to aim for start times that allow students the opportunity to achieve optimal levels of sleep (8.5–9.5 hours) and to improve physical (e.g., reduced obesity risk) and mental (e.g., lower rates of depression) health, safety (e.g., drowsy driving crashes), academic performance, and quality of life.

Despite the challenges that are macro level and systemic as well as individual, there are promising strategies to disrupt violence in disadvantaged areas. The strategies must be comprehensive, broad, and focused on the whole community and individual. Coordinated efforts that capitalize on the expertise and resources of multiple individuals and organizations are needed.

Fitting the Facts and Missing Puzzle Pieces

Living in areas that are characterized by multiple social and biological ills leads to a cycle of poverty, violence, and inequality. In fact, criminologists such as Graham Ousey have implored other scholars of crime and violence to expand their view and consider various social problems that occur in impoverished areas (Ousey, 2017). For example, while homicide is higher in disadvantaged areas—and has been a consistent concern of criminologists—other social ills like infant mortality and sexually transmitted infections (STIs) overlap with homicide in these areas. If we are to address crime, we must take a more full-community and full-person approach that is intentional about ameliorating multiple overlapping and intertwined social problems.

Recent research adds additional backing to the notion that social problems tend to cluster within fairly small spaces. Rutgers University and University of Arkansas criminologists connected area violence, socioeconomic status, and academic performance. Areas with a high percentage of individuals living in disadvantage were more likely to have lower mathematic and language arts proficiency rates. This was also true for exposure to area levels of violence. The greater the number of violent crimes near a school, the lower the proficiency rates of that school (Boxer, Drawve, & Caplan, 2020). While this study contributed to better understanding of the link between these social problems using innovative spatial methods, the findings may not be entirely surprising given the topics discussed thus far in the chapter. Exposure to violence, as well as experiencing resource deprivation, is associated with several health and social problems (see Felker-Kantor, Wallace, & Theall, 2017; Zimmerman & Posick, 2016) that, in turn, contribute to worse educational outcomes. Low educational outcomes, then, turn into worse adult outcomes (e.g., underemployment, health problems, criminal behavior), all of which reduce the probability that the next generation of children in those areas will be born healthy, develop appropriately, and succeed. A vicious cycle is perpetuated.

At the same time, these social problems are particularly pernicious. They are deeply entrenched within our society and will not be lessened, let alone eliminated, easily. As Rosenfeld (1989) pointed out, Merton's strain theory came under attack in the 1960s and 1970s when the economy was booming but crime was also rising. In fact, policies geared directly to reducing poverty did not seem to influence crime. This failure may, in part, have been a result of the difficulty in removing poverty or inequality in a capitalist society. Additionally, Rosenfeld suggested that simply reducing poverty would not necessarily reduce crime in Merton's model, as long as the cultural imperatives directing people to value money above all else remain strong. Thus, from this perspective, culture and structure must both be addressed.

While alleviating the social ills mentioned in this chapter is a herculean task, there is reason to be optimistic—if a biopsychosocially informed policy agenda is implemented. Getting the foundation wrong will likely miss the mark completely, leading to wasted dollars and, more importantly, wasted lives. By carefully developing large-scale programs along with local grassroots efforts in disadvantaged communities, a host of problems may be alleviated.

Finally, we know that not everyone is influenced in the same ways by the environment. One idea discussed, and returned to in Chapter 8, is called the "differential-susceptibility" hypothesis (Simons et al., 2011). The main idea is that certain genetic alleles make some people more susceptible to environmental influence (Simons et al., 2011). This is an intriguing possibility, but it remains unclear why most people in disadvantaged areas do not engage in serious crime or delinquency. Thus, one major missing puzzle piece is a better understanding of the ways people vary in how the environment influences them.

We are confident, though, that a biopsychosocial focus on the effects of living in disadvantaged areas will bring us closer to understanding not only how the environment matters but also how to improve conditions in a way that will bring the most benefits. Traditional sociological approaches have told us much about why disadvantage often increases rates of crime (and other social ills), but less so how. Knowledge of how the environment gets under the skin is improving every day, allowing a fuller picture of one of Braithwaite's primary facts of crime.

5

Peer Associations and Social Learning Influences in Criminal Behavior

Kevin grew up in one of the most violent neighborhoods in America. Speaking of his Brownsville neighborhood in the middle of Brooklyn, Kevin relates, "I could find someone with a gun before I could find someone with a diploma" (Bazelon, 2019, p. xv). He often hung out with friends in the neighborhood—particularly late at night. Kevin was routinely exposed to violence either directly—such as getting jumped going to the store or getting sliced with a razor blade in his community—or indirectly, such as hearing about friends and acquaintances getting shot. He and his friends were continually involved in violence—as either victims or offenders.

Kevin and his friend group often retaliated against people who harmed them throughout their teen years. He recounts, "I sometimes chilled with people who did wild shit" (Bazelon, 2019, p. xvii). One wild thing they did was get a gun. The plan was not to get the gun to go on the offensive; rather, it was to protect themselves from the craziness of the street. The gun was often kept out, as it was one night when Kevin was with his friend Mason. Mason was leaving his apartment when plainclothes police officers arrived.

Kevin panicked. He did not want to see his friend get in trouble. He did not want the gun to be found. He picked it up and put it into his waistband, but not before the officers saw him. It was a stupid thing to do. But as Emily Bazelon (2019, p. xx), the author of *Charged* who tells Kevin's story, states, "Young people do rash and impulsive things." Rash, indeed. And it would end up costing Kevin.

Bazelon is insightful here. Young people, as discussed in Chapter 3, often act impulsively, without thinking. Perhaps this is not surprisingly by this point in the book, but young people, especially, do rash and impulsive things in front of their friends. Scholars have long known that adolescence is a time of heightened risky behavior and have speculated on why that is the case. Today, our understanding of why risky behavior increases in adolescence relies on both social and biological factors that converge in adolescence.

Braithwaite (1989, p. 48) approaches the peer effects in the criminological research straightforwardly, writing as his tenth fact that "young people who have friendships with criminals are more likely to engage in crime themselves." Part of the explanation for this fact is related to the establishments of subcultures. He states earlier in the book that "subculture formation arising in part from the fact that the society creates types of outcasts with a common fate who face the same problems" (Braithwaite, 1989, p. 21). Cultures arise when like people are treated similarly to one another—often through labeling, ostracizing, and stigmatization. These individuals who are ostracized meet together and commit acts of deviance together. And if one thing about crime is almost certain, it is that people tend to offend with each other.

Traditional Theoretical Approaches

Some of the earliest explanations of behavior fall under the rubric of learning theories. As social creatures, it makes a whole lot of sense to assume we learn most of what we know and how to behave from other people. Just like Kevin, many people act like those around them and are influenced by their peers. We learn a lot from those around us, including attitudes, behaviors, and values. In criminology, the earliest theoretical contribution in this vein comes from sociologist Edwin Sutherland.

In response to a scathing critique of criminology in the early twentieth century regarding its lack of knowledge and organizing principles, Sutherland developed a differential association theory of crime.

Sutherland developed nine principles of learning that he combined to establish his social learning theory. In Sutherland's theory, (1) criminal behavior is learned, (2) in interaction with others, (3) especially those close to the individual, (4) including the techniques of committing crime and the motives and drives for committing crime. The (5) motivations are definitions unfavorable to legal codes, and (6) a person becomes delinquent when the definitions favorable to breaking the law exceed the definitions for not breaking the law. These definitions may (7) vary in frequency, duration, priority, and intensity, and (8) these definitions favorable to crime are learned just like any other type of learning, even for prosocial behavior. Finally, (9) criminal behavior is an expression of general needs and values but is not explained by those needs and values (since this would also be true of noncriminal behavior) (Sutherland, 1947).

Sutherland's differential association theory may have saved what is now the field of criminology. Had it not been for him, the academy might very well have turned its back on the theoretical explanation of crime through the field of criminology. A huge amount of credit is due to Sutherland. Regardless, there were some gaps in his theory. For instance, what are the specific mechanisms by which definitions are learned? Here, criminologist Ronald Akers makes his entrance and adds the ingredient of behavioral theory to Sutherland's perspective.

Akers was theorizing about crime causation around the same time that operant and respondent conditioning was all the rage (i.e., 1960s–1970s). Akers, along with a psychologist (Burgess & Akers, 1966), reimagined Sutherland's differential association theory via the lens of behavioral psychology. Sutherland's nine propositions became seven. Later, Akers refined the theory even more, distilling his social learning theory into four components. These components focused more fully on the motivations and reinforcements for crime. These four new social learning principles are presented specifically here: (1) criminal behavior is learned according to the principles of operant conditioning; (2) criminal behavior is learned both in nonsocial situations that are reinforcing or discriminative and through social interactions in which the behavior of other persons is reinforcing or discriminative for criminal behavior; (3) the principle part of learning criminal behavior occurs in those groups that are the individual's major source of reinforcements; and (4) the learning of criminal behavior, including specific techniques, attitudes, and avoidance procedures, is a function of the effective and available reinforcers and the existing reinforcement contingencies (Akers, 2009). These new propositions were more sociopsychological than Sutherland's and set up a strong foundation for biopsychosocial perspectives, as mentioned in the next section of this chapter.

Akers went on to expand on his social learning theory, including several levels of analysis. His main argument is that exposure to criminal models, or reinforcers, is dependent on background factors (e.g., race and class) as well as the area in which one lives. The social structure, to Akers, is composed of four components: (1) differential social organization (how society is organized according to demographics and cultural factors, (2) differential location in the social structure (the individual's demographic characteristics), (3) theoretically derived structural variables (here he is referring to factors such as anomie or disorganization), and (4) differential social location (the various groups one belongs to) (Akers, 2009, p. xxvii). These components of the social structure influence the individual-level social learning factors that explain crime. The individual factors are (1) differential association (who one hangs out with), (2) imitation (models we use to guide our own behavior), (3) definitions (attitudes and views toward crime), and (4) differential reinforcement (if we are reinforced for crime, we will continue to engage in it). The model proposes that structure influences individual social learning factors, which then lead to crime (Akers, 2009).

One can see in Akers's formulation that learning to engage in crime includes direct interaction with peers but also indirect interaction and attitudes. However, to focus on a simpler level, the "peer effect" is one of the most long-standing controversies in criminology. Having delinquent friends is strongly correlated with one's own delinquency. And we know that much delinquency on the part of youth happens in the company of peers. What explains this? Social learning theorists argue that peers *influence* each other and that there are several theoretical ways they are thought to do so.

Even within perspectives that attribute causality to peers, the mechanisms by which peers influence behavior remain contested. One explanation draws on routine activities theory, which, in essence, suggests that crime will occur if the right ingredients (motivated offender, suitable target for victimization, and lack of guardians) come together at the same time and place. The unstructured socialization perspective notes that when adolescents get together in groups without adult supervision or any form of structure to their activities, trouble is likely to ensue (Osgood et al., 1996). One study tested various ways unstructured socialization could affect delinquency, finding that such socializing increased reinforcement for delinquency, acceptance of crime, and contact with delinquent peers (Hoeben & Weerman, 2016).

In probably the most comprehensive treatment of peer effects on criminal behavior, Mark Warr's influential book *Companions in Crime* argued that "the social nature of criminal behavior is not merely an incidental feature of crime, but is instead a potential key to understanding its etiology and some of its most distinctive features" (Warr, 2002, p. 4). In trying to explain how peers may affect crime, Warr argued that peers are socializers. They provide models for behavior and reinforcement. The peer effect, to Warr, can also help explain several "facts" of crime, including the age-crime curve, in which criminal behavior increases through adolescence and early adulthood and then decreases. Why does crime increase and then decrease? Adolescence is a time when peers take on more salience in our lives. And as we enter adulthood, we enter institutions (e.g., jobs, marriages) that cut us off from peers. Similarly, the reason that marriage and crime are often negatively related is due to the reduced time with peers that occurs after getting married.

Thus, from a learning perspective, peers can influence behavior in numerous ways. They can encourage delinquency by, for example, pressuring someone to go along with a motor vehicle theft. They can distort decision-making, which is the essence of the groupthink hypothesis (Janis, 1972). Peers can also teach each other delinquent attitudes, which may be linked to deviant behavior—this was the key idea behind Sutherland's differential association theory, only he used the term "definitions."

However, we should point out that it is by no means accepted wisdom that peers are a strong influence on an individual's behavior. For example, a competing explanation of the finding that those engaged in delinquency often have delinquent friends is that peers who are alike in both attitudes and behavior tend to hang out together. Control theorists have responded to learning theorists that the peer effect is spurious, or not causal. The debates between control theorist Travis Hirschi and learning theorist Ron Akers have been long standing in criminology (see Posick & Rocque, 2018). Hirschi's classic *Causes of Delinquency* (1969) was one of the first expositions of a theoretical perspective accompanied by data to test it. Not only did Hirschi test whether his "social bond" theory was empirically valid, but he also tested it against social learning (and strain) theories, declaring his theory the winner.

The debates between control and learning theorists have served to clarify the theoretical position of each side but have not really settled many scores. In our book *Great Debates in Criminology* (Posick & Rocque, 2018), we concluded that while control theory seemed a bit more empirically supported, research on both learning and control theory provided support for each perspective. Nonetheless, each also has left much to be desired in terms of understanding antisocial behavior. We pointed to a study, now over 10 years old, that indicated that while differential association theory fared the best in terms of explaining variance in crime, it still left over half the variation unexplained.

Biopsychosocial Contributions

Recall Kevin again. When the cops busted in and he hid the gun, what did his peers actually do in that moment? Did they physically force him to hide the gun? Did they yell some instructions to him? No, he did it all on his own. What does this mean? It means that, in the moment, Kevin's brain made the decision to hide the gun. His past associations with peers did not directly force him to do anything; he had already trained his brain to act.

It is somewhat surprising that learning theories in criminology have largely ignored biology as the learning process itself is so heavily influenced by the brain. This may be because learning theories have been so firmly placed in sociological explanations of behavior, and that they have traditionally assumed a "blank slate" view of behavior in which a person is born without any predetermined ways of behavior. The emphasis on the environment, in terms of models and peers, would seem to contradict the biosocial argument that the environment is less important in understanding behavior. Whatever the reasons, a biopsychosocial approach is essential to understand the learning process as well as the influence of peers, family members, and others on behavior.

However, research using behavioral genetic models—which partition variance in outcomes between genetic and environmental factors, the latter of which is further partitioned into shared and nonshared environments—may support a learning approach. The reason is that these models use twins to calculate the portion of variance in behavior attributed to each factor. Generally, about 50 percent of the variance in crime is due to genetics. With respect to the environment, these studies have indicated that it is not the shared environment (e.g., parents, home life) that accounts for the lion's share of the variance in behavior but rather the nonshared environment (e.g., peers) (Beaver, 2015). As Judith Rich Harris (2009) argues in her influential book *The Nurture Assumption*, children do not become who they are from their parents but from their peers. This theory is called group socialization, and it is built on the idea that people behave differently (and learn different things) in different contexts. We may behave for our parents but be wild with our friends.

Homophily and Selection into Environments

Take a second and think about the friends you hang out with. Do they play similar sports? Do they have similar hobbies? Do they enjoy the same food or TV shows as you do? Your answer is probably yes, at least to some of these questions. This is not by chance. People tend to hang out with people who are like themselves. It makes sense, as we enjoy people's company when we share interests and can talk about similar things. Surely we also have friends who differ from ourselves, too. However, we probably share more than we think, such as race, socioeconomic status, and educational background.

Psychologist Robert Plomin gave a great example of selection into environments on the *Making Sense* podcast hosted by neuroscientist Sam Harris. He mentioned his two grandchildren. His granddaughter loved reading. At night, he would read books to her, and she loved this interaction. It would not be surprising if she turned into an avid reader, maybe a writer—probably someone with great reading comprehension. His grandson, however, hated reading. He did not want to read or be read to. In fact, Plomin mentioned that it would border on being cruel to force his grandson to listen to an entire Harry Potter book. So he was read to much less. It would not be surprising if he opted for physical activity over reading later in life.

Much has been said about the benefits of being read to in the early life course. And it probably does make a difference. But children's behavior will elicit their social exposure. Plomin's granddaughter was always likely to be a good reader because she was predisposed by her genes and biology to love reading. In turn, reading was something that bonded her to her parents. Plomin's grandson, not so much. However, other activities might have bonded them, such as sports or music (he did not comment on that).

Learning and the Brain

Learning, of course, necessarily has to include the brain. Nothing new will be learned and nothing will be retained if the brain is not engaged. The biological sciences long ago identified the major parts of the brain responsible for learning and determined which processes that occur in the brain are linked to social learning. Parts of the brain are implicated in motivating and reinforcing behavior as well. Lack of knowledge of the brain in learning theories of behavior severely limits opportunities to understand and treat antisocial behavior.

Proctor and Niemeyer (2020) offer a revised social learning perspective that acknowledges the brain basis of animal learning. Central to their argument is that autobiographical memory is essential in specifying the link between learning and behavior. Autobiographical memory includes both episodic (information about one's self in a historical context) and semantic (more generalized knowledge) memory. Referring to Sheldon and colleagues (2018), the authors state, "The medial temporal lobe, hippocampus, ventrolateral and medial prefrontal cortices, lateral temporal lobes, posteromedial cortical regions, and posterior inferior parietal lobes as the distributed network of brain regions that are consistently shown to underlie autobiographical memory" (Proctor & Niemeyer, 2020, p. 5). In both personal and general memory, the brain is implicated. Further, the "medial prefrontal cortex has consistently been shown to be critical to the self-referential aspects of autobiographical memory, while the precuneus and lateral temporal cortex are crucial to visual imagery processing and conceptual processing, respectively" (2020, p. 6). Learning, processing, and using information are clearly linked to brain functioning, as illustrated by brain research. We agree with the assessment of the authors that "social learning theory curiously omits any discussion of memory or the neuroanatomy and physiology of learning and memory, two areas where profound scientific discoveries have occurred in cognitive psychology and neuroscience over the last fifty years" (2020, p. 3).

The Genetics of Learning (Reward and Punishment)

Genes—many that code brain-based structure and function—are part of the learning process. Genes that impact the dopamine system, the opioid system, enzymatic degradation, and the acetylcholine system are all essential for learning. First, the dopamine system is linked to reward processing in the brain. Genes including DRD2, DRD4, DAT1, and COMT are central to processing in the prefrontal cortex.

Scientists at the National Institute of Neurological Disorders and Stroke estimate that roughly one-third of the 20,000 genes in the human genome are expressed in the brain (NINDS, 2019). In other words, human behavior, decision-making, and even how we learn are under some genetic influence. This is not to say that the behaviors we display, the decisions we make, and the things we learn are completely scripted by genetics. Indeed, these things are clearly influenced by the environment in which we are operating. Without external realities to present us with choices, there would be no way for genetic influences to affect decision-making. Similarly, without appropriate models, teachers, and mentors, we could not learn the behaviors, traits, and skills that come to define our actions. Similarly, though, without genetic potential for learning, we could not successfully mimic the behaviors of our peers, and, thus, theoretical accounts of offending that rely on learning would be unnecessary.

Criminologist Bryanna Fox (2017) showed how biology can be incorporated into social learning theory, focusing on genetics. Fox argued that genetic research can offer greater insight into how the components of social learning theory work. Peer association, for example, is not random but is partly a result of the tendency of individuals to search for environments that match their "genetic predispositions" (2017, p. 25). A similar process may be involved in selecting models for imitation, another social learning theory concept. Thus, part of the reason people associate with or imitate others with varying delinquent tendencies is because those people are, in some ways, like them (which is related to the discussion in the previous section). However, that does not mean the peers do not have influence on behavior, as control theorists claim. Additionally, according to Fox, genes can help us understand why particular people vary in terms of how they "define" behavior and the reinforcement they receive from such behavior. In the end, Fox's exposition does not radically change social learning theory, but it does help fill some of its gaps.

Considering Peer Influences and Learning in Crime Prevention and Intervention

As we have seen, peers matter when it comes to criminal behavior. The actual mechanisms by which peers influence behavior, however, remain somewhat murky. In the second edition of *The Nurture Assumption* (2009), Harris's theory is that peers socialize us but in the group sense, not in the individual sense. In other words, it's not just who you hang around with but your social group at large that matters. If it were as simple as ensuring people do not hang around with deviant peers, the policy implications that stem from the peer effect would be more straightforward.

However, the evidence does seem to suggest that individual peers are influential. And the policy implications stemming from a group socialization theory are not, in our view, incompatible with those from an individual peer effect. On the individual level, policies that seek to disrupt peer groups are one method of preventing crime and delinquency. For example, in David Kirk's influential work on the effects of Hurricane Katrina, which devastated New Orleans in the fall of 2005, he has shown that when individuals were released from prison back to their homes (and peer groups), they fared worse than those who were forced to relocate (Kirk, 2020). Kirk has also been integral in designing studies showing experimentally that relocating ex-offenders helps them stave off recidivism.

Other policy implications of an individual-level peer effect, particularly within adolescent groups, is increased supervision. As we noted prior, the research on peers is clear that unstructured socialization is linked to delinquency. After-school programs, clubs, and other extracurricular events may help reduce unstructured socializing and, therefore, delinquency. Evaluations of such programs are mixed, however (Barkan & Rocque, 2020). As Hirschi (1969) argued, involvement in delinquency takes so little time that virtually all free time would have to be spent in prosocial activities for these strategies to be effective.

On the group level, an argument could be made that we must change reinforcement and models for delinquency and crime. That, however, may be easier said than done. In his work on harmful male socialization, Jackson Katz has shown how cultural messages about what it means to be a man may be linked to violence. In his *Tough Guise 2*, Katz says, "we need to stop chasing symptoms and take a good look at a truth that's been hiding in plain sight all along: that when we talk about violence in America, whether it's real or imaginary, we're almost always talking about violent masculinity" (Media Education Foundation, 2013, p. 1).

There are two problems with grounding policy on media socialization theories. First, the media may not be inclined to self-censor, as it were. There is a reason the media utilize such violent imagery, and that is because it sells. It may therefore fall on other institutions to address exposure to violent media for young males. Second, whether violent media is causally related to increased aggression is not clear (Boxer, Groves, & Docherty, 2015; Ferguson & Kilburn, 2009; Ferguson, 2015). Research on desistance, or decline in crime over the life course, has suggested that a decreasing role of peers may play a part in why people stop committing crimes. This may be a more fruitful avenue for policy makers to pursue than media restrictions.

Fitting the Facts and Missing Puzzle Pieces

Theoretically, peers have figured prominently in theories of crime since the emergence of sociological criminology. The first truly social theory of crime and deviance used association with deviant others as the primary cause of crime as its lynchpin. Not long after differential association theory was developed, control theorists began questioning the relevance of peers. Nonetheless, having delinquent peers remains one of the strongest correlates of delinquency in the literature (Warr, 2002). That is not in question; what is in question is the meaning of this correlation.

Sociologists who align themselves with learning theories have offered their own suggestions for why peers matter in our own behavior. They have suggested that peers influence attitudes and reinforce behavior in ways that make delinquency more likely. Empirical evidence has tended to support the social learning theory of crime and delinquency (Akers, 2009). But gaps remain, including how learning happens and who is most vulnerable to the influence of peers. However, innovative research in the social sciences has been able to clarify some aspects of how peers influence us. For example, one point of contention is whether delinquent peers offer role models that are then imitated or whether peers affect our attitudes, which then leads to delinquency. Warr and Stafford (1991) examined both peer attitudes and peer behavior, finding that it was really peer behavior that affected one's own behavior. However, without taking the body into account, a complete understanding of how peers influence us is not possible.

Additionally, if peers influence us, it is unclear why media effects are nebulous. As mentioned in the previous section, despite early research on media effects, recent work is equivocal. If peers' behavior directly influences our own, why would the media not have such a clear-cut effect? We believe a biopsychosocial approach will come closest to helping us understand the nuances of learning and how the brain processes models. Work such as Proctor and Niemeyer's (2020) updating of social learning theory from a neurological basis will likely do more to advance this theoretical perspective and empirical "fact" than the last 30 years of theorizing and tests.

It is vital to get at the core of how learning takes place—not only for theoretical clarity but also for policy. Braithwaite's observation of the peer effect remains just as relevant today as it was in 1989. Crime and delinquency happen in the context of peers and others who engage in such behavior. The question of why and how that learning happens is still open, but it is necessary to interrogate it further so that improvements in prevention and rehabilitation programs can be made. We argue that incorporating biology into the largely environmental social learning theory will help substantially in this regard.

6

Social Relationships, Control, and Criminal Behavior

Pennsylvania state trooper Dylan Adams was sitting in his cruiser on March 8, 2020, waiting for speeding drivers or other activity he would have to address. While Adams was waiting, 39-year-old Jerry Glynn Lee sped by him "at a very high rate of speed." Adams turned on his lights and pulled up behind Lee. Lee did not stop (Czech, 2020).

Pretty soon, Adams and Lee were in a chase exceeding 80 miles per hour, and there were no signs Lee intended to give himself up. On a turn, Lee partially lost control and crashed into a fence. This did not stop him, and he continued to run through a field. Adams pursued Lee, jumping over two fences in the process. At the second fence, Adams was able to fire his Taser at Lee, but it missed. Lee made his way toward a heavily wooded area.

Just before getting to the woods, Adams fired a second Taser shot; once again, it missed. Then something strange happened. Lee stopped and turned toward his pursuer. He said, "You're going to have to shoot me, I have nothing to lose." Luckily, Adams did not have to do that. He was able to tackle Lee and get handcuffs on him. As he went back through the field, it was evident that Lee had dropped marijuana and methamphetamines (Czech, 2020).

Speeding and possession of marijuana and meth are certainly serious—but to risk one's life? To flee and resist arrest? These are much more serious charges. Why risk it? Oddly, Lee told Adams, he had nothing to lose. Why not do it? He could potentially get away, and even if not, who cares. This says much for control theory, one of the most empirically supported theories of crime.

Control theory states that crime needs no specific motivation and that we will commit crime when there are few restraints on our behavior. These controls are generally thought to come from the people (e.g., friends, family, teachers) and institutions (e.g., work, school, military) we come into contact with and care about strongly. When we do not have these ties, or if they are weak, nothing is really stopping us from committing crime. This means, obviously, that humans are by nature self-interested and need to be controlled or we would all be engaging in behavior that is advantageous to us but perhaps harmful to others. For Lee, it appeared he had little stopping him from committing crime and little to lose if he got into trouble—or even died.

Braithwaite wrote about several facts of crime that deal with social control concepts and variables. First, Braithwaite (1989, p. 46) mentioned that "crime is committed disproportionately by unmarried people." Braithwaite noted that the literature has been relatively silent on this "fact." Since then, much research has been conducted on understanding the relationship between marriage and crime (Laub & Sampson, 2003; Sampson, Laub, & Witmer, 2006; Skardhamar et al., 2015; Warr, 1998). Second, Braithwaite (1989, p. 47) declared that "young people who are strongly attached to their school are less likely to engage in crime." Relationships with teachers can restrain criminal tendencies, and negative labeling in school might account for the majority of the IQ-delinquency link (Hirschi & Hindelang, 1977).

Next, Braithwaite (1989, p. 48) wrote that "young people who do poorly at school are more likely to engage in crime." Finally, he stated that "young people who are strongly attached to their parents are less likely to engage in crime" (Braithwaite, 1989, p. 48). Bringing these together, he added that "attachments and commitments (interdependencies as we conceptualize it) reduce crime when people make use of them to engage in reintegrative shaming" (Braithwaite, 1989, p. 29). Reintegrative shaming is obviously a key to all of Braithwaite's ideas and, in itself, is likely informed by biopsychosocial perspectives.

This chapter introduces control theory, especially in the form of bonds and self-control (internalized bonds). Social bonds have been extensively theorized about and empirically tested. Biosocial factors related to the establishment and maintenance of social bonds and self-control is a growing but still nascent topic. We push this agenda forward and suggest that a biopsychosocial framework is essential for understanding the formation of all sorts of bonds, how bonds are depleted or destroyed, and how bonds can be maintained through time.

Traditional Theoretical Approaches

While a control perspective in criminology was popularized in the late 1960, the idea of social control is actually much older. Social control theory in criminology is based upon an image of human nature (that is, how would humans be if society did not exist?). Several such images are linked to Enlightenment thinkers such as Rousseau, Hobbes, and Locke (Friend, n.d.). In Hobbes's *Leviathan*, he makes the case that without society, people would have "continual fear and danger of violent death; and the life of man, (would be) solitary, poor, nasty, brutish, and short" (Hobbes, [1651] 1887, p. 64). This is because people are naturally self-interested, and, without society, there are no restraining structures to hold back our impulses. Note this does *not* mean that people are evil. Why? To be evil, one must be amoral and ignore social norms. If there is no society in the sense that we think of it today, one cannot ignore norms or morals that do not exist (unless, of course, these refer to religious or spiritual ones).

One of the first formal discourses on control theory was put forth by one of the founders of sociology, Emile Durkheim. When comparing varying rates of maladies, such as suicide, across cultural contexts, he noticed that certain societies shared a common feature. Countries that failed to provide their citizens with clear goals and values that could be achieved were characterized by a normlessness he called anomie. The more anomie in a society, the more social ills. With respect to suicide, in particular, Durkheim showed how social organization at the group level correlated with the taking of one's own life—an act that, to this day, continues to be chalked up mostly to individual problems. Durkheim discussed several kinds of suicide, but the anomic suicide was related to murder in that both have the same causes (Durkheim, [1897] 2005).

What is it about anomie that leads to poor outcomes like suicide and crime? One answer was that people justify poor behavior using "neutralizations." Gresham Sykes and David Matza called this justification "techniques of neutralization." If a person has an excuse for acting poorly, this diminishes the control on their behavior. This was expanded upon brilliantly by Ruth Kornhauser in her book, *Social Sources of Delinquency: An Appraisal of Analytic Models*. The normlessness that Durkheim discusses in his work, including *Suicide* ([1897] 2005), leads to cultural attenuation. In other words, it is not that people in anomic societies develop different cultures or value systems in response to normlessness; rather, they take the current value systems and slightly modify them. Crime is an easy way to obtain material goods and solve certain problems, and people will fall back on these mechanisms if there are no other ways to achieve success.

Much later, in the 1990s, criminologists would apply macro-level control theory to crime rates. In their landmark book *Crime and the American Dream*, Steven Messner and Richard Rosenfeld (1994) argued that the United States is a somewhat exceptional case in that it proscribes monetary wealth through a healthy economic institution as a value of society at the expense of other important institutions, such as family and education. This imbalance—where the economy is valued above all other institutions—leads to less social cohesion and control, resulting in high crime rates.

Around the same time as Kornhauser was appraising different theoretical approaches to the study of crime and settling on control theory, another theorist was looking more specifically at a micro-level control perspective that could explain why one person—and not necessarily a whole society—acts more criminally than another. In *Causes of Delinquency*, criminologist Travis Hirschi (1969) proposed that the reason people commit crime is not because they were pressured into it or taught to do so but because there were no factors preventing them from acting out their own self-interest in the form of antisocial behavior. These factors preventing someone from committing crime are "bonds."

For Hirschi, four major mechanisms operate together to establish one's bond to society. The first is attachment. This is the existence of a prosocial relationship with a person or institution. The stronger the bond, and the more of them there are, the more attachments people have that they will not want to break. Hirschi focused on attachment to mothers, fathers, and teachers in his work. The second is commitment. This refers to how strongly a person is committed to a conventional way of thinking and behaving. A person with strong commitment adheres to conformity. Having a strong commitment, or "stake," in conformity is directly relevant to the story at the outset of this chapter. Recall that Lee engaged in deviance in part because he had nothing to lose. Commitment is the "thing" that tells us not to act in ways that could jeopardize what we have. This is similar to what Jackson Toby referred to as having "stakes in conformity" (Toby, 1957).

The third bond that binds us to conventional society is involvement. The more time a person spends engaging in prosocial activities, the less time they have to engage in antisocial activity, Hirschi suggested. Fourth is belief. The more a person buys into a life of conformity to prosocial values, the less they will act counter to those values. This bond is connected to what's called authority, which is when individuals have power because society believes they deserve it. Those who believe in the moral validity of the law are much more likely to follow it. Interestingly, Hirschi tested his theory using data from a survey of students and found much support for the idea that when social bonds are weak, people are more likely to engage in delinquency. One point of surprise for him, though, was that involvement did not seem to be related to delinquency. In the end, he surmised that taking part in prosocial activities generally does not occupy all of youths' time, and so there will still be opportunity to get into trouble if they so desire.

Hirschi, along with his student Michael Gottfredson, expanded the control perspective to include self-control. In 1990, *A General Theory of Crime*, released by Gottfredson and Hirschi, made the bold claim that it is the ability of people to self-regulate their behavior that prevents them from committing crime. Through stable, effective parenting, a child will develop self-control and commit to conformity instead of delinquency. Later, in 2004, Hirschi described self-control as the bonds with family that have been instilled in a person that they carry with them through the day.

At about the same time that Gottfredson and Hirschi were developing self-control theory, their former students were working on a version of social bond theory that would extend throughout the life span. This "age-graded theory of informal social controls"

(Sampson & Laub, 1993) applied the logic of social bonds from childhood through adolescence to adulthood. One of the key arguments in Sampson and Laub's work was that marriage was a major factor in reducing crime among those who had been found delinquent in childhood. The researchers utilized data from Sheldon and Eleanor Glueck's classic *Unraveling Juvenile Delinquency* study (Glueck & Glueck, 1950) to show that marriage may promote desistance from crime, or when crime slows down and eventually fizzles out in adulthood. Sampson and Laub's work has been instrumental in sparking a large amount of scholarship examining the so-called marriage effect on crime, with much research indicating that marriage does indeed reduce crime, even on the aggregate level (Rocque et al., 2015a).

The story seems straightforward: marriage is a social bond that provides supervision and psychological motivation to go on the straight and narrow. Yet not all research has been supportive of this idea (see Giordano, Cernkovich, & Rudolph, 2002). Some work has also indicated that the literature on marriage and crime does not take into account selection processes, suggesting, for example, that individuals who are likely to marry are also more likely to desist from crime and that marriage is not the cause of either (Skardhamar et al., 2015).

Overall, research has tended to support various iterations of control theory—and self-control theory in particular (Pratt & Cullen, 2000; Rocque, Posick, & Piquero, 2016). At the same time, numerous gaps remain. For example, while Gottfredson and Hirschi (1990) argued that self-control was the primary cause of crime, scholarship has indicated that, in fact, tests of the theory leave much crime and delinquency to be explained (Weisburd & Piquero, 2008). The lack of relationship between involvement and crime is also somewhat puzzling, and that puzzle continues in the form of an unclear literature on extracurricular activities and crime. Finally, the way self-control develops—which, in Gottfredson and Hirschi's view, was primarily driven by parents—has come into focus as biopsychosocial research has offered evidence that self-control is more biological than previously thought.

Biopsychosocial Contributions

Social control perspectives have enhanced the explanation of crime immensely. Control theory begins on the premise that all people are naturally inclined toward self-interest and in that self-interest are oriented toward antisocial behavior. The theory describes the most important bonds to people and society and the various ways these bonds form, change, and are maintained throughout the life course. Self-control theory puts control over behavior within the individual. In this sense, it has become more biopsychosocially relevant. Yet the ways social bonds influence us are also related to the body. We argue that there are biological and psychological aspects of the development of bonds/self-control, how bonds/self-control may come to be weakened over time, and how bonds/self-control are maintained through personal resiliency. In addition, neurological research has expanded on how self-control develops in ways that make it clear that "control" is social and biologically housed. The biopsychosocial approach, therefore, is more comprehensive and indicates more inroads for prevention and intervention.

Establishing Bonds and Self-Control

Why do bonds develop in the first place? And how are they linked to behavior? Certain research has suggested that there is an evolutionary basis for early bonding. Pederson (2004) shows that in mammals, mother/infant bonding is an adaptation necessary for survival. Interestingly, Pederson wrote that bonding influences the stress response, as discussed in the next chapter. There may also be a neurological component to bonding such that certain protective behaviors of mothers toward infants "appear to be hard-wired and not at all learned" (2004, p. 108). Interestingly, Pedersen reviewed work on mammals showing that there is a neurological component to "pair bonding" in adults as well. Life-course criminology has shed light on adult bonds, showing that marriage may be a primary factor in encouraging desistance from crime (Sampson, Laub, & Wimer, 2006). Others have argued that the human brain evolved to facilitate important interpersonal skills that are useful for relationships (Turner, 2013).

While bonding may be hardwired, the lack of bonds developed by some individuals may be linked to neurological difficulties. Think about a person you know from school who spent a lot of time by themselves and had few friends. What was it that led them to not have a large peer group? Did they tend to annoy others? Did they bully others or always pick fights? Did they not pick up on social cues? It is possible the people you are thinking of engaged in one or more of these behaviors or had some of these traits. The result is weak or nonexistent bonds. Some people have a more difficult time than others in developing and maintaining relationships. This is often the result of biological and brain-based deficits and how they interact with a person's surroundings.

Moffitt's (1993) dual taxonomy theory offers a useful framework for understanding how this works. In her theory, Moffitt demonstrated that most adolescents engage in some delinquency. It is normative, in other words. Yet most of these delinquents eventually age out. They are adolescent-limited offenders. Crime is no longer appealing, and the motivations for such behavior largely disappear for these folks once they reach adulthood. A small percentage, however, are persistent offenders. These are individuals who suffer from neuropsychological deficits and do not develop normal, healthy relationships with those around them. According to Moffitt, "children with neuropsychological problems evoke a challenge to even the most resourceful, loving, and patient families" (1993, p. 682). These difficulties result in strained interactions with parents and others, which makes things worse. Disadvantage then accumulates over the life course; these "difficult" kids are not likely to develop great relationships with their teachers, another source of social control for Hirschi. The main point here is that biological and psychological risk factors affect interactions with others that increase the risk of deviance. Here, though, the biopsychological antecedents affect the lack of bonds, which then exacerbate an already bad situation.

Thus, we see that the establishment of bonds appears to be related to evolution as well as components of the brain. In addition, neurological difficulties help us understand why some people do not establish strong bonds early and throughout their life. For a variety of reasons, these folks, according to theoretical accounts like those of Moffitt and others (see, e.g., Patterson, 2016), spark negative interactions with caregivers early on. For Moffitt (1993), neuropsychological difficulties may create difficult personalities, which leads parents to become exasperated, straining their relationships with the child. To the extent that bonds are important for controlling behavior, then, a biopsychological factor increases the likelihood for delinquency through its effect on social relationships.

What about self-control? Where does that come from? Recall that Gottfredson and Hirschi (1990) argued that parenting instills self-control in early childhood. If parents do not do their job, children will not develop high self-control, which will be consequential throughout their lives. Biopsychological research, however, has had something to say about this. In terms of whether parents are the sole cause of self-control, research has shown otherwise (Cullen et al., 2008). For example, studies have indicated that one's neighborhood influences self-control (Pratt et al., 2004), and so do genetics (Wright et al., 2008; Wright & Beaver, 2005). Lacking self-control, the criminologist Matt DeLisi has argued, "is a brain-based disorder" (2014, title). Self-control is housed in the prefrontal cortex and develops over time. Environmental and neuropsychological factors can impact the development of self-control, of course, but much of the variance in self-control also appears to be genetic (DeLisi, 2014).

Weakening Bonds/Self-Control

The previous section discussed, primarily, establishing or failing to establish bonds. What about maintaining social bonds and self-control? Is it possible for a person who has strong relationships and high levels of self-control to lose them? The research suggests this may be the case. Both social bonds and self-control are biopsychosocial in nature and can be influenced by biopsychosocial mechanisms.

Self-control has recently been likened to a muscle. Just like your biceps will tire and give way after too many arm curls, your self-control will also weaken and give out when put to the test. Even the strongest people on the planet cannot bench press weights forever— although they will last much longer than most of us. Relating this to self-control suggests that people with amazing levels of self-control can be broken down when enough stress is put on their patience— they'll eventually give in. Further, if self-control becomes weak, that giving-in point becomes easier to reach. The key is to not miss those gym sessions!

Often referred to as "ego depletion," diminishing self-control over time can cause a person to act irrationally or antisocially. Baumeister, Vohs, and Tice (2007, p. 351) comment:

> We observed that self-control appeared vulnerable to deterioration over time from repeated exertions, resembling a muscle that gets tired. The implication was that effortful self-regulation depends on a limited resource that becomes depleted by any acts of self-control, causing subsequent performance even on other self-control tasks to become worse.

Baumeister and colleagues note that a major component of ego depletion appears to be blood glucose levels. Glucose is an essential energy resource that is required for appropriate physiological functioning as well as decision-making. As glucose is used in the body, self-regulation appears to weaken as well. There is evidence that restoring glucose in the bloodstream can bring energy back up and increase the ability to self-regulate (see also Gailliot et al., 2007).

Other research has clarified the neurological basis for self-control. In Todd Heatherton's 2011 review article, he argued that self-control is a social phenomenon that entails the ability to think about what you are doing, to understand that others are judging your behavior (which means you are thinking about others' thoughts and feelings), and to know when you are in danger of being excluded and, as a result, one can change your behavior. Heatherton then shows how each of these abilities is linked to particular parts of the brain. For example, research has indicated that the medial prefrontal cortex is implicated in information processing about the self (Heatherton, 2011). This corresponds with other work previously mentioned indicating that the prefrontal cortex is where self-control is housed in the brain.

Social Bonds: Selection?

It is important to note that selection/homophily may help us understand why we develop bonds with particular people and groups. Selection is incorporated into both learning and control theories but for different reasons. Learning theories suggest that peers first start to hang out for a variety of reasons and that they become more alike over time because they are learning from each other. A friend might motivate or chastise a certain behavior, which would impact that person's actions. Over time, friends establish group norms and act in accordance with these norms.

Control theory also incorporates homophily but is related to the adage "birds of a feather flock together." Individuals form friendships because they are already alike. In learning theory, people might act delinquently because they learned to be antisocial from their friends. In control theory, people are already delinquent and will attach to other delinquents. Of course, a bit of both can be true. But it still remains the case that a biopsychosocial perspective can inform both.

We discussed peer effects in the previous chapter; here we focus on bonding framed from a control perspective. Take the following scenario. Say you are very good at playing basketball. And you like it quite a bit. It's very likely that you will seek out other basketball players (or maybe just other athletic people) to be your friends and share in your hobbies. Similarly, if you like to drink heavily, you will likely choose friends who also drink. Sure, you may get *even better* at basketball after learning from your friends or become an *even heavier* drinker after going out with your drinking buddies, but there was a reason you established those friendships in the first place, and your biology is probably part of it.

Your genetic makeup (or, more broadly, your biological makeup) plays a large part in determining your interests, values, attitudes, beliefs, traits, and behaviors. Polderman and colleagues (2015) found that everything from conduct disorder to height to mental health have a genetic basis. Genes influence traits and behaviors, and individuals seek out those with similar traits and behaviors. Furthermore, it is found that close friends are genetically similar and that antisocial behavior is particularly influenced by genetic predisposition shared by friends (Guo, 2006).

Genes or other biological processes may also help explain the "marriage effect." In other words, marriage may provide a protective element against criminal conduct, but it may also be that processes that make someone "marriageable" in the first place are also related to decreases in crime. Skardhamar and colleagues' useful review of the marriage effect in essence concluded that we cannot assume causality within the literature on marriage and crime and that it may be "that desistance 'triggers' marriage rather than vice versa" (2015, p. 437). A biopsychosocial approach may help us understand the social *and* biopsychological factors that associate marriage and crime.

Considering Bonding and Self-Control in Crime Prevention and Intervention

Luckily, though low self-control has a genetic and neurological basis, there are several interventions that can increase self-regulation and assist with reserving energy and avoiding depletion over time. Just like one can use weights to strengthen a specific muscle, one can also use self-control to strengthen it. Paying attention to habits or tendencies and then changing behavior is one way to strengthen self-control. For example, working on better posture, emotion regulation, or dieting is linked to more self-regulation. Developing and participating in an exercising plan, studying schedule, or money-management program leads to great self-regulation (Baumeister et al., 2006). These interventions are nonintrusive, lead to multiple benefits for the individual, and are fairly easy to implement—and evidence shows they work!

Building up self-regulation is important, as is avoiding depletion. Training and practices that build awareness and attention can improve the retention of self-control. Often referred to as mindfulness practices, these techniques train the brain to focus and become aware of emotions. Participants in a study who exerted self-control but also meditated were able to complete self-control tasks equally as well as control participants who did not have depleted self-control (Friese, Messner, & Schaffner, 2012). Finally, to the extent that self-control levels are related to physiological factors (e.g., glucose), a healthy diet will also be important in reducing crime (certain work on fish oil has shown there *may* be an effect on aggression, and there is reason to think it may reduce impulsivity [e.g., Garland & Hallahan, 2006], but the jury is still out, as research has not found such a link; see Dean et al., 2014; Ginty et al., 2017).

Relating self-control and social control, recent research has shown that strategies that focus on improving relationships with youth can improve child outcomes. For example, parenting programs seek to create better interactions between child and parent. One of the pathways to delinquency for youth with neuropsychological impairment is poor parental relationships that are caused, in part, by difficult child temperament. If those relations can be improved, thus strengthening the bond, theoretically the risk of delinquency would be decreased. Meta-analyses of parenting programs have found that they can reduce problematic child behaviors (Hoeve et al., 2009; Piquero, Jennings, & Diamond, 2016).

School-based programs have also emerged that help children learn self-control. Interestingly, Gottfredson and Hirschi (1990) were quite adamant that the school was not an environment where self-control was likely to be taught for a variety of reasons. Yet meta-analyses have shown that programs in schools can result in substantial increases in youth self-control or reductions in impulsivity (Piquero et al., 2016; Robinson et al., 1999). However, in Piquero et al.'s (2016) study, programs in schools had less of an effect than those in clinics.

Fitting the Facts and Missing Puzzle Pieces

A biopsychosocial approach certainly illuminates much about how social bonds and self-control develop and how they are related to antisocial behavior. Early iterations of social control theories did not really specify why bonds may vary for particular individuals, just that they are important for restraining behavior. Scholarship on evolutionary adaptations may shed light on the intrinsic nature of parental bonds. And biopsychosocial work on "evocative" interactions (e.g., child behavior evoking negative reactions from parents) could explain why some children may not form strong bonds over the life course with others.

Additionally, self-control does not appear to be purely the result of strong parenting practices, as Gottfredson and Hirschi (1990) asserted. In fact, some research, controlling for genetic effects, suggests that parenting may not be all that important for instilling self-control (Wright & Beaver, 2005). In other words, low self-control is a "brain-based disorder" (DeLisi, 2014), according to some scholarship. This does not, however, mean that self-control cannot be enhanced, as studies have shown clearly that programs seeking to improve self-control work.

There remain several missing puzzles with respect to the literature on social control and self-control. It is unclear how practitioners and policy makers can utilize evidence that low self-control and social bonds are, at least in part, based on brain deficits, or heritable. It is possible that screening tools may identify those who could benefit from intensive intervention, however, and that information could be used to guide supervision and treatment. Of course, there is the very real threat of stigmatization and the use of biological data for nefarious purposes, so any collection of such data must be protected to the greatest extent possible.

Second, we do not know how nutrition programming might influence behavior in general or impulsivity/self-control specifically. It seems reasonable to suggest that misbehavior may be the result of—among other things—an inadequate diet or nutritional deficits. This is especially true for fish oil, which has been shown to be related to reduced aggression in experimental research (see Rocque, Welsh, & Raine, 2012). As yet, we do not know enough about this connection or about whether certain nutritional interventions may positively influence self-control.

Third, it seems fair to say that while there is evidence that social bonds in the family are protective for youth behavior, there remains a debate concerning just how much parents matter (Posick & Rocque, 2018). In the end, the final assessment may simply be the unsurprising conclusion that both the body and the environment are important in influencing children's outcomes. Yet for the purposes of interventions, it seems prudent to continue to probe the age-old nature-nurture question with respect to both self-control and social control.

Relatedly, while there are literally dozens of studies showing a negative relationship between marriage and crime, because we cannot simply randomly assign offenders to marriage versus nonmarriage groups, we cannot rule out spuriousness in that relationship. We believe more research should be conducted examining the biopsychosocial changes before and after marriage to better understand how this relationship works.

In the end, there is much evidence that human beings must be restrained in some way, either psychologically or socially, to reduce antisocial behavior. This idea includes several of Braithwaite's "facts" of crime. Traditional sociological approaches have been useful but somewhat limited in advancing our understanding of just why control is necessary and how it operates. A biopsychosocial approach, we submit, goes further and helps illuminate some of the remaining gaps.

7

Stress and Strain in Criminal Behavior

Patrick Sherrill had long been on the radar of those who knew him. He was someone to avoid. He did odd things with animals in his yard, and he snuck around at night, sometimes looking into neighbors' windows with binoculars. He just seemed off, earning the nickname "Crazy Pat." Patrick jumped around from job to job, finding some success in the military. His last job—and the last job for more than a dozen of his coworkers—was at a post office in Edmond, Oklahoma.

Patrick was a part-time letter carrier. But for some reason, he could not quite get the hang of it. A colleague, Vincent Furlong noted, "He just didn't know how to carry mail. He just couldn't get a handle on it" (Dallas Times Herald, 1986, A2). Obviously, Patrick was not a very good mail carrier. He was also, others said, known to open up mail and look through it, a bit of a no-no. Something was off with Patrick, but no one really knew what.

So it should have been no surprise when Patrick found himself, in the late summer of 1986, in a bit of hot water with his supervisors. He was not very talented, and he was not popular with his coworkers. "They chewed him out," Furlong said (Dallas Times Herald, 1986, A2). It looked likely that Patrick was about to be fired. Patrick had long been angry and frustrated with his life, and his anger and frustration boiled over on the morning of August 20. At seven in the morning, Patrick walked into the post office with a mailbag filled with firearms and started shooting. He did not say anything as he went about his work, according to witnesses. When police arrived and tried to negotiate with him, they had no luck. That is because Patrick decided to add his own name to the list of 14 lives he took that morning (Bovsun, 2010). What was wrong with Patrick that made him act the way he did? How could anyone have known he had the potential to commit such heinous crimes?

The general consensus was that the frustration and stress Patrick was facing just built up to the point that he snapped. A person can only take so much. One colleague said, "My suspicion was that he held things in and the pressure built up. There's no logical reasoning to cover what happened other than something snapped" (Dallas Times Herald, 1986, A2). Experts feared that jobs that demand high performance may be too much for some folks, who eventually will snap as well. Thus was coined the phrase "going postal."[1] Others may be completely fine in these high-stress positions.

Clearly many of us face stress and strain throughout life, but almost no one resorts to this type of violence. But can stress and strain help us understand more "everyday" antisocial behavior? When looking for answers about "why they do it," perhaps one reason is that people are sometimes pushed into bad actions. Interestingly, this idea of being pushed into crime is one of the "seminal trio" (Posick & Rocque, 2018) criminological theories. In this chapter, we discuss how perspectives related to strain and stress have long been used to explain antisocial behavior and then show how recent biosocial scholarship elucidates the ways stress or strain work in the body to make antisocial behavior more likely to occur.

Braithwaite's twelfth fact of crime is relevant to a discussion of how stress and strain may lead to antisocial behavior. Braithwaite argued that people at the bottom of the social class order in society and those who experience discrimination are more likely to engage

---

1. Sources used for this narrative: *Dallas Times Herald*, 1986; Bovsun, 2010; *Los Angeles Times*, 1986.

in crime. We covered social class and poverty in depth in Chapter 4. Here we discuss how such social statuses may lead to antisocial behavior by focusing on stress and strain. Stress and strain, looked at this way, are intervening mechanisms linking social factors to crime.

Traditional Theoretical Approaches

Our book on great debates in criminology (Posick & Rocque, 2018) argued that the "seminal trio" of criminological theory includes (1) learning theory, (2) control theory, and (3) strain theory, following other theory typologies (e.g., Hirschi, 1969). Each of these perspectives views crime as emerging from different causal mechanisms, driven by varying images of human nature. For example, control theories, most clearly specified by Ruth Kornhauser and Travis Hirschi (Hirschi, 1969; Kornhauser, 1978), see human beings as inherently self-interested, and since crimes are generally self-serving, their commission does not need explaining. It is obvious why someone would want to take another person's money—it enriches the thief. From that perspective, then, explaining crime is not the problem; the problem, rather, is to explain why most of us refrain from taking another person's money (even if we could get away with it). The answer is that we are "controlled" by social forces such as our conscience and our relationships with others that we do not want to jeopardize.

Learning theory, stemming from Sutherland's differential association theory (Sutherland, 1939), takes a different view of human nature. Implicit in the theory is that humans are neither self-interested nor naturally altruistic. Some have argued that this is a "blank slate" perspective, which suggests that someone's environment will determine his or her orientation. Learning theorists, though, take issue with this notion and do not claim that humans are without any natural tendencies (Akers, 2009). Nonetheless, what is important to understand is that learning theories, at their core, suggest that people engage in acts of crime and deviance if they are taught such behavior and attitudes. Some call this a "pull" perspective—that is, people are pulled into deviance from a neutral starting point.

Strain theory takes the opposite stance on human nature relative to control theories. Strain theories imply that humans are basically good and would treat each other well if left to their own devices. Taking advantage of others, hurting them, or even neglecting them is contrary to human nature. How, then, do we explain the reality that people do take advantage of others and hurt and neglect them? Something must have happened to offenders to push them toward antisocial behavior. When they are frustrated or upset, they may react in antisocial ways. That is the basis for strain theory.

In criminology, strain theory can be traced to Robert Merton's paper, "Social Structure and Anomie," published in the *American Sociological Review* in 1938. Only a small part of the analysis was focused on what we may think of as crime as the larger focus of the paper was on how societal goals can become disjointed from the population's ability to obtain those goals and how people react in that situation. Merton drew from Emile Durkheim's concept of anomie, often translated as "normlessness," which Durkheim used to explain suicide rates. In Merton's version, anomie was the societal state in which there was a disjuncture between its goals and the means to obtain those goals.

An example can help here. In the United States, the American dream is one of the primary societal goals and a reason that others immigrate to the United States. The American dream, roughly translated, is related to financial success: owning a house, car, and so on. To Merton, societal goals must be equally available to those to whom the goals are directed. Since the American dream is universal, it is directed at all segments of society. In addition, there are what Merton called culturally prescribed "means" to attain the goals. These are, in a sense, the rules of the game. To achieve the cultural dream, we are supposed to follow a particular path: go to school, get a stable job, earn money, and, thus, be successful. Yet in some instances, the rules of the game are underemphasized or not equally available to everyone. How, exactly, does one achieve the American dream if they do not have access to the culturally prescribed means? This is confusing. Thus, anomie ensues.

This is the macro, or societal, aspect of Merton's theory. The micro, or individual-level, aspect comes in when he describes how people respond to anomie. In short, he suggested that they feel "strain" and may cope with that strain in one of four ways. First, they may conform to the norm of seeking the goal in the approved ways. Second, they may reject the goal and accept the means—this would be akin to a person continuing to work hard in a dead-end job with no possibility of becoming wealthy. Third, they may reject both the goals and the means, essentially dropping out of society and giving up the dream. Fourth, people may reject both the goals and means and replace them with unique goals and means, such as joining a cult with different—countercultural—goals and unique means to achieve those goals. Finally, and most relevant to our purposes, they may accept the goals (e.g., they still want to get rich) but reject the means. In other words, it becomes about winning at all costs—the rules of the game are not as important. This, in essence, is cheating or criminal conduct. As Merton (1938, p. 675) put it:

> In competitive athletics, when the aim of victory is shorn of its institutional trappings and success in contests becomes construed as "winning the game" rather than "winning through circumscribed modes of activity," a premium is implicitly set upon the use of illegitimate but technically efficient means. The star of the opposing football team is surreptitiously slugged; the wrestler furtively incapacitates his opponent through ingenious but illicit techniques; university alumni covertly subsidize "students" whose talents are largely confined to the athletic field. The emphasis on the goal has so attenuated the satisfactions deriving from sheer participation in the competitive activity that these satisfactions are virtually confined to a successful outcome.

Since Merton's initial statement (and subsequent books), others have offered new or revised versions of strain theory. For example, Albert Cohen (1955), in his *Delinquent Boys*, argued that a great deal of male juvenile delinquency is not an attempt to subvert rules to gain wealth but rather a rejection of conventional norms. It is a symbolic thumbing of the nose at middle-class values, such as private property. This helps us make sense of violence and graffiti. Five years later, Cloward and Ohlin (1960) extended strain theory to take into account the opportunities groups have for coping strategies. For example, opportunities for underground profit (e.g., drug trade) are available in some relatively organized areas. In others, there is no such opportunity, and so violence may be chosen.

General Strain Theory

By far the most intricate revision of strain theory is Robert Agnew's general strain theory (GST). In 1992, Agnew published an article describing a social psychological approach to understanding how stress and strain may lead to antisocial behavior. Importantly, Agnew built upon Merton's foundation, recognizing that failing to achieve one's goals is a key source of strain that can lead to criminal coping. Within this type of strain were three substrains: (1) disjunctions between aspirations and expectations, (2) disjunctions between aspirations and achievements, and (3) disjunctions between fair outcomes and actual outcomes (1992, pp. 51–53). He then added two more types of strain that may be conducive to crime. First, he proposed that presentation of noxious stimuli—which refers to something unpleasant happening, such as bullying—is a crime-conducive type of strain. Second, he included removal of positive stimuli, which refers to when people lose something they valued highly, such as a relationship or a job.

Agnew's version of strain theory is notable not only for its expansion of the types of strain that matter but also in his attention to how those strains affect us psychologically. The link was emotions—strain can make us feel mad or sad. If we are mad and blame our frustrations on others, we are likelier to lash out. Finally, Agnew pointed out that strains that are more consequential, and more recent, last longer and that those that happen in close proximity to other strains may be more criminogenic (Agnew, 2001).

In the nearly 30 years since Agnew published his exposition, numerous tests have supported his claims that strain is linked to crime and delinquency (see, e.g., Agnew & White, 1992; Paternoster & Mazerolle, 1994). The theory has also continually been refined into its current state (Agnew, 2001; Agnew & Brezina, 2019). It has achieved empirical success in linking strain to crime, yet, like other theories, it only explains a small portion of why people commit crime in the first place. One reason is that strain has traditionally been studied and applied in a purely sociological or sociopsychological context. Pulling in biological concepts will usher in a new understanding of social and biological strain and antisocial behavior.

Biopsychosocial Contributions

A biopsychosocial approach to the role of stain on the body and subsequent antisocial behavior is one of the more natural connections in this book. Exposure to noxious stimuli naturally has an impact on the body, and those impacts influence a host of physiological changes in the body. Those changes are sometimes long lasting and potentially affect more than just the individual themselves.

Stress and strain affect the brain in ways that could relate to criminal or antisocial behavior. Vaske and Boisvert (2015) reviewed the ways stress impacts brains. First, there is an effect on what is called the HPA axis. Second, stress can actually affect the structure of the hippocampus, amygdala, and prefrontal cortex. Finally, stress can influence neurotransmitters such as serotonin and dopamine. All these influences have implications for crime. This section explores some of ways strain (both internal/biological strain and external/environmental strain) can impact the body and result in antisocial behavior.

Heart Rate and Brain Activity

Biopsychosocial research has a daunting task ahead of itself. Strain and stress arguably affect all biosystems, including the digestive, cardiovascular, and muscular systems (Healthline, 2021). For example, stress can increase heart rate and is a risk factor for heart disease (Vrijkotte et al., 2000). Anyone who has gone through a particularly stressful situation or period in life can attest to the overwhelming effect it can have on the body—from splitting headaches to an upset stomach, shaking limbs, excessive tiredness, and depression. Certainly, these feelings impact behavior, from short outbursts to frequent irritation and violent reactions. Strains are social, but their impacts are most certainly biosocial.

Biosocial researchers have recently documented how physiological systems are related to antisocial behavior. One frequently documented relationship is between resting heart rate and antisocial (especially violent) behavior. Resting heart rate is one's baseline before any exertion, or stress, is placed upon the body. To measure resting heart rate, a person is often asked to sit for several minutes or lie down in order for the body to rest and not be overly influenced by any specific or particular event that might increase or decrease this rate.

In this line of research, the stress placed on the body is not environmental but biological. The prevailing hypothesis is that those who have low resting heart rates may have higher risk thresholds—they do not react the same way to danger or negative consequences (which often come with antisocial acts) as those with "normal" or high resting heart rates. The wisdom here is that having a low resting heart rate enables people to engage in risky activity without feeling overly anxious by raising their heart rate. Related but distinct is the idea that a low resting heart rate results in an uncomfortable body state where the person feels sluggish and understimulated. Antisocial behavior is exciting and stimulating, which can elevate a low resting heart rate into the "normal" range where people are most comfortable. In this case, those with low resting heart rates seek out opportunities to elevate their heart rate—sometimes through sports and other times through delinquent or criminal activity.

Research consistently finds that low resting heart rate is associated with higher levels of antisocial behavior regardless of sex and type of antisocial behavior (Portnoy & Farrington, 2015). But why is it that low resting heart rate increases criminal activity? Criminologist Jill Portnoy and her collaborators (2014) find that it is the sensation seeking, and not fearlessness, that leads to antisocial behavior. Stress is actually *sought out* by individuals who are hoping that it stimulates their body and results in a comfortable body state.

Interestingly, the effects of chronic environmental stress on heart rate may actually increase resting heart rate (Bedi & Arora, 2007), which suggests stress may reduce antisocial behavior. Indeed, those with higher heart rates are less likely to engage in risky behavior (Farrington, 1997). This would not comport with strain theories, as Agnew argued that prolonged stress was more likely to lead to criminal coping. In sum, the link between heart rate and stress (and stress and heart rate) is complex and may not have clear behavioral implications.

HPA Axis

Of particular importance when considering the link between stress and crime is the effect of stress on the nervous system. The nervous system has several components, but here we are concerned with the parasympathetic and sympathetic nervous systems. The sympathetic nervous system is activated when we feel stress, and it directs our bodies to react in the way the body sees as most "appropriate" in that moment. Hormones, such as adrenaline and cortisol, are one mechanism that helps regulate the body's response. Have you ever been walking late at night and heard a rustling in the bushes? Or perhaps you fell victim to a practical joker who likes to spook you when you are not prepared. You likely felt a rush when the hormones adrenaline and cortisol filled your body and prepared you to act. This is the fight-or-flight response to a short-term stressor (APA.org, 2020). This response is an evolutionary adaptation that helps protect us from danger. It is useful when there is a threat that must be managed. However, this system may be disrupted by frequent and/or severely traumatic negative experiences.

The key physiological process that responds to environmental stressors includes the HPA axis. The HPA axis is directly related to the fight-or-flight response noted earlier. As we wrote previously (Rocque, Posick, & Felix, 2015, p. 90, citations omitted):

> When individuals encounter threatening situations, the body reacts in a manner meant to prolong survival. This "stress response" begins with the hypothalamus, which sends signals to the rest of the body to prepare for action. These physiological reactions include the release of corticotrophin-releasing factor (CRF) and adrenocorticotropic hormone (ACTH), which in turn influence the release of glucocorticoids which facilitate physical reactions to threats. The response helps prepare the body to take action to address the threat; the hormonal activity increases awareness and physical preparedness to engage in "fight or flight."

All these difficult-to-pronounce terms are simply describing the physical feeling you get when you are scared or stressed. However, this response is supposed to be short in duration. Think back to the last time you were scared or very stressed. You probably felt a rush of energy—some call this "nervous energy." It is invigorating but also uses up a lot of your body's resources. Then you probably felt a bit of a crash. This system is not intended to be utilized for long periods of time or repeatedly. If chronic stress occurs, the system can begin to malfunction. There are actually two systems being engaged here. The first, the sympathetic nervous system, is the alert-and-readiness system—that fight-or-flight response. The second, the parasympathetic nervous system, is responsible for returning us to "homeostasis," or our normal state. Both these systems must be properly functioning for us to be healthy. A psychologist has explained it this way: "Think of your sympathetic nervous system and your parasympathetic nervous system like your car's gas and breaks. You need both effectively for your car to run properly" (Cleveland Clinic, 2019). If frequent exposure to stress throws off this system, your body (car) will not operate well.

What happens when you are chronically exposed to stress? Overuse of the fight-or-flight system, as we have suggested, can affect the structure but also the functioning of the brain. Some work shows that too much stress can lead to a quicker activation of the fight-or-flight response than is healthy (Shonkoff & Phillips, 2000). What this means is that lower-risk situations may be viewed as more threatening than they are. Threats are seen everywhere. Criminological research views the misinterpretation of risk or threats as a predictor of violence (Bernard, 1990). Another response may be that people become less sensitive to stress and therefore fail to react when they should. Walsh and Yun (2014) refer to these two adaptations as hyper- and hypocortisolism, respectively. Rocque, Posick, and Felix's (2015) proposed model of environmental effects on the body via the HPA axis is shown in Figure 7.1.

Brain Structure and Function

When people study the brain, they often differentiate between structure and function. Structure refers to the physical makeup of the brain (e.g., the amount of gray and white matter) while function refers to the processes that are carried out in the brain (e.g., neurotransmission). We now have the technology to monitor both in living humans. Functional magnetic resonance imaging (fMRI) scans are used to examine how brains are functioning by looking at blood flow. Other types of technologies, such as positron emission topography (PET)

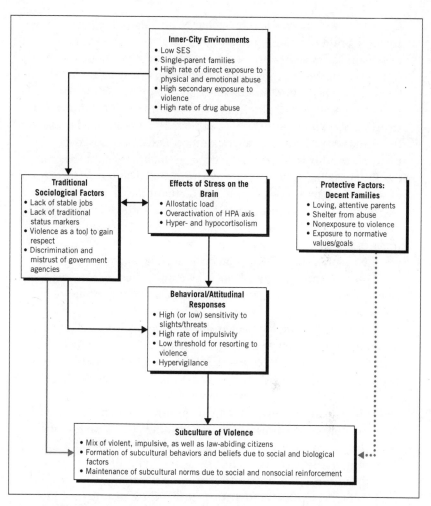

Figure 7.1. A Biopsychosocial Model of Environmental Effects of Stress on the Body and Behavior
(*Source*: A version of this figure was published in Rocque, Posick, & Felix, 2015. Image used with permission from Taylor & Francis.)

scans and near-infrared spectroscopy (NIRS), also use blood flow to examine brain functioning (Devlin, 2021). Brain structure is examined using technologies such as MRI and computerized tomography (CT) scans. CT scans create numerous images or slices of the brain that are then assembled to get a fuller picture of brain structure.

Research suggests that stress can affect both the functioning and structure of the brain. For example, early stress has been found to negatively impact the prefrontal cortex, hippocampus, and amygdala. The prefrontal cortex is the executive decision-making area of the brain (McEwen, 2000; McEwen, Nasca, & Gray, 2016). Damage to this area of the brain may reduce self-control and the ability to regulate emotions. The hippocampus relates to memory and, when damaged, may result in faulty memory. Victims of crime often have stress that impacts their ability to recall their victimization experience, reducing the chances that they will be believed. The amygdala regulates emotion and impulse control, and any damage here results in poor emotion regulation. Clearly, each of these areas is important for behavioral control.

Additionally, work has shown that early stress from child abuse or domestic violence has a negative relationship with adult intelligence (Koenen et al., 2003; Perez & Widom, 1994). This likely sets children up for failure, as intelligence is linked to myriad positive life outcomes (Ritchie, 2015). Other work has shown that early life stress generally impairs cognitive development, which is important for all facets of interpreting information and forming behavioral responses that are appropriate in a given situation (Petchtel & Pizzagalli, 2011).

Finally, research has shown that stress and strain affect neurotransmitters and hormones, such as serotonin and dopamine (Kumar et al., 2013; Mahar et al., 2014; Mora et al., 2012). These neurotransmitters are all implicated in antisocial behavior. For example, low serotonin and high dopamine levels have been found to be linked to crime (Rafter, Posick, & Rocque, 2016). High levels of dopamine—the neurotransmitter that is activated when we experience positive events—can lead to "an obsessive search for rewards" (Rafter et al., 2016, p. 268). Researchers have found this imbalance in psychopathic individuals (Buckholtz et al., 2010). Low levels of serotonin are related to mental illnesses such as depression and anxiety (Healthline.com, 2020), which is why these disorders are often treated with selective serotonin reuptake inhibitors (SSRIs). Some work has shown that depression is associated with antisocial behavior (Ozkan, Rocque, & Posick, 2019).

Adverse Childhood Experiences

One relatively recent focus in criminology that relates to stress and strain are what have become known as adverse childhood experiences. Initially, ACEs were examined in medical and health-care settings. Researchers found that early trauma led to significant medical problems later in life (e.g., obesity, smoking, heart disease) (Felitti et al., 1998). The story of how Dr. Vincent Felitti stumbled upon ACEs is illuminating and is related to our efforts in this book. In the 1980s, Felitti was running a clinic to help people lose weight. He quickly discovered that many patients were dropping out of the study with no apparent cause; in fact, many of the dropouts had successfully lost a lot of weight! So he left the lab and began talking to people. He found out that a large proportion had been sexually abused as kids or had suffered some other kind of trauma. The obesity was caused by their attempts to cope with their anxiety. It was not the obesity that was the problem, it was early trauma—that was what needed to be addressed (Stevens, 2012) For Felitti, it was going beyond the lab and engaging with people to fully understand the problem at hand—something all scientists would be wise to do!

If ACEs are linked to poor health outcomes, might they also be linked to later antisocial behavior? After all, poor health behaviors are a coping mechanism for trauma, as might be antisocial behavior. Criminologists, in line with the claims of strain theory, have consistently found that ACEs are related to later offending (Baglivio et al., 2015; Craig et al., 2017; Fox et al., 2015). In fact, early exposure to all types of trauma and victimization have been associated with later antisocial behavior. In fact, the overlap of early victimization and later antisocial behavior is one of the most supported in the criminological research (Posick, 2013). Figure 7.2 illustrates the ways in which ACEs may affect a variety of outcomes for individuals, including health and behavior.

Most research in criminology has argued that stress and strain influence behavior because they are psychological coping mechanisms. For example, Agnew (2001) argued that some types of strain provide

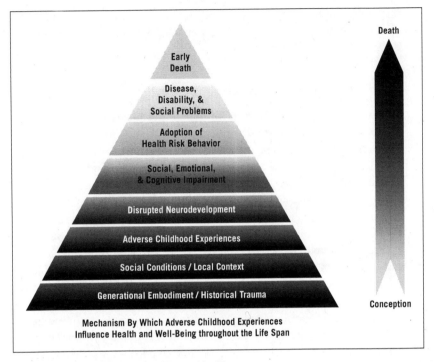

Figure 7.2. Influence of ACEs on Health
(*Source*: Centers for Disease Control and Prevention.)

rationales for criminal coping. He draws on Anderson's (2000) work on inner-city street codes to show that the types of strains young African American males experience can only be alleviated via extralegal means (e.g., violence). Growing up in areas that are plagued by disadvantage, poverty, discrimination, and few opportunities for individual and collective growth puts extreme strain on residents. As mentioned in Chapter 4, one coping mechanism that may alleviate strain and gain essential resources to at least continue living is criminal behavior. There is evidence that this indeed may be the case (Brezina, 1996).

At the same time, there are so many types of strain and so many potential factors that affect whether strain leads to crime that GST has become quite complex, incorporating social bonds, self-control, and personality traits (Agnew, 2006). Despite dozens and dozens of studies on the topic, the role of the body is relatively underemphasized in criminological work on stress and strain (Vaske & Boisvert, 2015). This is unfortunate given the explosion in research demonstrating that physiological and neurological factors link stress and behavior.

Integrating Biological Stress Response into Criminological Theory

There has been a tremendous amount of research of late on "toxic" stress and childhood outcomes (Bucci et al., 2016). Early childhood adverse experiences have severe health consequences. But what about behavior? One way to integrate this work on toxic stress and the body with antisocial behavior is to look at theories of urban areas and crime (also covered in Chapter 4). Well-known subcultural theories posit that certain areas have norms that are favorable to criminal behavior. It may be that violence is encouraged, or not specifically discouraged, in certain neighborhoods and communities. Anderson's "code of the street" theory is instructive here. Anderson (2000) was trying to explain the high rates of violence among African American men in urban areas. He argued that structural disadvantage and a lack of trust in the criminal justice system combine to create a situation where violence is used to gain status as well as to protect oneself from others. Wolfgang and Feracutti (1967) provided an early version of a subcultural theory to explain why seemingly innocuous encounters may prove deadly. In short, subcultural theories suggest that particular geographic locations have certain features that give rise to subcultures—norms and values, rules for behavior, and so forth—that are conducive to violence.

In both Anderson's and Wolfgang and Feracutti's versions, for those not living in the area, it may be difficult to understand why small insults or fights quickly become deadly. The subcultural approach is that norms emerged to support the quick resort to violence for protection but also as a way to gain status. Additionally, Anderson, in particular, delineated between "street" and "decent" folks. That is, not everyone buys into the code of the street that is so conducive to deadly violence.

Our argument is that chronic exposure to stress may help explain why violence is resorted to more often and more quickly in certain areas (where subcultures are said to exist) than others. In the revised version of the subculture theory, we attempt to solve two problems with these approaches. First, there is little attention paid to how or why subcultures form. Anderson argued that the shift to a service economy left many urban areas in the lurch, removing jobs and sources of stable income. This is certainly documented, and it devastated urban areas. However, why did norms approving or at least not disapproving of violence as a response to threats emerge? This is not clear. In fact, as we pointed out (Rocque, Posick, & Felix, 2015b, p. 89), violence is seen as protective but often actually increases the risk of being attacked. Ultimately, it is a false sense of protection. The biosocial perspective provides an answer to this conundrum. Poverty, ACEs, and other strains likely increased tremendously during this period. To the extent that these strains make people more likely to see threats and react with violence because of neurological effects, this could explain the origin of a subculture of violence.

Second, if everyone who lives in an area is exposed to the subculture, why are some people law abiding? Anderson (2000) explained this via the effects of familial socialization—some families are committed to middle-class values. These are the "decent" folks as opposed to the "street" folks who buy into the subculture. How do these "decent" folks insulate themselves, though, and how do subcultural values not permeate? The biosocial perspective again provides an answer. Not everyone is equally exposed to violence, poverty, lack of social protection, and other risk and protective factors. To those folks, negative effects of stress on the brain are likely lessened due to less exposure. This is a brief example of one way biosocial work can help supplement existing powerful theories.

General strain theory is one of the more comprehensive theories of antisocial behavior. As described prior, it was initially developed to extend Merton's strain theory by incorporating a vast literature on psychological reactions to stress. Of course, much of these psychological reactions are linked to biological mechanisms, but biological research has thus far not generally been incorporated directly into the theory. The biosocial mechanisms reviewed in this chapter help explain why chronic strain and strains long in duration are more likely to lead to criminal coping, as Agnew has argued. Chronic strain is related to overactivation of the fight-or-flight response system and can lead to becoming hyperresponsive to stress. In addition, as we have shown, stress can impair the prefrontal cortex—the part of the brain used for decision-making. Criminal coping may reduce strain, but it is generally thought to be a response with negative consequences (Gottfredson & Hirschi, 1990). Impairment of any kind in the brain's structure—or the way the brain functions—that harms one's ability to make sound decisions may be one reason some choose criminal coping. However, Agnew has argued that the link between strain and crime is negative emotions. That is, strain may lead to anger or depression, which then lead to antisocial behavior. As mentioned prior, research has shown that strain may affect the amygdala and the neurotransmitters that regulate emotions. Thus, at least one of Agnew's psychological links has a strong biological basis.

Another theory that is relevant to this discussion is self-control theory. In 1990, Michael Gottfredson and Travis Hirschi published the classic *General Theory of Crime*, which outlined self-control as the primary cause of all crimes and "analogous" acts. Self-control, they argued, is the ability to restrain impulses and think about the consequences, and the impact on others, of behavioral choices. Self-control, the authors posited, is learned early on in life, with the help of parents. If parents or caretakers do not teach children that deviance is wrong, the children will not develop high levels of self-control and will be prone to behavior with short-term benefits but long-term negative consequences throughout their lives.

The notion that parental socialization is responsible for instilling self-control, however, has come under increased scrutiny in the literature. It does not appear that parenting variation accounts for variation in self-control across people or that parenting affects delinquency through self-control (Burt, Simons, & Simons, 2006; Hay, 2001). Other researchers have noted that self-control is largely confined to the brain, particularly to the prefrontal cortex. As DeLisi noted, "self-control is a brain-based disorder" (2015, p. 173). While some of the variation in self-control is likely genetic (Beaver et al., 2009), brain injuries may also affect self-control (Isacescu & Dankert, 2016), as the famous Phineas Gage case illustrates (DeLisi, 2015). And, as noted, chronic stress affects the prefrontal cortex, thus likely affecting self-control. Some research has supported the notion that stress reduces self-control (Duckworth, Kim, & Tsukayama, 2013). Thus, biological research can help make sense of another prominent criminological theory. One of the stickier points for self-control theory is why people vary in their levels of impulse control. Stress and strain's effects on the brain go a long way toward helping us better understand this variation.

Incorporating the Body into Stress and Criminological Policy

Incorporating the body, particularly the brain, into work examining stress and crime opens up new avenues for policy and practice. For example, exposure therapy has been used to good effect to help individuals affected with PTSD (Rothbaum & Schwartz, 2002). Exposure therapy intends to have individuals directly confront the trauma that has harmed them so that they are better able to deal with the triggers. Could a variant of exposure therapy allow individuals who are dealing with chronic stress also avoid antisocial coping? This remains to be seen, but it is not unreasonable to assume so. Additionally, cognitive behavioral therapy, one of the more effective forms of treatment for criminal behavior (Lipsey, Landenberger, & Wilson, 2007), may be used to help reduce the negative consequences of stress and strain.

With respect to ACEs, health-care providers have developed treatment programs to help mitigate long-term effects. Some programs work to give parents the tools needed to buffer their children from trauma (Baker, 2016). In addition, there are several programs that have been proven effective in reducing antisocial behavior in youth. For example, the Blueprints for Healthy Youth Development project, housed at the University of Colorado, includes lists of programs that have been demonstrated to reduce delinquency. Some are model programs, which means they include at least two randomized trials showing effectiveness lasting at least a year, and others are model plus programs, which go further, including independent evaluation (independent from the program developers). Promising programs are those that indicate effectiveness but have not yet had two randomized trials. There are a few promising programs within the Blueprints list that focus on trauma. The Child First program is described as follows:

> A two-generation home visitation program which works to heal and protect young children and their families from the devastating effects of chronic stress and trauma. It provides psycho-therapeutic services and intensive care coordination,

while building adult reflective and executive capacity, to prevent or diminish serious emotional disturbance, developmental and learning disabilities, and abuse and neglect among young children.[2]

We mentioned CBT as a treatment approach that may help with the effects of strain. CBT is a form of therapy that seeks to link problematic cognitions or thoughts to consequent behavior. This way, the link between the two can be broken. In short, CBT helps people think carefully about decisions and manage their behavior. Yet most scholarship on CBT seems to overlook the neurological connections to experiences, cognitions, and behavior. One paramount paper explored just these connections. Jamie Vaske and her colleagues (2011) argued that CBT may work to reduce offending because of its effects on brain functioning.

Controlling the nonimmediate responses to stress, however, may generally involve more cognitive-based coping strategies, such as reappraisal and thought suppression. Reappraisal occurs when individuals reframe the stressful event in a less negative perspective or when they objectify the stressful event to mitigate any harm the event may cause. Thought suppression occurs when individuals try to avoid thinking a particular thought or when they consciously try to stop ruminating over a problem. These processes, Vaske et al. demonstrated, are linked to several areas of the brain. To the extent that CBT helps coping with stress, then, it also likely affects neural processes. Other mechanisms of CBT, such as improving problem-solving skills, are also relevant to how people deal with stress and, as Vaske and colleagues show, are linked to the brain.

Finally, knowledge about the brain, stress, and behavioral response could inform police and criminal justice decision-making. The bulk of this discussion is covered in the next chapter. To set the stage, encounters with criminal justice officials, including police, prosecutors, judges, corrections officers, and the like, are extremely stressful—especially for adolescents. We often think of "delinquents" and "criminals" as acting aggressively or evasively and resisting or not cooperating with the criminal justice system and its actors. This may be due to

---

2. See https://www.blueprintsprograms.org/programs/715999999/child-first/.

a culture of distrust, but it also has to do with the way the body reacts when in a stressful situation. Training and understanding are absolutely necessary when criminal justice actors interact with potential offenders and victims who come into contact with the system.

Fitting the Facts and Missing Puzzle Pieces

It is clear that stress and strain have a major role to play in criminal behavior. Merton, Agnew, and others have done the field a great service by showing how strain leads to situations in which criminal coping may occur. Agnew drew on a vast psychological literature to make the connection among strain, negative emotion, and crime. In addition, strain may be an intervening mechanism between disadvantage (discussed in Chapter 4) and criminal behavior. Thus, stress is relevant for Braithwaite's twelfth fact. However, as this chapter has shown, there is a missing biological element to much of this work. Stress and strain affect the body in a multitude of ways. While much of this chapter focused on the physiological and neurological consequences of strain, relating that work to criminological theory and policy interventions, a lot remains unknown. For example, stress is known to have numerous physiological effects that have different behavioral outcomes. We examined some of the effects on the heart, but the connection among stress, the heart, and crime is not well understood. Other biological effects should be considered as well. What exactly leads to hyper- and hypocortisolism, and how does each lead to certain antisocial behaviors? Further, how do genetic predispositions for factors like brain structure and function interact with environmental factors to influence behavior? With advances in both methodologies and technologies, these questions may be answered in the near future.

All the factors that place stress on the body, how they change the body, and which ones are most potent have yet to be fully uncovered and understood. For instance, new research has begun to explore the role (or lack thereof) of food insecurity (Jackson & Vaughn, 2017), environmental toxins (Martin & Wolfe, 2020), and ACEs (Connolly, 2020) on a host of negative life outcomes and overall well-being. Yet exactly how these stressors impact the brain and body is currently being investigated.

Along with stress risk factors, resiliency factors are also increasingly being investigated by researchers. These resiliency factors reduce the impact of exposure to stress and harm and assist in recovery. Some resiliency factors are biological. Caspi and collaborators (2002) found that having a polymorphism in an MAOA gene, which results in heightened levels of activity, insulated people against later antisocial behavior even in the presence of the stress brought on by abuse. Other psychosocial factors also insulate against negative life outcomes in the presence of stress, including supportive friends and family and strong bonds to school and work. Having a positive life outlook in general can increase reliance and shorten recovery time after stress and trauma (Grych, Hamby, & Banyard, 2015).

A somewhat controversial area is the role of stress and trauma on altering the expression of genes. Epigenetics refers to the altering of the transcription of genes but not the underlying genetic code itself. Epigenetics is a fairly recent area of study that has many proponents and popular support but also many detractors, who question the accuracy of the research base on epigenetics and its utility above and beyond genetics.

As two of us have argued, epigenetics is indeed new, and many aspects—especially the intergenerational transmission of stress—require more studies and replication to say with a high level of certainty how accurate the idea really is (Rocque & Posick, 2017). However, the idea has some promise when considering recent epigenetic research. Epigenetic changes have been found in individuals who have experienced stress in the past. Bullying research specifically has found epigenetic changes in individuals who were exposed to peer abuse (Mulder et al., 2020). What epigenetics can offer above and beyond genetics research and how it may inform prevention and intervention efforts will be seen in upcoming years.

As mentioned in Chapter 3, there is also emerging evidence that these epigenetic changes may be transmitted across generations. The children and grandchildren of survivors of famine (Zimmet et al., 2018), concentration camps (Yehuda et al., 2016), and the 9/11 terrorist attacks (Yehuda et al., 2009) are affected by these incidents. Of course, many more studies are needed, and over longer periods of time, to confirm these findings. Regardless, to date, there is consistent empirical evidence that stress has widespread and lasting impacts on both individuals and families.

8

Criminal Justice and Law in Criminal Behavior and Crime Rates

I n the late 1960s and early 1970s, the relationship between the criminal justice system and communities was under fire. Riots and protests in the name of civil rights ripped through cities, enflaming hostilities between the police and citizens. For example, in the Watts area of Los Angeles, the killing of an African American during a traffic stop led to riots in August of 1965 in which 34 people died. Other riots followed that were sparked by racial incidents, including the assassination of Dr. Martin Luther King Jr.

During the same time, confidence in government itself was plummeting, including trust in the ability of the state to reform those involved in criminal careers (Cullen, 2013). This idea came to a head in the mid-1970s, when the lack of confidence in the government coincided with research that questioned the ability of the prison system to rehabilitate. The famous *Martinson Report* cast considerable doubt about the effectiveness of rehabilitation programs that existed. Robert Martinson, in an essay about the report, famously declared that "with few and isolated exceptions, the rehabilitative efforts that have been reported so far have had no appreciable effect on recidivism" (Martinson, 1974, p. 25).

What do crises in policing and offender rehabilitation have to do with biosocial criminology? Quite a bit, it turns out. The ways people interact with the police, handle stress, and react to those interactions are consequential for policing outcomes and later behavior. Additionally, since Martinson's words were written, much has been discovered about what works to reduce offending among those convicted of crimes. At the same time, is it unclear how treatment programs work and for whom they work best. Recently, research is revealing that genetics can tell us about why certain people may be more susceptible to treatment than others. In this chapter, we review work on police/citizen interactions and justice and the effectiveness of the criminal justice system, with an emphasis on corrections. This chapter is organized differently than previous chapters to facilitate the discussion of traditional and biopsychosocial perspectives in various components in the criminal justice system. We cover traditional, biopsychosocial, and policy implications in policing and then move on to corrections before discussing remaining gaps in knowledge on these topics.

The criminal justice system and crime rates are related to two of Braithwaite's facts. First, in fact eleven, Braithwaite wrote that people who believe in the validity of the law are more likely to comply. The idea that the police need legitimacy has gained much traction in criminology since Braithwaite's book was published. Recent advances in effective correctional treatment may influence the legitimacy of the system but also relate to Braithwaite's thirteenth fact, which focused on crime rates. When Braithwaite's book was written, crime had been increasing generally since the end of World War II, but shortly thereafter, there began a precipitous crime decline that has yet to be explained fully. Thus, we add to Braithwaite's "fact" regarding increasing crime rates after World War II the "fact" of the crime decline since the early 1990s. Our approach is to show how traditional perspectives are helpful but not complete and that biological and psychological perspectives can help fill the gaps.

Police/Community Relations and Traditional Criminology

It has long been thought that public safety and policing are intimately intertwined. The more police in an area, the logic has often gone, the less crime. This seems obvious from a pure deterrence perspective. Anyone who has slammed on the brakes upon viewing a police car in the distance can understand the logic. Yet in the 1970s, policing had become overwhelmingly formal and less communal. Certain research (e.g., Kelling et al., 1974) showed that, in actuality, increasing random patrols did not actually affect levels of crime. For a time, it seemed that police were, in contrast to popular opinion and common sense, not able to appreciably affect crime rates (see Gottfredson & Hirschi, 1990).

Around this time, scholars began to substantively focus on encounters with law enforcement rather than simply the outcome (arrest/no arrest) (see Reiss, 1971 for an earlier examination). The idea of procedural justice—the way citizens felt they had been treated and whether they had been respected by law enforcement officers—was examined most notably by Tom Tyler. In his book *Why People Obey*, first published in 1990, Tyler described the idea of police legitimacy, which is the belief in the moral validity of the police. This form of authority was introduced by sociologist Max Weber in his analysis of various governmental types of power. When a leader has "authority," that means the public accepts the legitimacy of his or her power. Importantly, legitimacy of the police, Tyler found, is associated with greater compliance. In other words, when the public view the police as legitimate—that they deserve the power they have—crime is reduced. Procedural justice is associated with legitimacy such that when people feel fairly treated, they are more likely to trust law enforcement (Wolfe et al., 2016). Systematic reviews have indicated that police legitimacy is associated with increased rates of compliance, as well (Mazerolle et al., 2013). Overall, when trust is established, police are relied upon to help control crime, and coproduction of crime control between the police and the community can be realized.

The primary explanation for the effects of procedural justice and legitimacy has to date been psychological and sociological. Relying on coercion is not effective because people can always escape the supervision of the police. Voluntary compliance and cooperation are ideal, then, which indicates a feeling of "responsibility" on the part of the public. As Tyler (2004, p. 87) put it, "People, in other words, feel responsible for following the directives of legitimate authorities." The idea of compliance with norms being engendered through socialization, however, can be traced to the work of sociologists Talcott Parsons and Emile Durkheim. Both of these authors, considered "structural functionalists," suggested that social order is possible because citizens are socialized to accept norms and values. That is, they obey not because they are forced to, or because they see the utility of doing so, but because they think it is the appropriate way to behave. In effective socialization, then, norms are internalized and subconsciously affect the way we think and act. This is similar to the control perspective discussed in Chapter 6.

Biopsychosocial Criminology and Interactions with Police

While positive police-community relations are seen by most to be important for crime control, establishing these relationships is easier said than done. As of this writing, these relationships are severely threatened with calls to "defund" and abolish the police. Shootings and murders have increased in areas with the greatest conflict between police and the community.

Reports of police officers shooting and killing people of color are not new, as the introduction to this chapter makes clear. A series of police killing of minorities has set the stage for widespread distrust of policing and the criminal justice system as a whole. The Walter Scott shooting exemplifies these interactions. On April 4, 2015, Officer Michael Slager pulled over Walter Scott for a busted taillight. At first, the stop was routine. Officer Slager approached Scott's car, and they exchanged the necessary information. As Slager returned to his vehicle, Scott opened his door and took off on foot. After an altercation, Scott separated himself from Officer Slager by about 15 to 20 feet.

At this point, Officer Slager unholstered his service weapon and shot eight rounds. He hit Scott five times: once on his ear, once on his buttocks, and three on his back. One of the shots in the back struck Scott's lung and heart. He was pronounced dead at the scene. Another incident involving 25-year-old Freddie Gray is eerily similar. Gray also fled from police although he had not done anything wrong. He was chased down and caught. He later died in police custody.

A scroll through any comment section of the Scott and Gray stories reveals several individuals questioning these two men's actions. Why would they run from the police? If they were not doing anything wrong, why did they try to escape the stop? It was revealed that

Scott had a warrant out for his arrest regarding missed child support payments. But other than this fairly minor issue, Scott had no serious charges against him. Gray had no issues with the criminal justice system. Their flights seemed purely irrational.

However, their flights were not irrational. In times of overwhelming stress (such as being stopped by the police and fearing apprehension or physical harm), the body has a few choices it can make: it can freeze, fight, or flee. In the case of these two men, the response was to flee, probably driven by fear of the police. One could point to the socialization factor—a long-standing distrust of police due to unfair treatment and overpolicing. This surely has an impact on individuals. So, too, does the totality of stress brought on by poverty, abuse, exposure to violence and environmental toxins, and discrimination. In cases like those involving Scott and Gray, changes in the hormone cortisol might be chiefly responsible for their actions when confronted with the police. This is discussed at length in this chapter, which largely extends much of what was discussed in Chapter 7 and other previous chapters.

Being treated fairly and with respect is important for trust and legitimacy. Clearly, then, being treated poorly, unfairly, or even violently would have the opposite effect. Research has long shown that there are severe racial splits in terms of how the public views the police, with nonwhites having far less trust (Posick et al., 2013). The history of policing and race is rife with injustice and oppression, from the days of the slave patrol to the current examples of police brutality dominating the news cycle. Some have argued that police have been historically used as a tool of racial control (see Alexander, 2010) in the United States. Thus, it is no surprise that attitudes toward police are less positive for nonwhites. But nonwhites' negative interactions with the police have not simply resulted in colder attitudes and less trust toward the police. Several times throughout history, anger and mistrust, often sparked by a particular interaction, have boiled over into unrest and outright conflict.

Black and African Americans often report being discriminated against by the criminal justice system and by law enforcement officers in particular. Perceived discrimination is known to have persistent and widespread physiological impacts on people. A large-scale review of the relationship between perceived discrimination and cardiovascular disease (CVD) revealed that discrimination places stress on the cardiovascular system, especially through the HPA axis, resulting in higher rates of CVD among African Americans (Lockwood et al., 2018).

Allostatic load, or the "negative effects of prolonged stress" (Rocque et al., 2015b, p. 85; see McEwen, 1998) also increases the risk of dysregulation in the body. Feelings of chronic discrimination are related to dysregulation in various physiological system functionings, including cardiovascular regulation, lipid and glucose functioning, inflammation reaction, as well as sympathetic nervous system, parasympathetic nervous system, and the hypothalamic pituitary adrenal axis (Ong, Williams, Nwizu, & Gruenewald, 2017). Changes in these systems can lead to a host of serious, long-term negative health conditions that disproportionately impact black and African Americans.

Experiencing discrimination can lead to changes in behavior, including a higher risk of antisocial and aggressive behavior. Across several samples, individuals who reported discrimination were more likely to be neurotic and less likely to be trusting, organized, and disciplined (Sutin, Stephan, & Terracciano, 2016). Perceived discrimination increased antisocial behavior in two samples of Puerto Rican youth both in the United States and in Puerto Rico (Rivera et al., 2011).

Overt racism and/or discrimination does not even need to be part of an encounter with police to have an effect. Youth who encounter the police experience shifts in sleep patterns—for the worse. They get less sleep, and the quality of that sleep is poorer than those who do not encounter the police. The more intrusive the encounter, the worse off the individual is after the contact (Jackson et al., 2019).

The main point of this section is that interactions with law enforcement and the criminal justice system matter. Every encounter can have negative effects on people. That is not to say we should avoid using police to address problems in society, but we should be judicious when we do. Any contact with the criminal justice system is stressful and can have long-term impacts on people and their bodies. These contacts also reduce trust in law enforcement and belief that the police are there to be helpers. In turn, this increases crime and, ultimately, crime rates.

Correctional Treatment and
Traditional Criminology

The United States is, for better or worse, the birthplace of the modern prison. Prior to the widespread use of prisons as punishment, of course, there were cells in which people might be kept while awaiting trials (in the United Kingdom, these were called gaols), and wrongdoers could be banished to dungeons. But for the most part, the notion that the standard sanction for breaking the law would be varying periods of time locked up in a cell is relatively new. The United States' experiment with incarceration was so groundbreaking, in fact, that representatives from France toured the nation's major prisons to report back to their country on the innovation (de Beaumont & de Tocqueville, [1833] 2018).

The initial intention of prisons as a form of social control was not pure punishment, however. The term "penitentiary" was used for a reason; it implied that the goal of prisons was at least partly to invoke change in the individual. Specifically, incarcerated persons were to be kept in isolation, given only a Bible, and made to think about what they had done until they were resolved to change. In other words, the whole idea was for offenders to "give penance." Thus, prisons were meant to be therapeutic—to rehabilitate individuals who had traversed the wrong side of the tracks. However, as Stohr, Walsh, and Hemmens (2013) show, that goal was often displaced in favor of security needs and warehousing.

By the mid-1900s, prisons had come to include programs meant to provide those incarcerated with the skills and education thought to be associated with decreased criminal conduct. Rehabilitation was the primary focus of corrections. As Cullen (2013, p. 312) has pointed out, "The very use of the term 'corrections'—whether in reference to correctional institutions or to community corrections—signaled the ideological dominance of the rehabilitative ideal."

This all changed in the 1970s, however, when a variety of factors combined to reduce public trust in government and institutions meant to help people. The Vietnam War had engendered animosity toward the government in general. With respect to prisons, specifically, events such as the Attica prison riot of 1971 served to shift distrust from foreign-based affairs to the system of punishments at home. Attica, a revolt of prisoners against horrible conditions that start-ed somewhat accidentally, ended with police and corrections officers in essence waging war on the rioters, killing 39 on the fourth day of the uprising (Gopnick, 2016).

Attica led to many changes—some good, some not so good (Chin-lund, 2011). Gopnick (2016) argues that the fear inspired by Attica led, in part, to greater restrictions on prisoners and eventually to mass incarceration—a move toward warehousing individuals rather than trying to help them. Rehabilitation programs, meant to help people, came under fire for additional reasons. In the mid-1970s, a report showed that there was little if any evidence that treatment pro-grams reduced recidivism (Martinson, 1974). This study, of more than 200 correctional treatment programs, seemed to be the nail in the re-habilitation coffin.

It appeared, then, that the idea that prisons could help their con-stituents was to be abandoned. However, not long after the *Martinson Report*, researchers began to try to rescue, or "reaffirm," rehabilita-tion (Cullen & Gilbert, 1982). The *Martinson Report* became known as the "nothing works" study. Soon, a "what works" movement would emerge in criminology, and it showed demonstrably that some types of programs *do* work to reduce recidivism and improve attitudes. Today, much is known about treatment approaches, including the types that seem most beneficial for particular groups. There are websites devoted to information on what works, such as Blueprints for Healthy Youth Development, the Office of Juvenile Justice and Delinquency Preven-tion (OJJDP)'s Model Program Guide, and the National Institute of Justice's Crime Solutions. Today, rehabilitation is one of the top prefer-ences among the American public compared to more harsh penalties (Baker et al., 2015), and Americans currently do not believe prisons reduce crime because they do not offer treatment (Clarke, 2018). Thus, the legitimacy of rehabilitation appears to be relatively high, which, as Braithwaite (1989) argued, is important for effectiveness.

Programs that appear to be particularly effective include family-based therapy for juveniles and cognitive behavioral therapy ap-proaches, the latter of which seeks to break the connection between antisocial thoughts and subsequent behavior. Reviews of CBT have indicated that it is effective in reducing later antisocial behavior (Lipsey & Landenberger, 2007). However, the mechanisms by which treatment works (or does not work) are often unclear. The focus, for much of the "what works" era, has been to discover what works, not how they work.

Biopsychosocial Criminology and How Correctional Treatment Gets Under the Skin

At the beginning of the "what works" movement, the push to empirically demonstrate that treatment can and does work to reduce recidivism was led by a group of Canadian psychologists. In the late 1980s, they argued that criminology had ignored psychology—specifically, personality traits—in favor of sociology, going so far as to suggest the field engaged in "knowledge destruction" (Andrews & Wormith, 1989). These scholars then went on to show that treatment programs that followed certain principles were effective in reducing recidivism (Andrews et al., 1990). Soon, the "psychology of criminal conduct," a theoretical perspective focusing on major risk factors for crime, was born (Andrews & Bonta, 1998); this perspective developed into an approach to understanding the factors that help correctional programs become more effective. The risk-need-responsivity (RNR) approach is now one of the more well-known frameworks for developing and evaluating correctional programs.

The RNR approach is somewhat simplistic, suggesting that programs should focus on criminogenic risk factors, criminogenic needs/deficits, and responsivity or learning styles. However, the key is that the risk factors must be empirically grounded and known to be related to antisocial behavior. The factors identified include antisocial peers, antisocial attitudes, and substance use/abuse. The RNR framework also includes a popular risk- and needs-assessment tool used by correctional departments across North America called the Level of Service Inventory-Revised (with a similar tool developed for youth called the Level of Service, Case Management Inventory).

The correctional revolution has taken place alongside a boom in knowledge on how to prevent crime and delinquency in the first place. The "what works" movement was not just about reducing recidivism but also preventing crime in childhood and adolescence. The Blueprints for Healthy Youth Development clearinghouse, for example, provides information on programs that have been demonstrated effective using rigorous methods. Model programs are those that have undergone at least two randomized trials or one randomized trial and one quasi-experimental study and a long-term (at least a year) follow-up. Model plus programs include an "independent" evaluation by scholars other than the program developers. Examples of model plus programs are Functional Family Therapy (FFT) and Multisystemic Therapy (MST), which use slightly different frameworks for working with at-risk youth and their social environments to improve behavior. These programs focus on promoting "healthy development," as the Blueprints clearinghouse name suggests.

It is safe to say that much is known about why certain crime prevention and correctional approaches work or do not work to reduce antisocial behavior. At the same time, much is unknown, particularly on the biological end of the spectrum. Recent work has suggested that biosocial criminology may help fill gaps in our understanding of how and why certain approaches are effective. In a series of works, one of us has argued that effective crime prevention and rehabilitation programs work in part because they address biological risk factors such as intelligence, cognitive development, and physical health (Rocque, Welsh, & Raine, 2012). For example, parenting programs often seek to address cognitive deficits. Other approaches are more clearly biologically focused, such as the use of fish oil to reduce aggression.

Why does CBT work? CBT is specifically about identifying links between antisocial thoughts and subsequent antisocial behavior. Thus, it is primarily thought to work via psychological mechanisms. However, Jamie Vaske and her colleagues (2011) made a fascinating case for understanding how CBT may work via neurological mechanisms. They first reviewed what CBT programs focus on improving, such as problem-solving skills. Then they discussed the neurological basis for these skills, suggesting that CBT may "work" in large part by changing the functioning of important brain regions such as the prefrontal cortex, orbitofrontal cortex, cingulate cortex, and insula. There is some research that has shown CBT does improve brain functioning, supporting Vaske and colleagues' arguments.

Later, Vaske (2017) expanded the discussion of how biosocial criminology can help explicate the mechanisms through which treatment works by focusing on stress- and regulation-response systems. Parenting programs, she argues, may have important effects on stress

142 \ Chapter 8

in both mothers and their children. As we reviewed earlier (Chapter 7), stress is theoretically and empirically linked to antisocial behavior. Vaske also discussed the findings that genetic variants may be important in understanding who responds to treatment.

The genetic variant finding is intriguing because we know not everyone benefits equally from programs or interventions. According to Vaske (2017, p. 1050), "Approximately 15 percent to 50 percent of individuals do poorly" in evidence-based practices. By this she meant they do not respond well or do not make it through the entirety of the program. The "responsivity" component of the RNR approach is meant to address the different learning styles and adaptations to treatment for each individual. Variations in motivations, learning styles, and suitability to temperament may explain some of the reasons not everyone responds to programs with strong evidence bases. However, genetic variations may also help fill this gap in our knowledge.

The work of biosocial researchers is instructive on the ways the environment interacts with genetic variants, called alleles. In biosocial research, one of the more popular approaches to studying both the biological and the social is called gene-by-environment interaction. This method came to prominence with the work of Avshalom Caspi and colleagues (2002), who discovered that "individual differences at a functional polymorphism in the promoter of the monoamine oxidase A (MAOA) gene" differentiated which children were more likely to be aggressive after maltreatment. In other words, they were motivated by the finding that not every maltreated child becomes violent later. They found that those with at-risk genetic variants are more likely to be violent in response to maltreatment. Thus, two risk factors, one genetic and one environmental, increased the odds of a negative outcome. This is the dual risk or diathesis-stress hypothesis describing how genes interact with the environment.

A competing theory is differential susceptibility (Belsky & Pluess, 2009). This theory suggests there are not truly "risk" genetic variants but rather genetic variants that make individuals more susceptible to environmental effects. In other words, genetic variants help explain why the environment is more impactful for some than others. This could go a long way toward helping us understand why correctional treatment may work for some and not others (see Beaver, Jackson, & Flesher, 2014; Simons & Lei, 2013).

Crime Trends in the United States

In the United States, crime rates, generally measured with "official" sources of data such as arrests or police contacts, have fluctuated quite a bit over the past 50 years. When Braithwaite was writing, crime had increased in the United States and other nations (except Japan) since World War II, hence his thirteenth fact. In the United States, criminologists did try to tackle why crime was increasing in the 1960 and 1970s despite generally good economic conditions (see Cohen & Felson, 1979). Crime continued to fluctuate in the United States until the early 1990s, when rates began to decline across the world. Figure 8.1 shows U.S. violent crime rates since 1985, which illustrates that after the early 1990s peak, the "crime drop" was not just immediate, but profound, dipping lower than they had been since the early 1970s (James, 2018).

How have traditional criminological perspectives sought to explain the "great American crime decline" (which also happened to have occurred in places like Canada [Glowacki, 2016] and the United Kingdom [Cobain, 2014])? There have been several competing explanations and much empirical evidence brought to bear on under-

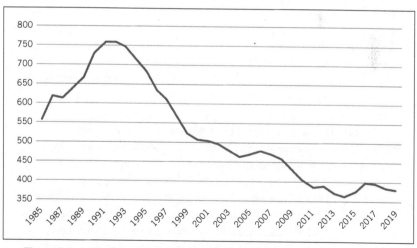

Figure 8.1. U.S. Violent Crime Rates per 100,000, 1985–2019
(*Source*: Federal Bureau of Investigation, Crime Data Explorer,
https://crime-data-explorer.fr.cloud.gov/explorer/national/united-states/crime.)

standing the crime decline. Economist Steven Levitt (2004), from *Freakonomics* fame, examined popular factors that had been posited to account for the crime drop. He argued that police presence, expansion of incarceration, a slowing of the crack cocaine crisis, and abortion were important whereas the economy, gun policies, the death penalty, changes in the age of the population, and changes in police strategies were not important factors in sparking the crime decline. One of those factors, abortion, may need further discussion. In a study published in 2001, Donahue and Levitt advanced the still-controversial argument that *Roe v. Wade* (1973), which legalized abortion in the United States, contributed to the crime decline basically by increasing the odds that unwanted and potentially disadvantaged children would not be born at all. The timing of when *Roe v. Wade* occurred and when this cohort would be at the peak of criminality matched the beginning of the crime decline.

A Biopsychosocial Approach to Understanding Crime Rates

Despite all the research on the crime decline, it is safe to say that traditional criminological approaches have not been able to adequately explain it. Most of these explanations have ignored biology. Some have indirectly included the body by including age as a risk factor, since at least part of the reason age is related to criminal behavior is due to biology and psychology (see Chapter 3). In addition, for the most part, biosocial explanations of crime have remained on the micro level, focusing on individuals rather than macro units such as nations. Yet this field has much to say, we think, about crime rates.

One of the more interesting hypotheses concerning crime rates has to do with environmental lead levels. Lead used to be an ingredient in things such as gasoline and paint. In gas stations now, all varieties are "unleaded." This change began in the 1970s and was completed by the mid-1990s (Energy Information Administration [EIA], 2020). Paints used around the home have not contained paint since the late 1970s (Centers for Disease Control and Prevention [CDC], 2020). Lead can have detrimental effects on development, particularly with respect to the brain, in ways that may increase the likelihood of antisocial behavior. The hypothesis is that as lead was removed from the environment, brains were able to develop in a healthier manner and crime subsequently declined. Kevin Drum, of *Mother Jones*, put forth this thesis, arguing that lead may have been instrumental to explain both the increase in crime in the 1960s and 1970s and the decline in the 1990s. Drum pointed to a relatively ignored economic paper that argued that lead from the exhaust from cars could account for 90 percent of the variation in violent crime (Nevin, 2000). Drum reviewed other pieces that showed state-level correlations between environmental lead and crime and correlations in other countries (Drum, 2013).

It was a fascinating hypothesis, and it continues to garner attention. However, the link may not be as clear as originally thought. One report by the Brennan Center for Justice examining causes of the crime decline concluded that lead may have had a bit of an effect in the 1990s but virtually none in the 2000s (Roeder et al., 2015). One study conducted using longitudinal data from New Zealand, which measured lead levels in participants at age 11, found no association with crime in adulthood (Beckley et al., 2018). The hypothesis remains intriguing, but whether and how much lead in the environment has affected crime rates remains an open question.

Other factors mentioned in the Brennan report included a reduction in the use of alcohol. This factor, the authors estimated, can account for 5–10 percent of the decline in crime in both the 1990s and 2000s. Alcohol has been linked to criminal behavior through its effects on the body as well as the social aspects of drinking. Salas-Wright and Todic (2014) make the biosocial case for understanding why and how substances are related to crime, including biological risks for substance misuse as well as the biological effects of substances on brain functioning. The problem with this explanation for crime rates is that alcohol use dipped a bit in the 1990s but increased after (Roeder et al., 2015).

In the end, compelling explanations of crime rates are likely to be found in a combination of factors at the individual and social levels. These factors also cannot be viewed in isolation but must be seen as integrated. For example, the effects of alcohol are not the same for everyone but vary by individual-level and cultural factors (Adan, Forero, & Navarro, 2017; Castro et al., 2014; Secretary of Health and Human Services [SHHS], 2000).

Fitting the Facts and Missing
Puzzle Pieces

In this last substantive chapter of fitting the facts of crime, there may be just as many questions left as answers. In the United States, and really all over the world, police-community relationships have gone through ups and downs. How can biopsychosocial perspectives inform these changes in trends? Rehabilitation has made a comeback from its "demise" in the 1970s. How do we know which approaches, and for whom, are likely to succeed? We have seen much promise in biopsychosocial explanations. Likewise, crime rates fluctuate. In the United States, crime rates rose in general after World War II, peaked in the early 1990s, and then fell precipitously for the next two decades. Some biosocial mechanisms, like lead exposure and substance use, can partially explain these rises and drops but certainly not all changes in crime rate trends.

Criminology is making strides in multilevel analyses that combine structural-environmental factors and individual factors in explaining antisocial phenomena, but there is much room to improve the understanding of how structure can influence individual behavior and how individuals combine to create and maintain cultures, values, and social institutions. In particular, as we learn more about police and citizen relationships, rehabilitation approaches, and how crime rates are continuing to change, new perspectives will need to be developed to understand them. For example, there is much to be learned about why police relations are so important, and as we write this book, in 2020, police reform is again at the top of the news cycle, with calls to "defund" the police making the rounds. How can we utilize the most cutting-edge science to improve relationships between the community and police? Which tasks may be best handled by police, and which may be best executed by other professionals (e.g., social workers)? New information is also emerging about why programs work or do not work, and biopsychosocial mechanisms are likely to be at play. An ongoing analysis of an approach called focused deterrence—which seeks to enhance the effectiveness of programs by, for example, increasing the swiftness of punishments for infractions— is illustrative. This analysis examined individuals in a Washington State assessment of a "Certain and Swift" program. The researchers found that those who were "not deterred" were more likely to have a mental health or substance use problem (Campbell et al., 2016). In other words, not everyone is equally deterrable, and a biopsychosocial approach can help us identify why this is the case in ways that may improve future programs.

A decade ago, Laland, Odling-Smee, and Myles (2010) detailed how culture (which is determined by people) can shape population genetics. Laland and colleagues rely on niche construction theory, which suggests that organisms can modify elements of natural selection by adapting their behavior to collective norms. Humans, they believe, are the definitive niche constructors, selecting genes for traits that are specifically related to cultural norms. Thus, a coevolution emerges out of the interaction of genetics and culture; genes reflect culture, and culture reflects genes. Merging the insights from one of the most individualistic explanations of behavior—molecular genetics—and one of the most collective explanations of behavior—culture—is an exciting and important future avenue that researchers much travel.

9

Concluding Remarks on the Future of Biosocial Criminology

While criminology is a young field with many disagreements about the whats, wheres, and whys of crime, there *are* certain findings that are without controversy. These have been the foundation of this book. The "facts of crime" (Braithwaite, 1989) include: (1) crime is disproportionately committed by men, (2) crime is disproportionately committed by young people, (3) crime is disproportionately committed by unmarried people, (4) crime is disproportionately committed by people living in large cities, (5) crime is disproportionately committed by people who have experienced high residential mobility and who live in areas characterized by high residential mobility, (6) school commitment is linked to lower crime, (7) educational and occupational aspirations are linked to lower crime, (8) school success is linked to lower crime, (9) attachment to parents is linked to lower crime, (10) delinquent associations/peers are linked to higher crime, (11) believing in the legitimacy of the law is linked to lower crime, (12) being in an oppressed social category increases crime, and (13) crime rates have been increasing in the Western world since World War II.

Each of these facts remains relevant. However, recent work (since 1989, anyway) has added some nuance to the causes of crime. For example, it was true that crime was on the rise when Braithwaite wrote his book. However, since the early 1990s, crime in the United States and other similar nations underwent a massive and steady decline. Nonetheless, the facts used here to undergird our discussion are not in serious dispute among criminologists. What is in dispute, however, is our ability to explain and make sense of the facts. Why is crime committed by those in large cities, males, and young people?

By using the "facts of crime" to set the foundation for this book, we hope that readers have come to the conclusion that biology, psychology, and sociology matter in the study of criminal behavior and in understanding the consequences of exposure to violence. If you have read this far, we also hope you agree that the body and its surrounding environments are intimately and intricately intertwined such that one cannot be separated from the other in explaining almost every life outcome we can think of—especially behavior. To fully account for the facts linked to crime, students and scholars of criminology must incorporate information and variables from a wide range of biological and environmental factors.

As many of the stories that opened our chapters illustrate, determining why someone did something is no easy task. And we—the three of us who have written this book—certainly do not have all the answers. But criminal behavior is an activity that profoundly affects people and society. Violence costs lives and harms families and communities. It injures people and can send them to the emergency room, where they face financial costs and a recovery period. Violence has significant intangible costs, such as taking away a loved one from a family, school, church, or neighborhood, or it may take away a person's ability to walk. The tangible costs—from health care, to funeral costs, to criminal justice operations—are staggering. It is incumbent that we get prevention and intervention right—and that we continue to keep doing better.

We do not claim that a biopsychosocial approach fills all the gaps in our knowledge about the 13 facts of crime, but we do submit that where there are holes from traditional criminological perspectives, biopsychosocial work has often had something to offer. We emphasize here that our intention is not to privilege biology or suggest it is a "stronger" or more appropriate lens with which to examine crime and justice. Just as we believe a purely sociological approach is incomplete, we also believe too much emphasis on biology or psychology would be as well. We come to a closer understanding of the facts of crime, we argue, when we take seriously that life and our behavior throughout it involve the mind, body, and society. To finish the book, we review new methods to investigate the facts of crime as well as some other promising findings that are consistent across studies and time.

Genome-Wide Association Studies

When behavior genetics and early molecular genetic studies began to explore the biological underpinnings of antisocial behavior, genetics were explored as a conceptual whole (how much variation in a certain trait is genetic versus environmental) or through candidate gene studies that pinpoint a few sets of genes that are theoretically related to antisocial behavior (e.g., genes that regulate dopamine or serotonin). These studies have been responsible for affirming a partial genetic basis to just about every animal trait and behavior. These studies also enabled researchers to establish a set of principles from which to build when explaining behavior. As Robert Plomin and his collaborators (2016) highlight, there is much we know about the genetic and environmental foundations of behavior: that every trait is part genetic and part environmental, that no trait is 100 percent heritable, that traits are caused by many genes with small individual effects, and so on. Still, these studies were limited in identifying exactly which genes across the broad array of genes in the human genome are associated with antisocial behavior. This is beginning to change.

Recently, with advances in technology and the dropping cost of genetic testing, it is now possible to sequence the entire genome fairly quickly. This enables researchers to identify specific genes that influence certain behaviors. Genome-wide association studies, or GWAS, are growing in popularity and have made their way into the study of antisocial behavior. The National Human Genome Research Institute states, "A genome-wide association study is an approach that involves rapidly scanning markers across the complete sets of DNA, or genomes, of many people to find genetic variations associated with a particular disease" (National Human Genome Research Institute, 2020a). Through the identification of these genes, we can more carefully pinpoint prevention efforts for antisocial behavior and gauge the risk for exhibiting conduct disorders.

One of the first GWAS studies was conducted by Rautiainen and colleagues (2016), who identified two genetic variants that were expressly related to antisocial behavior: LINC00951 and LRFN2. It will be unsurprising to readers at this point that these two genes are expressed in the brain—mostly in the frontal cortex. Given the strong link between frontal lobe functioning and behavior, these two genes, then, are theoretically and empirically linked to behavioral outcomes. With this effort, researchers began to identify specific genes that, together with other genes and environment, impact antisocial behavior.

A large GWAS study was recently conducted by Tielbeek and colleagues (2017), who used five large population data sets to develop a broad measure of antisocial behavior across various age ranges. The large sample size also allowed the researchers to split the samples by sex to understand any heterogeneous effects across males and females. They found that antisocial behavior is polygenic (influenced by several genes making small effects on people's behavior) and that genetic risk may be different across sex. Again, this is crucial information for people to have when treating disorders and creating prevention and intervention programs. Later in this chapter, we discuss further the recent work on genetically informed prevention and intervention programs.

Polygenic Risk Scoring

Almost every single trait one can think of is influenced by genetic and environmental factors. This has been a mainstay of this book. And new empirical evidence suggests that most personality traits, like the ones that are implicated in antisocial behavior, are considered complex traits. While some genetic diseases, such as Down syndrome and cystic fibrosis, are single-variant outcomes, most social traits, like antisocial behavior, are the result of hundreds—if not thousands—of individual genetic variants that make small contributions to the explanation of a behavior.

With the advent of genome-wide studies, it is possible to calculate a risk score based on the cumulative number of genetic variants associated with a particular disorder. The score does not identify specific genes related to a disorder, but it does allow for a relative risk of having a specific disorder. The National Human Genome Research Institute (2020b) describes a polygenic risk score as such:

> A polygenic risk score tells you how a person's risk compares to others with a different genetic constitution. However, polygenic scores do not provide a baseline or timeframe for the progression of a disease. For example, consider two people with high polygenic risk scores for having coronary heart disease. The first person is 22 years old, while the latter is 98. Although they have the same polygenic risk score, they will have different lifetime risks of the disease. Polygenic risk scores only show correlations, not causations.

Polygenic risk scores have made headway into various fields of study. The leader of the use of this methodology, perhaps somewhat surprisingly, is education. High attention deficit hyperactivity disorder (ADHD) polygenic scores are known to reduce educational outcomes for children and their mothers (Stergiakouli et al., 2017). Polygenic scores for education have been linked to several negative emotional and behavioral problems (Jansen et al., 2018). Researchers have now begun to extend polygenic risk scores to understand the influence of cumulative genetic risk on antisocial behavior with some success (Sadeh et al., 2016; Wertz et al., 2018). However, this is a greatly underutilized method in biopsychosocial criminology. We believe this is a ripe new area of research that can bring to light new ways that genetics and social environments can inform prevention and intervention (Barnes et al., 2019).

Despite the promise of polygenic risk scores in assisting medical professionals in identifying individuals predisposed to a disease or disorder, most of this research has been conducted on individuals of European ancestry. A more diverse set of participants in polygenic scoring studies is needed to make more general claims about the risk that people and groups have toward certain diseases and disorders (Haga, 2010).

Epigenetics and Related Regulation Concepts

The genetic work being done using GWAS and polygenic risk scores is clarifying what genes are most likely related to which behaviors.

One aspect these types of studies are not necessarily equipped to account for is the regulation of genes. Gene regulation is a natural part of genetic expression, and several mechanisms influence such expression. The two discussed here are epigenetic and transcription factors.

Epigenetics, recall, is the regulation of genes through a change in *activation*, but not structure, of the gene. This generally occurs through two major methods: (1) DNA methylation, and (2) histone acetylation. DNA methylation reduces or slows down the expression of genes while histone acetylation increases or quickens the expression of genes. Environmental factors such as child maltreatment (Mc-Gowen et al., 2009) and poor health behavior of pregnant mothers (Oberlander et al., 2008) can increase or decrease DNA methylation and histone acetylation, modulating behavior over the life course.

Despite the promise of epigenetics, some say it is too early to put much stock into this area of research (see Moffitt & Beckley, 2015). The contribution of the field of epigenetics beyond what is offered by molecular genetics has yet to be seen for some researchers. Especially problematic for critics of epigenetic research is how environmental factors can penetrate the germ line and influence children across generations. Yet evidence of epigenetic inheritance is growing and should be considered moving forward (Yehuda & Lehrner, 2018). To further understand the facts of crime, it would appear important to know those factors that can influence genetic expression.

Along with epigenetic mechanisms that control expression of genes, transcription factors also influence the way that genes are expressed. A technical definition is given by Latchman (1993): "The process of transcription is the first stage of gene expression resulting in the production of a primary RNA transcript from the DNA of a particular gene. It therefore represents a critical first step in gene expression which is followed by a number of post-transcriptional processes such as RNA splicing and translation. These lead ultimately to the production of a functional protein" (p. 417). The specific proteins made through DNA transcription are what influences phenotypes. Many phenotypes, such as aggressive and violent behavior, may be the result of various differences in gene transcription (Damberg et al., 2001). Despite the importance of transcription, much more needs to be learned about the creation of specific proteins and how this, in turn, guides behavioral outcomes in people.

Sociogenomics

A push has been made to fully integrate genetic information (including GWAS, polygenic risk scores, epigenetics, etc.) with sociology/social psychology. This recent effort is often referred to as sociogenomics. In their 2005 article, Gene Robinson, Christina Grozinger, and Charles Whitfield described the aim of sociogenomics (2005, p. 257):

> The goal of sociogenomics is to achieve a comprehensive understanding of social life in molecular terms: how it evolved, how it is governed, and how it influences all aspects of genome structure, genome activity, and organismal function. Which genes and pathways regulate those aspects of development, physiology, and behavior that influence sociality, and how are they themselves influenced by social life and social evolution?

The effort, in sum, is to fully explore the genetic and environmental factors (and how they interact) that influence social behavior. In this piece, the authors focus on nonhuman animals. However, in the years since this publication, others have focused on the sociogenomics of humans.

Psychologist Brent Roberts has extended original sociogenomic models to understand the development of personality traits. In particular, he uses evolutionary theory to describe the development and maintenance of personality traits. Some personality traits are adaptive in that, even though they appear maladaptive today, they served to enhance the ability to survive and breed (Roberts, 2018). Evolutionary perspectives inherently combine biological and sociological viewpoints to understand change over time to improve reproduction and survival.

In 2017, Dalton Conley and Jason Fletcher released their book, *The Genome Factor: What the Social Genomics Revolution Reveals about Ourselves, Our History and the Future*. In this book, the sociogenomic era is brought to light with up-to-date findings on the role of biology and the environment on everything from educational success to marriage and social disadvantage. Through the sociobiology approach, Conley and Fletcher (2017) convincingly put the nature-versus-nurture debate to rest. If we are serious about behavior, we need to integrate and understand genetics and social history. They also provide a clear path for using genetic and social information in prevention and intervention—one that does not hinge on the eugenics of the past but, instead, coincides with efforts to establish social justice.

The Genome Factor, while comprehensive and up to date, is only the tip of the iceberg when it comes to sociogenetic research and what it can tell us. As sociogenomics grows in popularity, it will be necessary to drill down and start to understand which genes matter most for which behaviors and for whom. Are there differences by sex or race/ethnicity? Does age matter when it comes to genetic and social causes for behavior? What about effective intervention? What works best for whom? Are the interventions we deliver ethical? Are there downstream negative effects? All these questions are pertinent and need to be carefully considered moving forward.

Biopsychosocially Informed Prevention and Intervention

Sociogenomics and similar efforts naturally inform what we should do to address certain behavioral and health outcomes. As mentioned, this is new, and a vast number of questions remain. However, there are recent efforts to better understand what types of prevention programs work for which types of people. These efforts would not be possible without a biopsychosocial perspective that seeks to integrate information on the whole person.

One of the most effective treatment interventions for aggressive and violent behavior is cognitive behavioral therapy. Sukhodolsky, Kassinove, and Gorman (2004) conducted a meta-analysis on the effectiveness of CBT on aggression and found that CBT consistently reduced aggression across programs and studies. As we noted in the previous chapter, Vaske, Galyean, and Cullen (2011) argue that one of the reasons CBT works is likely because it strengthens brain-based skills, including social, coping, and problem-solving skills. These skills are largely influenced by parts of the brain in the prefrontal cortex. Similar findings also exist for mindfulness meditation, which also influences parts of the brain, including increasing the amount of gray matter (Hölzel et al., 2011). Additional practices that promote similar changes in the brain should be implemented in correctional contexts.

Psychologist Andrea Glenn is leading the way on research into biosocially informed prevention and intervention using sophisticated methodologies. Glenn and colleagues (2018b) evaluated the outcomes of Coping Power, a small-group intervention for aggressive youth. Previous evaluations of the project indicated there may be negative impacts—it may do more harm than good. The research team wondered if the difference might be due to the delivery of the program. Sometimes the program is delivered in groups and at other times individually. Some people may do better in groups and others solo. Indeed, this is what they found. Youth with a specific version of the oxytocin gene (OXTR) demonstrated reductions in aggression regardless of the intervention type (whether group or individual). Youth with a polymorphism (the G allele) showed little reduction in aggression after the group-based intervention and actually increased aggression long term while those receiving the individual format did reduce their aggressive behavior. This finding suggests that small variations in treatment (here, group versus individual delivery) can make huge differences for people given their genetic makeup.

While many genetically informed interventions are very noninvasive, some are not. A more controversial genetic intervention is clustered regularly interspaced short palindromic repeats, or, as it is much better known, CRISPR. CRISPR allows direct manipulation of genes through "gene editing." The National Institute of Health (Medline Plus, 2020) describes the CRISPR gene-editing process as follows:

> Researchers create a small piece of RNA with a short "guide" sequence that attaches (binds) to a specific target sequence of DNA in a genome. The RNA also binds to the Cas9 enzyme. As in bacteria, the modified RNA is used to recognize the DNA sequence, and the Cas9 enzyme cuts the DNA at the targeted location. Although Cas9 is the enzyme that is used most often, other enzymes (for example Cpf1) can also be used. Once the DNA is cut, researchers use the cell's own DNA repair machinery to add or delete pieces of genetic material, or to make changes to the DNA by replacing an existing segment with a customized DNA sequence.

In each chapter, we have given examples of how the biopsychosocial perspective can inform prevention and intervention. Most of these policies, practices, and programs focus on the environment or how biology can inform the delivery or focus of the intervention. We have not discussed direct genetic interventions. This is mostly because these types of interventions are new and need more research until they can be recommended. For example, CRISPR, while promising in treating some diseases, also has unintended consequences. The cutting of a gene was thought to "disable" the gene so it does not produce a protein. That may actually not be the case (Smits et al., 2019). Other downstream effects may also occur, limiting the current potential of gene editing for anything but the most serious diseases and disorders.

Additionally, any time genetic information is uncovered and accessed by researchers and medical professionals, and anytime it is voluntarily given to companies (such as 23 and Me and Ancestry.com), there is the potential for misuse of the data. Harvard University has outlined some of the risks and issues when dealing with sensitive genetic information. Their website indicates the following (Segert & Nathan, 2018):

> Although sharing one's own data is opt-in, there are no systems in place to protect the genetic privacy of relatives. Whenever a person makes the choice to publicize their own data, they implicitly publicize data pertaining to their relatives, as related individuals share portions of their genetic code. Data from relatives as far removed as third cousins can be used to identify individuals. As of right now, 60 percent of Americans with Northern European heritage can be identified by data a relative uploaded to a public database. This number is expected to rise to over 90 percent within a few years. Although far from being implemented, there have been calls for national forensic DNA databases in the US that include data for all citizens regardless of criminal history.

Genetic data can also be sold to third parties. One issue that has been particularly troubling is the potential for insurance companies to access individual genetic information. If an individual is determined to have risk factors for particular disorders or diseases, would that impact insurance premiums and the type of care received? These issues must be addressed before genetic screening is used widely.

Fitting More Facts

We based the foundation of this book on the "facts of crime" developed by criminologist John Braithwaite several decades ago. We believed these facts were the most empirically supported and studied by criminologists. However, there are other recurring and replicated findings in criminology that have come about since Braithwaite's writing in the late 1980s that we have not touched upon—or, if we have, it has been tangential. Future work should reorient to include these "facts" as they emerge and strengthen. We discuss these briefly here—highlighting paths for future work.

One well-known but controversial finding is the link between intelligence or academic achievement (not necessarily the same thing) and antisocial behavior. Certain criminologists have argued that intelligence and delinquency have been ignored by sociologically oriented scholars because of fears of stigmatization and that intelligence assessments are culturally biased (Hirschi & Hindelang, 1977; Nedelec, Schwartz, & Connolly, 2014). Intelligence, or IQ, has long been controversial because of the association between the use of intelligence concepts and eugenics. As a result, it has been primarily the domain of psychology or, more recently, biology. One reason sociologists shy away from the study of intelligence is the notion that assessment measures are culturally biased and do not actually capture intelligence. This suggests to us an opportunity to study intelligence tests as a product of more than psychological or biological factors. Sociologists should step up to the plate to help explicate exactly how environmental factors matter for intelligence and how environmental factors influence the relationship between intelligence and behavior.

Second, the effects of incarceration on later life outcomes remains nebulous. Some criminologists argue that incarceration is criminogenic and leads to poorer later health (Cullen, Jonson, & Nagin, 2011; Schnittker & John, 2007). At the same time, some work has indicated null effects of incarceration on later outcomes, or even positive effects (Beckley et al., 2019; Bhati & Piquero, 2007). Often the findings contradicting the expected negative impact of incarceration are explained in terms of selection bias with respect to previous research. However, it is possible that there are biopsychosocial mechanisms at play that could help better answer the question of whether incarceration harms and for whom it is likely to do so.

Third, childhood maltreatment has consistently been linked to poor health outcomes across the life course. Childhood abuse is related to various mental health conditions, including anxious arousal, depression, disassociation, avoidant behavior, and sexual dysfunction leading to thoughts of betrayal and powerlessness (Banyard, Williams, & Siegel, 2001). Child abuse also increases the likelihood of negative physical health problems, such as high blood pressure, liver problems, heart trouble, ulcers, circulation problems, and allergies (Springer et al., 2007). Directly relevant to criminology is the brute fact that exposure to victimization increases all varieties of offending, including property crime, violent crime, and drug use (Posick, 2013; Zimmerman & Posick, 2016).

To be sure, while prior childhood abuse or neglect is a risk factor for future poor health and behavior, it does not predetermine these outcomes (Fagan, 2001). It is likely that a host of social and biological factors either decrease the likelihood of negative behavioral outcomes, such as through variations in protective alleles (Caspi et al., 2002), or increase antisocial potential through risk alleles (Beaver, Barnes, & Boutwell, 2014). Considerably more research is needed to understand the "fact" that early maltreatment is a potent risk factor for later antisociality.

Fourth, a biopsychosocial approach to criminology can emphasize a larger focus on issues of environmental justice, including the conservation of water, land, air, and biodiversity. In a 2017 article appearing in *Biological Conservation*, Bennett and colleagues provided a blueprint for conducting conservation social science. They note, "The social sciences are one means through which researchers and practitioners can come to understand the human dimensions of conservation and natural resource management" (Bennett et al., 2017, p. 94). As global climate change and ecosystem collapse continue to have widespread impacts on people and communities, a transdisciplinary effort may be able to improve the health and well-being of all people and their diverse surroundings.

Finally, biopsychosocial factors may help unravel the theoretical ball of yarn that characterizes the current status of criminological theory. We opened this chapter with a discussion of how criminology has long recognized that theories continue to be developed with no proper way of discarding old, less effective perspectives. In the 1980s and 1990s, some criminologists suggested that one way to do so would be to combine theories—called theoretical integration—to reduce the glut (Bernard & Snipes, 1996). However, all this seemed to do was add more theories to the fold; the constituent parts of the integrated theories never went away! Others argued that theories need to be tested, and the winners will survive. Which theories fit the data better? Those are the theories we should continue to utilize (Hirschi, 1989; Posick & Rocque, 2018). Yet it is often the case that the standard social science methods of theory testing do not provide definitive tests. Some (e.g., Wright & Boisert, 2009) have argued that biosocial methods would allow more rigorous tests of theories. We are not advocating for social or biological scientific methods but rather that all three elements—bio, social, and psychological—be taken into account in tests; as a result, such tests would be more comprehensive.

Conclusion

To bring our book to a close, we wish to leave readers with an excerpt from *The Origins of You* by developmental psychologists Jay Belsky, Avshalom Caspi, Terrie Moffitt, and Ritchie Poulton (2020, p. 253):

> Experience also teaches us that even such better—meaning stronger—evidence will not be sufficient for many. This is because too many people today still distinguish body, mind, and behavior, somehow thinking that while the body is genetically influenced, this is not so in the case of the mind and behavior. We strongly advocate moving beyond such false distinctions. After all, evidence now indicates that gut bacteria are related to psychological functioning, no doubt via the vagal nerve connecting gut and brain. So treating the body and mind and thus the body and behavior as somehow fundamentally different seems a seriously outdated way of thinking about humans, genetics, and human development. Simply put, it is long past time to abandon the mind-body duality; we are dealing with a systemically integrated organism, not an

individual with separate parts that somehow follow entirely different rules.

The field of biopsychosocial criminology is relatively new, but it is a promising approach to the study of crime and criminality. While there is not much one can say for sure about the causes and consequences of antisocial behavior, there are some replicated findings that must be accounted for by theories of behavior. We have discussed what we believe are the most consistent findings in the criminological literature and how a biopsychosocial approach can explain these findings. What is most exciting is that this perspective is going to continue to explain behaviors and also raise new questions. We look forward to continuing to uncover "facts of crime" and using a comprehensive, empirical approach to understanding these facts.

References

Abt, T. (2019). *Bleeding out: The devastating consequences of urban violence—and a bold new plan for peace in the streets.* New York: Basic Books.

Adan, A., Forero, D. A., & Navarro, J. F. (2017). Personality traits related to binge drinking: A systematic review. *Frontiers in Psychiatry, 8,* 134.

Adler, F. (1975). *Sisters in crime: The rise of the new female criminal.* New York: McGraw-Hill.

Adolescent Sleep Working Group. (2014). School start times for adolescents. *Pediatrics, 134*(3), 642–649.

Agnew, R. (1985). Social control theory and delinquency: A longitudinal test. *Criminology, 23*(1), 47–61.

Agnew, R. (1992). Foundation for a general strain theory of crime and delinquency. *Criminology, 30*(1), 47–88.

Agnew, R. (2001). Building on the foundation of general strain theory: Specifying the types of strain most likely to lead to crime and delinquency. *Journal of Research in Crime and Delinquency, 38*(4), 319–361.

Agnew, R. (2003). An integrated theory of the adolescent peak in offending. *Youth & Society, 34*(3), 263–299.

Agnew, R. (2006). *Pressured into crime: An overview of General Strain Theory.* Los Angeles: Roxbury.

Agnew, R., & Brezina, T. (2019). General strain theory. In M. D. Krohn, N. Hendrix, G. P. Hall, & A. J. Lizotte (Eds.), *Handbook on crime and deviance* (pp. 145–160). New York: Springer.

Agnew, R., & White, H. R. (1992). An empirical test of general strain theory. *Criminology, 30*(4), 475–500.

Akers, R. L. (2009). *Social learning and social structure: A general theory of crime and deviance.* New Brunswick, NJ: Transaction Publishers.

Anderson, E. (2000). *Code of the street: Decency, violence, and the moral life of the inner city.* New York: W. W. Norton.

Andrews, D. A., & Bonta, J. (1998). *The psychology of criminal conduct* (2nd ed.). Cincinnati, OH: Anderson.

Andrews, D. A., & Wormith, J. S. (1989). Personality and crime: Knowledge destruction and construction in criminology. *Justice Quarterly, 6*(3), 289–309.

Andrews, D. A., Zinger, I., Hoge, R. D., Bonta, J., Gendreau, P., & Cullen, F. T. (1990). Does correctional treatment work? A clinically relevant and psychologically informed meta-analysis. *Criminology, 28*(3), 369–404.

APA.org. (2017). Ethnic and racial minorities and socioeconomic status. *American Psychological Association.* Available at https://www.apa.org/pi/ses/resources/publications/minorities.

APA.org. (2020). Flight-or-fight response. *APA Dictionary of Psychology.* Available at https://dictionary.apa.org/fight-or-flight-response.

Apel, R., & Kaukinen, C. (2008). On the relationship between family structure and antisocial behavior: Parental cohabitation and blended households. *Criminology, 46*(1), 35–70.

Applebaum, A. J. (2017). Survival of the fittest . . . caregiver? *Palliative & Supportive Care, 15*(1), 1–2.

Arnocky, S., Ribout, A., Mirza, R. S., & Knack, J. M. (2014). Perceived mate availability influences intrasexual competition, jealousy and mate-guarding behavior. *Journal of Evolutionary Psychology, 12*(1), 45–64.

Augustyn, M. B., & Ray, J. V. (2016). Psychopathy and perceptions of procedural justice. *Journal of Criminal Justice, 46*, 170–183.

Babcock, J. C., Green, C. E., & Robie, C. (2004). Does batterers' treatment work? A meta-analytic review of domestic violence treatment. *Clinical Psychology Review, 23*(8), 1023–1053.

Bagley, E. J., Fuller-Rowell, T. E., Saini, E. K., Philbrook, L. E., & El-Sheikh, M. (2018). Neighborhood economic deprivation and social fragmentation: Associations with children's sleep. *Behavioral Sleep Medicine, 16*(6), 542–552.

Baglivio, M. (2020). Adverse childhood experiences, delinquency, and health: Implications for juvenile justice systems. In M. G. Vaughn, C. P. Salas-Wright, & D. B. Jackson (Eds.), *Routledge international handbook of delinquency and health* (pp. 90–103). New York: Routledge.

Baglivio, M. T., Wolff, K. T., Piquero, A. R., & Epps, N. (2015). The relationship between adverse childhood experiences (ACE) and juvenile offending trajectories in a juvenile offender sample. *Journal of Criminal Justice, 43*(3), 229–241.

Baker, M. (2016). Undoing the harm of childhood trauma and adversity. *University of California San Francisco.* October 5, 2016. Available at https://

www.ucsf.edu/news/2016/10/404446/undoing-harm-childhood-trauma-and
-adversity.

Baker, T., Falco Metcalfe, C., Berenblum, T., Aviv, G., & Gertz, M. (2015). Examining public preferences for the allocation of resources to rehabilitative versus punitive crime policies. *Criminal Justice Policy Review, 26*(5), 448–462.

Banyard, V. L., Williams, L. M., & Siegel, J. A. (2001). The long-term mental health consequences of child sexual abuse: An exploratory study of the impact of multiple traumas in a sample of women. *Journal of Traumatic Stress, 14*(4), 697–715.

Barkan, S. E. (2011). *Sociology: Understanding and changing the social world.* Boston: Flat World Knowledge.

Barkan, S. E., & Rocque, M. (2018). Socioeconomic status and racism as fundamental causes of street criminality. *Critical Criminology, 26*(2), 211–231.

Barkan, S. E., & Rocque, M. (2020). *Crime prevention: Programs, policies, and practices.* Thousand Oaks, CA: Sage.

Barnes, J. C., & Beaver, K. M. (2012). Marriage and desistance from crime: A consideration of gene–environment correlation. *Journal of Marriage and Family, 74*(1), 19–33.

Barnes, J. C., Beaver, K. M., & Boutwell, B. B. (2011). Examining the genetic underpinnings to Moffitt's developmental taxonomy: A behavioral genetic analysis. *Criminology, 49*(4), 923–954.

Barnes, J. C., Liu, H., Motz, R. T., Tanksley, P. T., Kail, R., Beckley, A. L., . . . & Wertz, J. (2019). The propensity for aggressive behavior and lifetime incarceration risk: A test for gene-environment interaction (G×E) using whole-genome data. *Aggression and Violent Behavior, 49*, 101307.

Baumeister, R. F., Gailliot, M., DeWall, C. N., & Oaten, M. (2006). Self-regulation and personality: How interventions increase regulatory success, and how depletion moderates the effects of traits on behavior. *Journal of personality, 74*(6), 1773–1802.

Baumeister, R. F., Vohs, K. D., & Tice, D. M. (2007). The strength model of self-control. *Current Directions in Psychological Science, 16*(6), 351–355.

Bazelon, E. (2019). *Charged: The new movement to transform American prosecution and end mass incarceration.* New York: Random House.

Beaumont, G. de, & Tocqueville, A. de ([1833] 2018). *On the penitentiary system in the United States and its application to France* (E. K. Ferkaluk, Trans.). Cham, Switzerland: Springer Nature.

Beaver, K. (2015). Genetics and crime. In W. Jennings (Ed.), *The encyclopedia of crime & punishment* (pp. 668–672). Hoboken, NJ: Wiley.

Beaver, K. M., Barnes, J. C., & Boutwell, B. B. (2014). The 2-repeat allele of the MAOA gene confers an increased risk for shooting and stabbing behaviors. *Psychiatric Quarterly, 85*(3), 257–265.

Beaver, K. M., Barnes, J. C., & Boutwell, B. B. (Eds.). (2015). *The nurture versus biosocial debate in criminology: On the origins of criminal behavior and criminality.* Thousand Oaks, CA: Sage.

Beaver, K. M., DeLisi, M., Vaughn, M. G., & Wright, J. P. (2010). The intersection of genes and neuropsychological deficits in the prediction of adolescent delinquency and low self-control. *International Journal of Offender Therapy and Comparative Criminology, 54*(1), 22–42.

Beaver, K. M., Jackson, D. B., & Flesher, D. (2014). The potential use of genetics to increase the effectiveness of treatment programs for criminal offenders. *Recent Advances in DNA & Gene Sequences (Formerly Recent Patents on DNA & Gene Sequences), 8*(2), 113–118.

Beaver, K. M., Ratchford, M., & Ferguson, C. J. (2009). Evidence of genetic and environmental effects on the development of low self-control. *Criminal Justice and Behavior, 36*(11), 1158–1172.

Beaver, K. M., Wright, J. P., DeLisi, M., & Vaughn, M. G. (2008). Genetic influences on the stability of low self-control: Results from a longitudinal sample of twins. *Journal of Criminal Justice, 36*(6), 478–485.

Beckley, A. L., Caspi, A., Broadbent, J., Harrington, H., Houts, R. M., Poulton, R., . . . & Moffitt, T. E. (2018). Association of childhood blood lead levels with criminal offending. *JAMA Pediatrics, 172*(2), 166–173.

Beckley, A. L., Palmer, R. H., Rocque, M., & Whitfield, K. E. (2019). Health and criminal justice system involvement among African American siblings. *SSM-Population Health, 7*, 100359.

Bedi, U. S., & Arora, R. (2007). Cardiovascular manifestations of posttraumatic stress disorder. *Journal of the National Medical Association, 99*(6), 642–649.

Belsky, D. W., Domingue, B. W., Wedow, R., Arsenault, L., Boardman, J. D., Caspi, A., . . . & Harris, K. M. (2018). Genetic analysis of social-class mobility in five longitudinal studies. *Proceedings of the National Academy of Sciences, 115*(31), E7275–E7284.

Belsky, J. (1980). Child maltreatment: An ecological integration. *American Psychologist, 35*(4), 320–335.

Belsky, J., Caspi, A., Moffitt, T. E., & Poulton, R. (2020). *The origins of you: How childhood shapes later life.* Cambridge, MA: Harvard University Press.

Belsky, J., & Pluess, M. (2009). Beyond diathesis stress: differential susceptibility to environmental influences. *Psychological Bulletin, 135*(6), 885–908.

Bennett, N. J., Roth, R., Klain, S. C., Chan, K., Christie, P., Clark, D. A., . . . & Greenberg, A. (2017). Conservation social science: Understanding and integrating human dimensions to improve conservation. *Biological Conservation, 205*, 93–108.

Bernard, T. J., & Snipes, J. B. (1996). Theoretical integration in criminology. *Crime and Justice, 20*, 301–348.

Bernhardt, P. C. (1997). Influences of serotonin and testosterone in aggression and dominance: Convergence with social psychology. *Current Directions in Psychological Science, 6*(2), 44–48.

Bhati, A. S., & Piquero, A. R. (2007). Estimating the impact of incarceration on subsequent offending trajectories: Deterrent, criminogenic, or null effect. *Journal of Criminal Law & Crimnology, 98*(1), 207–254.

Bjork, J. M., Moeller, F. G., Dougherty, D. M., & Swann, A. C. (2001). Endogenous plasma testosterone levels and commission errors in women: A preliminary report. *Physiology & Behavior, 73*(1), 217–221.

Blackwell, B. S. (2000). Perceived sanction threats, gender, and crime: A test and elaboration of power-control theory. *Criminology, 38*(2), 439–488.

Blau, J. R., & Blau, P. M. (1982). The cost of inequality: Metropolitan structure and violent crime. *American Sociological Review, 47*(1), 114–129.

Book, A. S., Starzyk, K. B., & Quinsey, V. L. (2001). The relationship between testosterone and aggression: A meta-analysis. *Aggression and Violent Behavior, 6*(6), 579–599.

Botchkovar, E., Marshall, I. H., Rocque, M., & Posick, C. (2015). The importance of parenting in the development of self-control in boys and girls: Results from a multinational study of youth. *Journal of Criminal Justice, 43*(2), 133–141.

Botchkovar, E. V., & Broidy, L. (2013). Parenting, self-control, and the gender gap in heavy drinking: The case of Russia. *International Journal of Offender Therapy and Comparative Criminology, 57*(3), 357–376.

Boutwell, B. B., Nelson, E. J., Emo, B., Vaughn, M. G., Schootman, M., Rosenfeld, R., & Lewis, R. (2016). The intersection of aggregate-level lead exposure and crime. *Environmental Research, 148*, 79–85.

Bovsun, M. (2010). Mailman massacre: 14 die after Patrick Sherrill 'goes postal' in 1986 shootings. *New York Daily News.* August 15, 2010. Available at https://www.nydailynews.com/news/crime/mailman-massacre-14-die-patrick-sherrill-postal-1986-shootings-article-1.204101.

Bowler, R. M., Mergler, D., Sassine, M. P., Larribe, F., & Hudnell, K. (1999). Neuropsychiatric effects of manganese on mood. *Neurotoxicology, 20*(2–3), 367–378.

Boxer, P., Drawve, G., & Caplan, J. M. (2020). Neighborhood violent crime and academic performance: A geospatial analysis. *American Journal of Community Psychology, 65*, 343–352.

Boxer, P., Groves, C. L., & Docherty, M. (2015). Video games do indeed influence children and adolescents' aggression, prosocial behavior, and academic performance: A clearer reading of Ferguson (2015). *Perspectives on Psychological Science, 10*(5), 671–673.

Braithwaite, J. (1981). The myth of social class and criminality reconsidered. *American Sociological Review, 46*(1), 36–57.

Braithwaite, J. (1989). *Crime, shame and reintegration.* New York: Cambridge University Press.

Brezina, T. (1996). Adapting to strain: An examination of delinquent coping responses. *Criminology, 34*(1), 39–60.

Brody, G. H., Yu, T., Miller, G. E., & Chen, E. (2015). Discrimination, racial identity, and cytokine levels among African-American adolescents. *Journal of Adolescent Health, 56*(5), 496–501.

Broidy, L., & Agnew, R. (1997). Gender and crime: A general strain theory perspective. *Journal of Research in Crime and Delinquency, 34*(3), 275–306.

Brown, B. B., & Larson, J. (2009). Peer relationships in adolescence. In R. M. Lerner & L. Steinberg (Eds.), *Handbook of adolescent psychology* (pp. 74–103). Hoboken, NJ: Wiley.

Bucci, M., Marques, S. S., Oh, D., & Harris, N. B. (2016). Toxic stress in children and adolescents. *Advances in Pediatrics, 63*(1), 403–428.

Buckholtz, J. W., Treadway, M. T., Cowan, R. L., Woodward, N. D., Benning, S. D., Li, R., . . . & Zald, D. H. (2010). Mesolimbic dopamine reward system hypersensitivity in individuals with psychopathic traits. *Nature Neuroscience, 13*(4), 419–421.

Burgess, R. L., & Akers, R. L. (1966). A differential association-reinforcement theory of criminal behavior. *Social Problems, 14*(2), 128–147.

Burt, C. H., Simons, R. L., & Simons, L. G. (2006). A longitudinal test of the effects of parenting and the stability of self-control: negative evidence for the general theory of crime. *Criminology, 44*(2), 353–396.

Burton, V. S., Cullen, F. T., Evans, T. D., Alarid, L. F., & Dunaway, R. G. (1998). Gender, self-control, and crime. *Journal of Research in Crime and Delinquency, 35*(2), 123–147.

Campbell, A. (1999). Staying alive: Evolution, culture, and women's intrasexual aggression. *Behavioral and Brain Sciences, 22*(2), 203–214.

Campbell, A. (2008). Attachment, aggression and affiliation: The role of oxytocin in female social behavior. *Biological Psychology, 77*(1), 1–10.

Campbell, B. C., Dreber, A., Apicella, C. L., Eisenberg, D. T., Gray, P. B., Little, A. C., . . . & Lum, J. K. (2010). Testosterone exposure, dopaminergic reward, and sensation-seeking in young men. *Physiology & Behavior, 99*(4), 451–456.

Campbell, B. G. (2009). *Human evolution: An introduction to man's adaptations* (4th ed.). New Brunswick, NJ: Transaction Publishers.

Campbell, C., Niemeyer, R. E., & Proctor, K. R. (2016). When focusing deterrence fails: Examining differences of deterrence among offender types. November 2016. Paper presented at the Annual Meeting of the American Society of Criminology, New Orleans.

Carney, D. R., & Mason, M. F. (2010). Decision making and testosterone: When the ends justify the means. *Journal of Experimental Social Psychology, 46*(4), 668–671.

Carson, R. (1962). *Silent spring.* New York: Houghton Mifflin Harcourt.

Casey, B. J., Jones, R. M., & Somerville, L. H. (2011). Braking and accelerating of the adolescent brain. *Journal of Research on Adolescence, 21*(1), 21–33.

Caspi, A., McClay, J., Moffitt, T. E., Mill, J., Martin, J., Craig, I. W., Taylor, A., & Poulton, R. (2002). Role of genotype in the cycle of violence in maltreated children. *Science, 297*(5582), 851–854.

Castro, F. G., Barrera Jr., M., Mena, L. A., & Aguirre, K. M. (2014). Culture and alcohol use: Historical and sociocultural themes from 75 years of alcohol research. *Journal of Studies on Alcohol and Drugs* (Supplement s17), 36–49.

Centers for Disease Control and Prevention (CDC). (2020). *Childhood lead poisoning prevention.* November 24, 2020. Available at https://www.cdc.gov/nceh/lead/prevention/sources/paint.htm.

Chae, D. H., Nuru-Jeter, A. M., Adler, N. E., Brody, G. H., Lin, J., Blackburn, E. H., & Epel, E. S. (2014). Discrimination, racial bias, and telomere length in African-American men. *American Journal of Preventive Medicine, 46*(2), 103–111.

Chinlund, S. (2011). After Attica: Hope for prison? *The Nation.* September 9, 2011. Available at https://www.thenation.com/article/archive/after-attica-hope-prisons/.

Choy, O., Raine, A., Venables, P. H., & Farrington, D. P. (2017). Explaining the gender gap in crime: The role of heart rate. *Criminology, 55*(2), 465–487.

Christakis, N. A., & Fowler, J. H. (2009). *Connected: The surprising power of our social networks and how they shape our lives.* Boston: Little, Brown, and Company.

Clarke, M. (2018). Polls show people favor rehabilitation over incarceration. *Prison Legal News.* November 6, 2018. Available at https://www.prisonlegal news.org/news/2018/nov/6/polls-show-people-favor-rehabilitation-over-incarceration/.

Cleveland Clinic. (2019). What happens to your body during the flight or fight response? Your survival response explained. December 9, 2019. Available at https://health.clevelandclinic.org/what-happens-to-your-body-during-the-fight-or-flight-response/.

Cloward, R. A. & Ohlin, L. (1960). *Delinquency and opportunity: A theory of delinquent gangs.* New York: The Free Press.

Clutton-Brock, T. H. (1988). *Reproductive success: Studies of individual variation in contrasting breeding systems.* Chicago: University of Chicago Press.

Cobain, I. (2014). Tough case to crack: The mystery of Britain's falling crime rate. *Guardian.* August 31, 2014. Available at https://www.theguardian.com/uk-news/2014/aug/31/tough-case-mystery-britains-falling-crime-rate.

Cohen, A. K. (1955). *Delinquent boys: The culture of the gang.* New York: Free Press.

Cohen, L. E., & Felson, M. (1979). Social change and crime rate trends: A routine activity approach. *American Sociological Review, 44*(4), 588–608.

Collins, R. E. (2004). Onset and desistance in criminal careers: Neurobiology and the age-crime relationship. *Journal of Offender Rehabilitation, 39*(3), 1–19.

Conley, D., & Fletcher, J. (2017). *The genome factor.* Princeton, NJ: Princeton University Press.

Connolly, E. J. (2020). Further evaluating the relationship between adverse childhood experiences, antisocial behavior, and violent victimization: A sibling-comparison analysis. *Youth Violence and Juvenile Justice, 18*(1), 3–23.

Cosgrove, K. P., Mazure, C. M., & Staley, J. K. (2007). Evolving knowledge of sex differences in brain structure, function, and chemistry. *Biological Psychiatry, 62*(8), 847–855.

Côté, S., Vaillancourt, T., LeBlanc, J. C., Nagin, D. S., & Tremblay, R. E. (2006). The development of physical aggression from toddlerhood to pre-adolescence: A nation wide longitudinal study of Canadian children. *Journal of Abnormal Child Psychology, 34*(1), 68–82.

Craig, J. M., Piquero, A. R., Farrington, D. P., & Ttofi, M. M. (2017). A little early risk goes a long bad way: Adverse childhood experiences and life-course offending in the Cambridge study. *Journal of Criminal Justice, 53*, 34–45.

Cuddy, A. J., Wolf, E. B., Glick, P., Crotty, S., Chong, J., & Norton, M. I. (2015). Men as cultural ideals: Cultural values moderate gender stereotype content. *Journal of Personality and Social Psychology, 109*(4), 622–635.

Cullen, F. T. (2013). Rehabilitation: Beyond nothing works. *Crime and Justice, 42*(1), 299–376.

Cullen, F. T. & Gilbert, K. E. (1982). *Reaffirming rehabilitation.* Cincinnati, OH: Anderson.

Cullen, F. T., Jonson, C. L., & Nagin, D. S. (2011). Prisons do not reduce recidivism: The high cost of ignoring science. *The Prison Journal, 91*(3_suppl), 48S–65S.

Cullen, F. T., Unnever, J. D., Wright, J. P., & Beaver, K. M. (2008). Parenting and self-control. In E. Goode (Ed.). *Out of control: Assessing the general theory of crime* (pp. 61–74). Stanford, CA: Stanford Social Sciences.

Czech, T. (2020). "I have nothing to lose," suspected drug dealer tells state trooper during foot chase. *York Daily Record.* March 10, 2020. Available at https://www.ydr.com/story/news/crime/2020/03/10/i-have-nothing-lose-suspected-drug-dealer-tells-trooper/5012310002/.

Dabbs, J., & Hargrove, M. F. (1997). Age, testosterone, and behavior among female prison inmates. *Psychosomatic Medicine, 59*(5), 477–480.

Dallas Times Herald. (1986). Neighbors avoided the recluse who scowled, skulked about. In Ashbury Park Press, August 21, 1986, page A2.

Daly, K. (1994). *Gender, crime, and punishment.* New Haven, CT: Yale University Press.

Daly, M., & Wilson, M. (1988). Evolutionary social psychology and family homicide. *Science, 242*(4878), 519–524.

Daly, M., & Wilson, M. (1997). Crime and conflict: Homicide in evolutionary psychological perspective. *Crime and Justice, 22*, 51–100.

Damberg, M., Garpenstrand, H., Hallman, J., & Oreland, L. (2001). Genetic mechanisms of behavior—don't forget about the transcription factors. *Molecular Psychiatry, 6*(5), 503–510.

Davis, M., & Emory, E. (1995). Sex differences in neonatal stress reactivity. *Child Development, 66*(1), 14–27.

Day, A., Chung, D., O'Leary, P., & Carson, E. (2009). Programs for men who perpetrate domestic violence: An examination of the issues underlying the effectiveness of intervention programs. *Journal of Family Violence, 24*(3), 203–212.

Dean, A. J., Bor, W., Adam, K., Bowling, F. G., & Bellgrove, M. A. (2014). A randomized, controlled, crossover trial of fish oil treatment for impulsive aggression in children and adolescents with disruptive behavior disorders. *Journal of Child and Adolescent Psychopharmacology, 24*(3), 140–148.

De Coster, S., Heimer, K., & Cumley, S. R. (2013). Gender and theories of delinquency. In F. T. Cullen & P. Wilcox (Eds.), *The Oxford handbook of criminological theory* (pp. 313–330). New York: Oxford University Press.

Del Giudice, M., Gangestad, S. W., & Kaplan, H. S. (2016). Life history theory and evolutionary psychology. In D. M. Buss (Ed.), *The handbook of evolutionary psychology: Foundations* (p. 88–114). New York: John Wiley & Sons.

DeLisi, M. (2014). Low self-control is a brain-based disorder. In K. M. Beaver, J. C. Barnes, & B. B. Boutwell (Eds.), *The nature versus biosocial debate in criminology: On the origins of criminal behavior and criminality* (pp. 172–182). Thousand Oaks, CA: Sage.

Devlin, H. (2021). Introduction to FMRI. *Nuffield Department of Clinical Neurosciences.* Available at https://www.ndcn.ox.ac.uk/divisions/fmrib/what-is-fmri/introduction-to-fmri.

DeWit, E. L., Meissen-Sebelius, E. M., Shook, R. P., Pina, K. A., De Miranda, E. D., Summar, M. J., & Hurley, E. A. (2020). Beyond clinical food prescriptions and mobile markets: Parent views on the role of a healthcare institution in increasing healthy eating in food insecure families. *Nutrition Journal, 19*(1), 1–12.

Dionne, G., Tremblay, R., Boivin, M., Laplante, D., & Pérusse, D. (2003). Physical aggression and expressive vocabulary in 19-month-old twins. *Developmental Psychology, 39*(2), 261–273.

Domingue, B. W., Fletcher, J., Conley, D., & Boardman, J. D. (2014). Genetic and educational assortative mating among US adults. *Proceedings of the National Academy of Sciences, 111*(22), 7996–8000.

Dong, M., Anda, R. F., Felitti, V. J., Williamson, D. F., Dube, S. R., Brown, D. W., & Giles, W. H. (2005). Childhood residential mobility and multiple health risks during adolescence and adulthood: The hidden role of adverse childhood experiences. *Archives of Pediatrics & Adolescent Medicine, 159*(12), 1104–1110.

Donohue III, J. J., & Levitt, S. D. (2001). The impact of legalized abortion on crime. *The Quarterly Journal of Economics, 116*(2), 379–420.

Drum, K. (2013). Lead: America's real criminal element. *Mother Jones.* January/February, 2013. Available at https://www.motherjones.com/environment/2016/02/lead-exposure-gasoline-crime-increase-children-health/.

Duckworth, A. L., Kim, B., & Tsukayama, E. (2013). Life stress impairs self-control in early adolescence. *Frontiers in Psychology, 3*, 1–12.

Duke, S. A., Balzer, B. W., & Steinbeck, K. S. (2014). Testosterone and its effects on human male adolescent mood and behavior: A systematic review. *Journal of Adolescent Health, 55*(3), 315–322.

Durkheim, E. ([1897] 2005). *Suicide: A study in sociology.* London: Routledge.

Durrant, R., & Ward, T. (2015). *Evolutionary criminology: Towards a comprehensive explanation of crime.* London, UK: Academic Press.

Duwe, G. (2014). *Mass murder in the United States: A history.* Jefferson, NC: McFarland.

Duwe, G. (2020). Patterns and prevalence of lethal mass violence. *Criminology & Public Policy, 19*(1), 17–35.

Ellis, L. (1988). Criminal behavior and r/K selection: An extension of gene-based evolutionary theory. *Personality and Individual Differences, 9*(4), 697–708.

Ellis, L., Das, S., & Buker, H. (2008). Androgen-promoted physiological traits and criminality: A test of the evolutionary neuroandrogenic theory. *Personality and Individual Differences, 44*(3), 701–711.

Energy Information Administration (EIA). (2020). *Gasoline explained: A history of gasoline.* June 25, 2020. Available at https://www.eia.gov/energyexplained /gasoline/history-of-gasoline.php#:~:text=Unleaded%20gasoline%20 was%20introduced%20in,using%20leaded%20gasoline%20in%20vehicles.

Euling, S. Y., Herman-Giddens, M. E., Lee, P. A., Selevan, S. G., Juul, A., Sørensen, T. I., . . . & Swan, S. H. (2008). Examination of US puberty-timing data from 1940 to 1994 for secular trends: Panel findings. *Pediatrics, 121*(Supplement 3), S172–S191.

Fagan, A. A. (2001). The gender cycle of violence: Comparing the effects of child abuse and neglect on criminal offending for males and females. *Violence and Victims, 16*(4), 457–474.

Fagot, B. I., Rodgers, C. S., & Leinbach, M. D. (2000). Theories of gender socialization. In T. Eckes & H. M. Trautner (Eds.), *The developmental social psychology of gender* (pp. 65–89). New York: Psychology Press.

Farrington, D. P. (1986). Age and crime. *Crime and Justice, 7,* 189–250.

Farrington, D. P. (1997). The relationship between low resting heart rate and violence. In A. Raine, P. A. Brennan, D. P. Farrington, & S. A. Mednick (Eds.). *Biosocial bases of violence* (pp. 89–105). New York: Springer.

Farrington, D. P., Loeber, R., & Howell, J. C. (2012). Young adult offenders: The need for more effective legislative options and justice processing. *Criminology & Public Policy, 11*(4), 729–750.

Fausto-Sterling, A. (1993). The five sexes. *The Sciences, 33*(2), 20–24.

Felitti, V. J., Anda, R. F., Nordenberg, D., Williamson, D. F., Spitz, A. M., Edwards, V., & Marks, J. S. (1998). Relationship of childhood abuse and household dysfunction to many of the leading causes of death in adults: The Adverse Childhood Experiences (ACE) Study. *American Journal of Preventive Medicine, 14*(4), 245–258.

Felker-Kantor, E., Wallace, M., & Theall, K. (2017). Living in violence: Neighborhood domestic violence and small for gestational age births. *Health & Place, 46,* 130–136.

Ferguson, C. J. (2015). Clinicians' attitudes toward video games vary as a function of age, gender and negative beliefs about youth: A sociology of media research approach. *Computers in Human Behavior, 52,* 379–386.

Ferguson, C. J., & Kilburn, J. (2009). The public health risks of media violence: A meta-analytic review. *Journal of Pediatrics, 154*(5), 759–763.

Fieder, M., Huber, S., Bookstein, F. L., Iber, K., Schäfer, K., Winckler, G., & Wallner, B. (2005). Status and reproduction in humans: New evidence for the validity of evolutionary explanations on basis of a university sample. *Ethology, 111*(10), 940–950.

Fishbein, D., & Pease, S. E. (1994). Diet, nutrition, and aggression. *Journal of Offender Rehabilitation, 21*(3–4), 117–144.

Fitzpatrick, K. M., Harris, C., Drawve, G., & Willis, D. E. (2020). Assessing food insecurity among US adults during the COVID-19 pandemic. *Journal of Hunger & Environmental Nutrition*, 1–18.

Fox, B. (2017). It's nature and nurture: Integrating biology and genetics into the social learning theory of criminal behavior. *Journal of Criminal Justice, 49*, 22–31.

Fox, B. H., Perez, N., Cass, E., Baglivio, M. T., & Epps, N. (2015). Trauma changes everything: Examining the relationship between adverse childhood experiences and serious, violent and chronic juvenile offenders. *Child Abuse & Neglect, 46*, 163–173.

Fox, J. A., Levin, J., & Quinet, K. (2012). *The will to kill: Making sense of senseless murder.* Upper Saddle Ridge, NJ: Pearson.

Friend, C. (n.d.). Social contract theory. *Internet Encyclopedia of Philosophy.* Available at https://iep.utm.edu/soc-cont/.

Friese, M., Messner, C., & Schaffner, Y. (2012). Mindfulness meditation counteracts self-control depletion. *Consciousness and Cognition, 21*(2), 1016–1022.

Fuller-Rowell, T. E., Curtis, D. S., El-Sheikh, M., Chae, D. H., Boylan, J. M., & Ryff, C. D. (2016). Racial disparities in sleep: The role of neighborhood disadvantage. *Sleep Medicine, 27*, 1–8.

Gabrielli, W. F., & Mednick, S. A. (1984). Urban environment, genetics, and crime. *Criminology, 22*(4), 645–652.

Gailliot, M. T., Baumeister, R. F., DeWall, C. N., Maner, J. K., Plant, E. A., Tice, D. M., . . . & Schmeichel, B. J. (2007). Self-control relies on glucose as a limited energy source: Willpower is more than a metaphor. *Journal of Personality and Social Psychology, 92*(2), 325–336.

Garland, M. R., & Hallahan, B. (2006). Essential fatty acids and their role in conditions characterised by impulsivity. *International Review of Psychiatry, 18*(2), 99–105.

Giedd, J. N., Clasen, L. S., Lenroot, R., Greenstein, D., Wallace, G. L., Ordaz, S., . . . & Samango-Sprouse, C. A. (2006). Puberty-related influences on brain development. *Molecular and Cellular Endocrinology, 254*, 154–162.

Ginty, A. T., Muldoon, M. F., Kuan, D. C., Schirda, B., Kamarck, T. W., Jennings, J. R., . . . & Gianaros, P. J. (2017). Omega-3 supplementation and the neural correlates of negative affect and impulsivity: A double-blind, randomized, placebo-controlled trial in midlife adults. *Psychosomatic Medicine, 79*(5), 549–556.

Giordano, P. C., Cernkovich, S. A., & Rudolph, J. L. (2002). Gender, crime, and desistance: Toward a theory of cognitive transformation. *American Journal of Sociology, 107*(4), 990–1064.

Glenn, A. L., Lochman, J. E., Dishion, T., Powell, N. P., Boxmeyer, C., Kassing, F., Qu, L., & Romero, D. (2018a). Toward tailored interventions: Sympathetic and parasympathetic functioning predicts responses to an intervention for conduct problems delivered in two formats. *Prevention Science, 20*(1), 30–40.

Glenn, A. L., Lochman, J. E., Dishion, T., Powell, N. P., Boxmeyer, C., & Qu, L. (2018b). Oxytocin receptor gene variant interacts with intervention delivery format in predicting intervention outcomes for youth with conduct problems. *Prevention Science, 19*(1), 38–48.

Glowacki, L. (2016). 9 reasons Canada's crime rate is falling. *CBC.* July 26, 2016. Available at https://www.cbc.ca/news/canada/manitoba/9-reasons-crime-rate-1.3692193.

Glueck, S., & Glueck, E. (1940). *Juvenile delinquents grown up.* Washington, DC: Commonwealth Fund.

Glueck, S., & Glueck, E. T. (1950). *Unraveling juvenile delinquency.* Harvard, MA: Harvard University Press.

Goel, N., Workman, J. L., Lee, T. T., Innala, L., & Viau, V. (2014). Sex differences in the HPA axis. *Comprehensive Physiology, 4*, 1121–1155.

Gopnik, A. (2016). Learning from the slaughter in Attica. *The New Yorker.* August 29, 2016. Available at https://www.newyorker.com/magazine/2016/08/29/learning-from-the-slaughter-in-attica.

Gorman, J. M. (2006). Gender differences in depression and response to psychotropic medication. *Gender Medicine, 3*(2), 93–109.

Gottfredson, M. R., & Hirschi, T. (1986). The true value of lambda would appear to be zero: An essay on career criminals, criminal careers, selective incapacitation, cohort studies, and related topics. *Criminology, 24*(2), 213–234.

Gottfredson, M. R., & Hirschi, T. (1990). *A general theory of crime.* Stanford, CA: Stanford University Press.

Gove, W. R. (1985). The effect of age and gender on deviant behavior: A biopsychosocial perspective. In A. Rossi (Ed.), *Gender and the life course* (pp. 115–144). New York: Routledge.

Gray, P. B., Kahlenberg, S. M., Barrett, E. S., Lipson, S. F., & Ellison, P. T. (2002). Marriage and fatherhood are associated with lower testosterone in males. *Evolution and Human Behavior, 23*(3), 193–201.

Greenberg, D. F. (1977). Delinquency and the age structure of society. *Contemporary Crises, 1*(2), 189–223.

Greenberg, D. F. (1985). Age, crime, and social explanation. *American Journal of Sociology, 91*(1), 1–21.

Grych, J., Hamby, S., & Banyard, V. (2015). The resilience portfolio model: Understanding healthy adaptation in victims of violence. *Psychology of Violence, 5*(4), 343–454.

Guo, G. (2006). Genetic similarity shared by best friends among adolescents. *Twin Research and Human Genetics, 9*(1), 113–121.

Guo, G., Roettger, M. E., & Cai, T. (2008). The integration of genetic propensities into social-control models of delinquency and violence among male youths. *American Sociological Review, 73*(4), 543–568.

Haga, S. B. (2010). Impact of limited population diversity of genome-wide association studies. *Genetics in Medicine, 12*(2), 81–84.

Hagan, J., Gillis, A. R., & Simpson, J. (1985). The class structure of gender and delinquency: Toward a power-control theory of common delinquent behavior. *American Journal of Sociology, 90*(6), 1151–1178.

Hahn, T., Heinzel, S., Dresler, T., Plichta, M. M., Renner, T. J., Markulin, F., . . . & Fallgatter, A. J. (2011). Association between reward-related activation in the ventral striatum and trait reward sensitivity is moderated by dopamine transporter genotype. *Human Brain Mapping, 32*(10), 1557–1565.

Haider, S. (2016). The shooting in Orlando, terrorism or toxic masculinity (or both?). *Men and Masculinities, 19*(5), 555–565.

Hall, G. S. (1904). *Adolescence.* New York: D. Appleton.

Hamazaki, T., & Hamazaki, K. (2008). Fish oils and aggression or hostility. *Progress in Lipid Research, 47*(4), 221–232.

Harden, K. P., Mann, F. D., Grotzinger, A. D., Patterson, M. W., Steinberg, L., Tackett, J. L., & Tucker-Drob, E. M. (2018). Developmental differences in reward sensitivity and sensation seeking in adolescence: Testing sex-specific associations with gonadal hormones and pubertal development. *Journal of Personality and Social Psychology, 115*(1), 161–178.

Hare, R. D. (1993). *Without conscience: The disturbing world of the psychopaths among us.* New York: Guilford Press.

Harris, J. R. (2009). *The nurture assumption: Why children turn out the way they do.* New York: Simon and Schuster.

Hay, C. (2001). Parenting, self-control, and delinquency: A test of self-control theory. *Criminology, 39*(3), 707–736.

Healthline. (2020). Serotonin: What you need to know. August 19, 2020. Available at https://www.healthline.com/health/mental-health/serotonin.

Healthline. (2021). The effects of stress on your body. March 29, 2020. Available at https://www.healthline.com/health/stress/effects-on-body#Respiratory -and-cardiovascular-systems.

Heatherton, T. F. (2011). Neuroscience of self and self-regulation. *Annual Review of Psychology, 62*, 363–390.

Heissel, J. A., Sharkey, P. T., Torrats-Espinosa, G., Grant, K., & Adam, E. K. (2018). Violence and vigilance: The acute effects of community violent crime on sleep and cortisol. *Child Development, 89*(4), e323–e331.

Herman, A. I., Conner, T. S., Anton, R. F., Gelernter, J., Kranzler, H. R., & Covault, J. (2011). Variation in the gene encoding the serotonin transporter is associated with a measure of sociopathy in alcoholics. *Addiction Biology, 16*(1), 124–132.

Hermans, E. J., Putman, P., & van Honk, J. (2006). Testosterone administration reduces empathetic behavior: A facial mimicry study. *Psychoneuroendocrinology, 31*(7), 859–866.

Hirschi, T. (1969). *Causes of delinquency.* New Brunswick, NJ: Transaction Publishers.

Hirschi, T. (1989). Exploring alternatives to integrated theory. In S. F. Messner, M. D. Krohn, & A. E. Liska (Eds.), *Theoretical integration in the study of deviance and crime* (pp. 37–49). Albany, NY: SUNY Press.

Hirschi, T. (2004). Self-control and crime. In R. F. Baumeister & K. D. Vohs (Eds.), *The handbook of self-regulation: Theory, research and applications* (pp. 537–552). New York: Guilford Press.

Hirschi, T., & Gottfredson, M. R. (1983). Age and the explanation of crime. *American Journal of Sociology, 89*, 552–584.

Hirschi, T., & Hindelang, M. J. (1977). Intelligence and delinquency: A revisionist review. *American Sociological Review, 42*(4), 571–587.

Hobbes, T. ([1651] 1887). *Leviathan, or the matter, form, and power of a commonwealth, ecclesiastical and civil* (3rd ed.). London: George Routledge and Sons.

Hoeben, E. M., & Weerman, F. M. (2016). Why is involvement in unstructured socializing related to adolescent delinquency? *Criminology, 54*(2), 242–281.

Hoeve, M., Dubas, J. S., Eichelsheim, V. I., Van der Laan, P. H., Smeenk, W., & Gerris, J. R. (2009). The relationship between parenting and delinquency: A meta-analysis. *Journal of Abnormal Child Psychology, 37*(6), 749–775.

Hoffmann, J. P., & Cerbone, F. G. (1999). Stressful life events and delinquency escalation in early adolescence. *Criminology, 37*(2), 343–374.

Hölzel, B. K., Carmody, J., Vangel, M., Congleton, C., Yerramsetti, S. M., Gard, T., & Lazar, S. W. (2011). Mindfulness practice leads to increases in regional brain gray matter density. *Psychiatry Research: Neuroimaging, 191*(1), 36–43.

Hood-Williams, J. (2001). Gender, masculinities and crime: From structures to psyches. *Theoretical Criminology, 5*(1), 37–60.

Isacescu, J., & Danckert, J. (2018). Exploring the relationship between boredom proneness and self-control in traumatic brain injury (TBI). *Experimental Brain Research, 236*(9), 2493–2505.

Itomura, M., Hamazaki, K., Sawazaki, S., Kobayashi, M., Terasawa, K., Watanabe, S., & Hamazaki, T. (2005). The effect of fish oil on physical aggression in schoolchildren—A randomized, double-blind, placebo-controlled trial. *Journal of Nutritional Biochemistry, 16*(3), 163–171.

Jackson, D. B. (2016). The link between poor quality nutrition and childhood antisocial behavior: A genetically informative analysis. *Journal of Criminal Justice, 44*, 13–20.

Jackson, D. B., Fahmy, C., Vaughn, M. G., & Testa, A. (2019). Police stops among at-risk youth: Repercussions for mental health. *Journal of Adolescent Health, 65*(5), 627–632.

Jackson, D. B., Newsome, J., Vaughn, M. G., & Johnson, K. R. (2018). Considering the role of food insecurity in low self-control and early delinquency. *Journal of Criminal Justice, 56*, 127–139.

Jackson, D. B., & Vaughn, M. G. (2017). Household food insecurity during childhood and adolescent misconduct. *Preventive Medicine, 96*, 113–117.

Jackson, J., Bradford, B., Hough, M., Myhill, A., Quinton, P., & Tyler, T. R. (2012). Why do people comply with the law? Legitimacy and the influence of legal institutions. *British Journal of Criminology, 52*(6), 1051–1071.

Jacobson, K. C., & Rowe, D. C. (1999). Genetic and environmental influences on the relationships between family connectedness, school connectedness, and adolescent depressed mood: Sex differences. *Developmental Psychology, 35*(4), 926–939.

James, N. (2018). Recent violent crime trends in the United States. *Congressional Research Service.* June 20, 2018. Available at https://fas.org/sgp/crs/misc /R45236.pdf.

Janis, I. L. (1972). *Victims of groupthink: A psychological study of foreign-policy decisions and fiascoes.* Boston: Houghton Mifflin.

Jansen, P. R., Polderman, T. J., Bolhuis, K., van der Ende, J., Jaddoe, V. W., Verhulst, F. C., . . . & Tiemeier, H. (2018). Polygenic scores for schizophrenia and educational attainment are associated with behavioural problems in early childhood in the general population. *Journal of Child Psychology and Psychiatry, 59*(1), 39–47.

Jennings, W. G., & Reingle, J. M. (2012). On the number and shape of developmental/life-course violence, aggression, and delinquency trajectories: A state-of-the-art review. *Journal of Criminal Justice, 40*(6), 472–489.

Johnson, D. A., Jackson, C. L., Williams, N. J., & Alcántara, C. (2019). Are sleep patterns influenced by race/ethnicity—a marker of relative advantage or disadvantage? Evidence to date. *Nature and Science of Sleep, 11,* 79–95.

Johnson, S. B., Riis, J. L., & Noble, K. G. (2016). State of the art review: Poverty and the developing brain. *Pediatrics, 137*(4), e20153075.

Josephs, R. A., Mehta, P. H., & Carré, J. M. (2011). Gender and social environment modulate the effects of testosterone on social behavior: Comment on Eisenegger et al. *Trends in Cognitive Sciences, 15*(11), 509–510.

Josephs, R. A., Sellers, J. G., Newman, M. L., & Mehta, P. H. (2006). The mismatch effect: When testosterone and status are at odds. *Journal of Personality and Social Psychology, 90*(6), 999–1013.

Jovanovic, H., Lundberg, J., Karlsson, P., Cerin, Å., Saijo, T., Varrone, A., Halldin, C., & Nordström, A. L. (2008). Sex differences in the serotonin 1A receptor and serotonin transporter binding in the human brain measured by PET. *Neuroimage, 39*(3), 1408–1419.

Kelling, G. L., Pate, T., Dieckman, D., & Brown, C. (1974). *The Kansas City Preventive Patrol Experiment: A Technical Report.* Washington, DC: Police Foundation.

Kessler, R. C., Aguilar-Gaxiola, S., Alonso, J., Chatterji, S., Lee, S., Ormel, J., . . . & Wang, P. S. (2009). The global burden of mental disorders: An update from the WHO World Mental Health (WMH) surveys. *Epidemiologia e Psichiatria Sociale, 18*(1), 23–33.

Kim, P., Evans, G. W., Angstadt, M., Ho, S. S., Sripada, C. S., Swain, J. E., Liberzon, I., & Phan, K. L. (2013). Effects of childhood poverty and chronic stress on emotion regulatory brain function in adulthood. *Proceedings of the National Academy of Sciences, 110*(46), 18442–18447.

King, R. D., Massoglia, M., & MacMillan, R. (2007). The context of marriage and crime: Gender, the propensity to marry, and offending in early adulthood. *Criminology, 45*(1), 33–65.

Kirk, D. S. (2020). *Home free: Prisoner reentry and residential change after Hurricane Katrina*. New York: Oxford University Press.

Kirschbaum, C., Kudielka, B. M., Gaab, J., Schommer, N. C., & Hellhammer, D. H. (1999). Impact of gender, menstrual cycle phase, and oral contraceptives on the activity of the hypothalamus-pituitary-adrenal axis. *Psychosomatic Medicine, 61*(2), 154–162.

Koenen, K. C., Moffitt, T. E., Caspi, A., Taylor, A., & Purcell, S. (2003). Domestic violence is associated with environmental suppression of IQ in young children. *Development and Psychopathology, 15*(2), 297–311.

Konner, M. (2015). *Women after all: Sex, evolution, and the end of male supremacy*. W. W. Norton.

Kornhauser, R. R. (1978). *Social sources of delinquency: An appraisal of analytic models*. Chicago: University of Chicago Press.

Kreiss, K., Zack, M. M., Kimbrough, R. D., Needham, L. L., Smrek, A. L., & Jones, B. T. (1981). Cross-sectional study of a community with exceptional exposure to DDT. *JAMA, 245*(19), 1926–1930.

Kruttschnitt, C. (2013). Gender and crime. *Annual Review of Sociology, 39*, 291–308.

Kudielka, B. M., & Kirschbaum, C. (2005). Sex differences in HPA axis responses to stress: A review. *Biological Psychology, 69*(1), 113–132.

Kumar, A., Rinwa, P., Kaur, G., & Machawal, L. (2013). Stress: Neurobiology, consequences and management. *Journal of Pharmacy & Bioallied Sciences, 5*(2), 91.

Laland, K. N., Odling-Smee, J., & Myles, S. (2010). How culture shaped the human genome: Bringing genetics and the human sciences together. *Nature Reviews Genetics, 11*(2), 137–148.

Lankford, A. (2016). Public mass shooters and firearms: A cross-national study of 171 countries. *Violence and Victims, 31*(2), 187–199.

Latchman, D. S. (1993). Transcription factors: An overview. *International Journal of Experimental Pathology, 74*(5), 417–422.

Laub, J. H., & Sampson, R. J. (1991). The Sutherland-Glueck debate: On the sociology of criminological knowledge. *American Journal of Sociology, 96*(6), 1402–1440.

Laub, J. H., & Sampson, R. J. (2003). *Shared beginnings, divergent lives: Delinquent boys to age 70*. Cambridge, MA: Harvard University Press.

Lee, K.-C., Yu, C.-C., Hsieh, P.-L., Li, C., & Chao, Y.-F. C. (2018). Situated teaching improves empathy learning of the students in a BSN program: A quasi-experimental study. *Nurse Education Today, 64*, 138–143.

Levitt, S. D. (2004). Understanding why crime fell in the 1990s: Four factors that explain the decline and six that do not. *Journal of Economic Perspectives, 18*(1), 163–190.

Li, Y., Liu, H., & Guo, G. (2015). Does marriage moderate genetic effects on delinquency and violence? *Journal of Marriage and Family, 77*(5), 1217–1233.

Lipsey, M. W., Landenberger, N. A., & Wilson, S. J. (2007). Effects of cognitive-behavioral programs for criminal offenders. *Campbell Systematic Reviews, 3*(1), 1–27.

Lockwood, K. G., Marsland, A. L., Matthews, K. A., & Gianaros, P. J. (2018). Perceived discrimination and cardiovascular health disparities: A multi-system review and health neuroscience perspective. *Annals of the New York Academy of Sciences, 1428*(1), 170–207.

Los Angeles Times. (1986). Post office massacre: 15 dead after Okla. mailman's three-gun rampage: He faced job loss for poor-work reprimand. August 20, 1986. Available at https://www.latimes.com/archives/la-xpm-1986-08-20-mn -18500-story.html.

Lyngstad, T. H., & Skardhamar, T. (2013). Changes in criminal offending around the time of marriage. *Journal of Research in Crime and Delinquency, 50*(4), 608–615.

Mahar, I., Bambico, F. R., Mechawar, N., & Nobrega, J. N. (2014). Stress, serotonin, and hippocampal neurogenesis in relation to depression and antidepressant effects. *Neuroscience & Biobehavioral Reviews, 38*, 173–192.

Marlowe, M., Cossairt, A., Moon, C., Errera, J., MacNeel, A., Peak, R., . . . & Schroeder, C. (1985). Main and interaction effects of metallic toxins on classroom behavior. *Journal of Abnormal Child Psychology, 13*(2), 185–198.

Martin, T. E., & Wolfe, S. E. (2020). Lead exposure, concentrated disadvantage, and violent crime rates. *Justice Quarterly, 37*(1), 1–24.

Martinez, D., Orlowska, D., Narendran, R., Slifstein, M., Liu, F., Kumar, D., . . . & Kleber, H. D. (2010). Dopamine type 2/3 receptor availability in the striatum and social status in human volunteers. *Biological Psychiatry, 67*(3), 275–278.

Martinez-Alier, J., Temper, L., Del Bene, D., & Scheidel, A. (2016). Is there a global environmental justice movement? *Journal of Peasant Studies, 43*(3), 731–755.

Martinson, R. (1974). What works?-Questions and answers about prison reform. *The Public Interest, 35*, 22–54.

Maruna, S. (2001). *Making good: How ex-convicts reform and rebuild their lives.* Washington, DC: American Psychological Association.

Mathews, T. J., & Hamilton, B. E. (2016). Mean age of mothers is on the rise: United States, 2000–2014. *NCHS Data Brief, 232*, 1–8.

Matsueda, R. L., & Anderson, K. (1998). The dynamics of delinquent peers and delinquent behavior. *Criminology, 36*(2), 269–308.

Matza, D. (1964). *Delinquency and drift.* Piscataway, NJ: Transaction Publishers.

Mazerolle, L., Bennett, S., Davis, J., Sargeant, E., & Manning, M. (2013). Procedural justice and police legitimacy: A systematic review of the research evidence. *Journal of Experimental Criminology, 9*(3), 245–274.

Mazerolle, P. (1998). Gender, general strain, and delinquency: An empirical examination. *Justice Quarterly, 15*(1), 65–91.

Mazur, A., & Michalek, J. (1998). Marriage, divorce, and male testosterone. *Social Forces, 77*(1), 315–330.

McCormick, B. F., Connolly, E. J., & Nelson, D. V. (2020). Mild traumatic brain injury as a predictor of classes of youth internalizing and externalizing psychopathology. *Child Psychiatry and Human Development.* Available at https://doi.org/10.1007/s10578-020-00992-9.

McCuish, E., Lussier, P., & Rocque, M. (2020). Maturation beyond age: Interrelationships among psychosocial, adult role, and identity maturation and their implications for desistance from crime. *Journal of Youth and Adolescence, 49*(2), 479–493.

McEwen, B. S. (2000). Effects of adverse experiences for brain structure and function. *Biological Psychiatry, 48*(8), 721–731.

McEwen, B. S. (2012). Brain on stress: How the social environment gets under the skin. *Proceedings of the National Academy of Sciences, 109*(Supplement 2), 17180–17185.

McEwen, B. S., Nasca, C., & Gray, J. D. (2016). Stress effects on neuronal structure: hippocampus, amygdala, and prefrontal cortex. *Neuropsychopharmacology, 41*(1), 3–23.

McGowan, P. O., Sasaki, A., D'alessio, A. C., Dymov, S., Labonté, B., Szyf, M., . . . & Meaney, M. J. (2009). Epigenetic regulation of the glucocorticoid receptor in human brain associates with childhood abuse. *Nature Neuroscience, 12*(3), 342–348.

McNally, R. T. (1983). *Dracula was a woman: In search of the blood countess of Transylvania.* New York: McGraw-Hill.

Mead, M. (1963). *Sex and temperament in three primitive societies.* New York: Morrow.

Media Education Foundation. (2013). Tough Guise 2 Transcript. Available at https://www.mediaed.org/transcripts/Tough-Guise-2-Transcript.pdf?_ga= 2.31206906.432403819.1625762333-442868071.1625762333.

Medline Plus. (2020). What are genome editing and CRISPR-Cas9? U.S. National Library of Medicine, National Institutes of Health. September 18, 2020. Available at https://medlineplus.gov/genetics/understanding/genomicre search/genomeediting/.

Meldrum, R. C., Barnes, J. C., & Hay, C. (2015). Sleep deprivation, low self-control, and delinquency: A test of the strength model of self-control. *Journal of Youth and Adolescence, 44*(2), 465–477.

Merton, R. K. (1938). Social structure and anomie. *American Sociological Review, 3*(5), 672–682.

Mesoudi, A. (2011). *Cultural evolution: How Darwinian theory can explain human culture and synthesize the social sciences.* Chicago: University of Chicago Press.

Messerschmidt, J. W. (1993). *Masculinities and crime.* Hoboken, NJ: John Wiley & Sons.

Messner, S. F., & Rosenfeld, R. (1994). *Crime and the American dream.* Belmont, CA: Wadsworth.

Miller, J. (2002). The strengths and limits of 'doing gender' for understanding street crime. *Theoretical Criminology, 6*(4), 433–460.

Mischel, W., Shoda, Y., & Rodriguez, M. I. (1989). Delay of gratification in children. *Science, 244*(4907), 933–938.

Moffitt, T. E. (1993). Adolescence-limited and life-course-persistent antisocial behavior: A developmental taxonomy. *Psychological Review, 100*(4), 674–701.

Moffitt, T. E. (2005). The new look of behavioral genetics in developmental psychopathology: gene-environment interplay in antisocial behaviors. *Psychological Bulletin, 131*(4), 533–554.

Moffitt, T. E. (2018). Male antisocial behaviour in adolescence and beyond. *Nature Human Behaviour, 2,* 177–186.

Moffitt, T. E., & Beckley, A. (2015). Abandon twin research-embrace epigenetic research: Premature advice for criminologists. *Criminology, 53,* 121–126.

Mora, F., Segovia, G., Del Arco, A., de Blas, M., & Garrido, P. (2012). Stress, neurotransmitters, corticosterone and body–brain integration. *Brain Research, 1476,* 71–85.

Mosher, C. J., Miethe, T. D., & Phillips, D. M. (2002). *The mismeasure of crime.* Thousand Oaks, CA: Sage.

Mowen, T., & Brent, J. (2016). School discipline as a turning point: The cumulative effect of suspension on arrest. *Journal of Research in Crime and Delinquency, 53*(5), 628–653.

Mulder, R. H., Walton, E., Neumann, A., Houtepen, L. C., Felix, J. F., Bakermans-Kranenburg, M. J., . . . & Cecil, C. A. (2020). Epigenomics of being bullied: Changes in DNA methylation following bullying exposure. *Epigenetics, 15*(6–7), 750–764.

Munro, C. A., McCaul, M. E., Wong, D. F., Oswald, L. M., Zhou, Y., Brasic, J., . . . & Wand, G. S. (2006). Sex differences in striatal dopamine release in healthy adults. *Biological Psychiatry, 59*(10), 966–974.

Nagin, D. S., & Land, K. C. (1993). Age, criminal careers, and population heterogeneity: Specification and estimation of a nonparametric, mixed Poisson model. *Criminology, 31,* 327–362.

Nagin, D. S., & Paternoster, R. (1994). Personal capital and social control: The deterrence implications of a theory of individual differences in criminal offending. *Criminology, 32*(4), 581–606.

National Human Genome Research Institute. (2020a). Genome-wide association studies fact sheet. August 17, 2020. Available at https://www.genome

.gov/about-genomics/fact-sheets/Genome-Wide-Association-Studies-Fact
-Sheet.

National Human Genome Research Institute. (2020b). Polygenic risk scores. August 11, 2020. Available at https://www.genome.gov/Health/Genomics-and -Medicine/Polygenic-risk-scores.

National Institute of Neurological Disorders and Stroke (NINDS). (2019). Brain basics: Genes at work in the brain. August 13, 2019. Available at https://www .ninds.nih.gov/Disorders/Patient-Caregiver-Education/Genes-Work-Brain.

Nedelec, J. L., Schwartz, J. A., & Connolly, E. J. (2014). Intelligence as the quintessential biosocial variable: An examination of etiological factors and associations with criminal offending and criminal justice processing. In M. DeLisi (Ed.). *The Routledge international handbook of biosocial criminology* (pp. 463–485). New York: Routledge.

Needleman, H. L., Riess, J. A., Tobin, M. J., Biesecker, G. E., & Greenhouse, J. B. (1996). Bone lead levels and delinquent behavior. *JAMA, 275*(5), 363–369.

Nevin, R. (2000). How lead exposure relates to temporal changes in IQ, violent crime, and unwed pregnancy. *Environmental Research, 83*(1), 1–22.

Nishizawa, S., Benkelfat, C., Young, S. N., Leyton, M., Mzengeza, S. D., De Montigny, C., Blier, P., & Diksic, M. (1997). Differences between males and females in rates of serotonin synthesis in human brain. *Proceedings of the National Academy of Sciences, 94*(10), 5308–5313.

Oberlander, T. F., Weinberg, J., Papsdorf, M., Grunau, R., Misri, S., & Devlin, A. M. (2008). Prenatal exposure to maternal depression, neonatal methylation of human glucocorticoid receptor gene (NR3C1) and infant cortisol stress responses. *Epigenetics, 3*(2), 97–106.

Ong, A. D., Williams, D. R., Nwizu, U., & Gruenewald, T. L. (2017). Everyday unfair treatment and multisystem biological dysregulation in African American adults. *Cultural Diversity and Ethnic Minority Psychology, 23*(1), 27.

Op de Macks, Z. A., Moor, B. G., Overgaauw, S., Güroğlu, B., Dahl, R. E., & Crone, E. A. (2011). Testosterone levels correspond with increased ventral striatum activation in response to monetary rewards in adolescents. *Developmental Cognitive Neuroscience, 1*(4), 506–516.

Osgood, D. W., Wilson, J. K., O'Malley, P. M., Bachman, J. G., & Johnston, L. D. (1996). Routine activities and individual deviant behavior. *American Sociological Review,* 635–655.

Ostchega, Y., Porter, K. S., Hughes, J., Dillon, C. F., & Nwankwo, T. (2011). Resting pulse rate reference data for children, adolescents, and adults: United States, 1999–2008. Natl Health Stat Report (Aug 24), (41), 1–16.

Ousey, G. C. (2017). Crime is not the only problem: Examining why violence and adverse health outcomes co-vary across large US counties. *Journal of Criminal Justice, 50,* 29–41.

Ozkan, T., Rocque, M., & Posick, C. (2019). Reconsidering the link between depression and crime: A longitudinal assessment. *Criminal Justice and Behavior, 46*(7), 961–979.

Palmer, C. T., & Tilley, C. F. (1995). Sexual access to females as a motivation for joining gangs: An evolutionary approach. *Journal of Sex Research, 32*(3), 213–217.

Paternoster, R., & Bushway, S. (2009). Desistance and the "feared self": Toward an identity theory of criminal desistance. *Journal of Criminal Law and Criminology, 99*(4), 1103–1156.

Paternoster, R., & Mazerolle, P. (1994). General strain theory and delinquency: A replication and extension. *Journal of Research in Crime and Delinquency, 31*(3), 235–263.

Patterson, G. R. (2016). Coercion theory: The study of change. In T. J. Dishion, & J. J. Snyder (Eds.), *The Oxford handbook of coercive relationship dynamics* (pp. 7–22). New York: Oxford University Press.

Pechtel, P., & Pizzagalli, D. A. (2011). Effects of early life stress on cognitive and affective function: An integrated review of human literature. *Psychopharmacology, 214*(1), 55–70.

Pedersen, C. A. (2004). Biological aspects of social bonding and the roots of human violence. In J. Devine, J. Gilligan, K. A. Miczek, R. Shaikh, & D. Pfaff (Eds.), *Annals of the New York Academy of Sciences. Youth violence: Scientific approaches to prevention, 1036*(1), 106–127.

Peper, J. S., & Dahl, R. E. (2013). The teenage brain: Surging hormones—Brain-behavior interactions during puberty. *Current Directions in Psychological Science, 22*(2), 134–139.

Perez, C. M., & Widom, C. S. (1994). Childhood victimization and long-term intellectual and academic outcomes. *Child Abuse & Neglect, 18*(8), 617–633.

Pinker, S. A. (2002). *The blank slate: The modern denial of human nature.* New York: Penguin.

Piquero, A. R., Jennings, W. G., Diamond, B., Farrington, D. P., Tremblay, R. E., Welsh, B. C., & Gonzalez, J. M. R. (2016). A meta-analysis update on the effects of early family/parent training programs on antisocial behavior and delinquency. *Journal of Experimental Criminology, 12*(2), 229–248.

Piquero, N. L., & Sealock, M. D. (2004). Gender and general strain theory: A preliminary test of Broidy and Agnew's gender/GST hypotheses. *Justice Quarterly, 21*(1), 125–158.

Plomin, R., DeFries, J. C., Knopik, V. S., & Neiderhiser, J. M. (2016). Top 10 replicated findings from behavioral genetics. *Perspectives on Psychological Science, 11*(1), 3–23.

Polderman, T. J., Benyamin, B., De Leeuw, C. A., Sullivan, P. F., Van Bochoven, A., Visscher, P. M., & Posthuma, D. (2015). Meta-analysis of the heritability of human traits based on fifty years of twin studies. *Nature Genetics, 47*(7), 702–709.

Poole, J. C., Dobson, K. S., & Pusch, D. (2018). Do adverse childhood experiences predict adult interpersonal difficulties? The role of emotion dysregulation. *Child Abuse & Neglect, 80*, 123–133.

Portnoy, J., & Farrington, D. P. (2015). Resting heart rate and antisocial behavior: An updated systematic review and meta-analysis. *Aggression and Violent Behavior, 22,* 33–45.

Portnoy, J., Raine, A., Chen, F. R., Pardini, D., Loeber, R., & Jennings, J. R. (2014). Heart rate and antisocial behavior: The mediating role of impulsive sensation seeking. *Criminology, 52*(2), 292–311.

Posick, C. (2013). The overlap between offending and victimization among adolescents: Results from the second International Self-Report Delinquency Study. *Journal of Contemporary Criminal Justice, 29*(1), 106–124.

Posick, C., Farrell, A., & Swatt, M. L. (2013). Do boys fight and girls cut? A general strain theory approach to gender and deviance. *Deviant Behavior, 34*(9), 685–705.

Posick, C., & Rocque, M. (2015). Family matters: A cross-national examination of family bonding and victimization. *European Journal of Criminology, 12*(1), 51–69.

Posick, C., & Rocque, M. (2018). *Great debates in criminology.* New York: Routledge.

Pratt, T. C., & Cullen, F. T. (2000). The empirical status of Gottfredson and Hirschi's general theory of crime: A meta-analysis. *Criminology, 38*(3), 931–964.

Pratt, T. C., Turanovic, J. J., & Cullen, F. T. (2016). Revisiting the criminological consequences of exposure to fetal testosterone: A meta-analysis of the 2D:4D digit ratio. *Criminology, 54*(4), 587–620.

Pratt, T. C., Turner, M. G., & Piquero, A. R. (2004). Parental socialization and community context: A longitudinal analysis of the structural sources of low self-control. *Journal of Research in Crime and Delinquency, 41*(3), 219–243.

Proctor, K. R., & Niemeyer, R. E. (2020). Retrofitting social learning theory with contemporary understandings of learning and memory derived from cognitive psychology and neuroscience. *Journal of Criminal Justice, 66,* 101655.

Quetelet, A. ([1831] 1984). *Research on the propensity for crime at different ages* (S. F. Sylvester, Trans). Cincinnati, OH: Anderson.

Rafter, N. (2004). The unrepentant horse-slasher: Moral insanity and the origins of criminological thought. *Criminology, 42*(4), 979–1008.

Rafter, N., Posick, C., & Rocque, M. (2016). *The criminal brain: Understanding biological theories of crime.* New York: New York University Press.

Raine, A. (2013). *The anatomy of violence: The biological roots of crime.* New York: Vintage.

Raine, A., Lencz, T., Bihrle, S., LaCasse, L., & Colletti, P. (2000). Reduced prefrontal gray matter volume and reduced autonomic activity in antisocial personality disorder. *Archives of General Psychiatry, 57*(2), 119–127.

Raine, A., Yang, Y., Narr, K. L., & Toga, A. W. (2011). Sex differences in orbitofrontal gray as a partial explanation for sex differences in antisocial personality. *Molecular Psychiatry, 16*(2), 227–236.

Rautiainen, M. R., Paunio, T., Repo-Tiihonen, E., Virkkunen, M., Ollila, H. M., Sulkava, S., . . . & Tiihonen, J. (2016). Genome-wide association study of antisocial personality disorder. *Translational Psychiatry, 6*(9), e883–e883.

Reber, J., & Tranel, D. (2017). Sex differences in the functional lateralization of emotion and decision making in the human brain. *Journal of Neuroscience Research, 95*(1–2), 270–278.

Reiner, R. (2020). *Social democratic criminology.* New York: Routledge.

Reiss, A. J. (1971). *The police and the public.* Yale University Press.

Rice, K. M., Walker Jr., E. M., Wu, M., Gillette, C., & Blough, E. R. (2014). Environmental mercury and its toxic effects. *Journal of Preventive Medicine and Public Health, 47*(2), 74–83.

Ridley, M. (1993). *The red queen: Sex and the evolution of human nature.* New York: Penguin.

Ritchie, S. (2015). *Intelligence: All that matters.* London: John Murray.

Ritchie, S. J., Cox, S. R., Shen, X., Lombardo, M. V., Reus, L. M., Alloza, C., . . . & Liewald, D. C. (2018). Sex differences in the adult human brain: Evidence from 5216 UK Biobank participants. *Cerebral Cortex, 28*(8), 2959–2975.

Rivera, F., López, I., Guarnaccia, P., Ramirez, R., Canino, G., & Bird, H. (2011). Perceived discrimination and antisocial behaviors in Puerto Rican children. *Journal of Immigrant and Minority Health, 13*(3), 453–461.

Roberts, B. W. (2018). A revised sociogenomic model of personality traits. *Journal of Personality, 86*(1), 23–35.

Robinson, G. E., Grozinger, C. M., & Whitfield, C. W. (2005). Sociogenomics: Social life in molecular terms. *Nature Reviews Genetics, 6*(4), 257–270.

Robinson, T. R., Smith, S. W., Miller, M. D., & Brownell, M. T. (1999). Cognitive behavior modification of hyperactivity–impulsivity and aggression: A meta-analysis of school-based studies. *Journal of Educational Psychology, 91*(2), 195–203.

Rocque, M. (2015). The lost concept: The (re) emerging link between maturation and desistance from crime. *Criminology & Criminal Justice, 15*(3), 340–360.

Rocque, M. (2017). *Desistance from crime: New advances in theory and research.* New York: Palgrave Macmillan.

Rocque, M., Beckley, A. L., & Piquero, A. R. (2019). Psychosocial maturation, race, and desistance from crime. *Journal of Youth and Adolescence, 48*(7), 1403–1417.

Rocque, M., & Posick, C. (2017). Paradigm shift or normal science? The future of (biosocial) criminology. *Theoretical Criminology, 21*(3), 288–303.

Rocque, M., Posick, C., Barkan, S. E., & Paternoster, R. (2015a). Marriage and county-level crime rates: A research note. *Journal of Research in Crime and Delinquency, 52*(1), 130–145.

Rocque, M., Posick, C., & Felix, S. (2015b). The role of the brain in urban violent offending: Integrating biology with structural theories of 'the streets.' *Criminal Justice Studies, 28*(1), 84–103.

Rocque, M., Posick, C., & Piquero, A. R. (2016). Self-control and crime: Theory, research, and remaining puzzles. In K. D. Vohs & R. F. Baumeister, (Eds.), *Handbook of self-regulation: Research, theory, and applications* (3rd ed.) (pp. 514–532). New York: Guilford Press.

Rocque, M., Posick, C., & White, H. R. (2015). Growing up is hard to do: An empirical evaluation of maturation and desistance. *Journal of Developmental and Life-Course Criminology, 1*(4), 350–384.

Rocque, M., Serwick, A., & Plummer-Beale, J. (2017). Offender rehabilitation and reentry during emerging adulthood: A review and introduction of a new approach. In L. M. Padilla-Walker & L. J. Nelson (Eds.), *Flourishing in emerging adulthood: Positive development during the third decade of life* (chap. 12, pp. 510–531). New York: Oxford University Press.

Rocque, M., Welsh, B. C., & Raine, A. (2012). Biosocial criminology and modern crime prevention. *Journal of Criminal Justice, 40*(4), 306–312.

Roeder, O. K., Brooke-Eisen, L., Bowling, J., Stiglitz, J. E., & Chettiar, I. M. (2015). *What caused the crime decline?* Columbia Business School Research Paper No. 15-28. Available at http://dx.doi.org/10.2139/ssrn.2566965.

Rosenfeld, R. (1989). Robert Merton's contributions to the sociology of deviance. *Sociological Inquiry, 59*(4), 453–466.

Rothbaum, B. O., & Schwartz, A. C. (2002). Exposure therapy for posttraumatic stress disorder. *American journal of psychotherapy, 56*(1), 59–75.

Roy, A. L., McCoy, D. C., & Raver, C. C. (2014). Instability versus quality: Residential mobility, neighborhood poverty, and children's self-regulation. *Developmental Psychology, 50*(7), 1891–1896.

Ruigrok, A. N., Salimi-Khorshidi, G., Lai, M. C., Baron-Cohen, S., Lombardo, M. V., Tait, R. J., & Suckling, J. (2014). A meta-analysis of sex differences in human brain structure. *Neuroscience & Biobehavioral Reviews, 39*, 34–50.

Sadeh, N., Wolf, E. J., Logue, M. W., Lusk, J., Hayes, J. P., McGlinchey, R. E., . . . & Miller, M. W. (2016). Polygenic risk for externalizing psychopathology and executive dysfunction in trauma-exposed veterans. *Clinical Psychological Science, 4*(3), 545–558.

Salas-Wright, C. P., & Todic, J. (2014). Alcohol and drug misuse as a biosocial source of crime. In M. DeLisi (Ed.). *Routledge international handbook of biosocial criminology* (pp. 558–570). New York: Routledge.

Sampson, R. J., & Laub, J. H. (1992). Crime and deviance in the life course. *Annual Review of Sociology, 18*(1), 63–84.

Sampson, R. J., & Laub, J. H. (1993). *Crime in the making: Pathways and turning points through life.* Cambridge, MA: Harvard University Press.

Sampson, R. J., Laub, J. H., & Wimer, C. (2006). Does marriage reduce crime? A counterfactual approach to within-individual causal effects. *Criminology, 44*(3), 465–508.

Sampson, R. J., & Lauritsen, J. L. (1994). Violent victimization and offending: Individual-, situational-, and community-level risk factors. In A. J. Reiss &

J. A. Roth (Eds.), *Understanding and preventing violence* (vol. 3, pp. 1–114). Washington, DC: National Academy Press.

Sampson, R. J., Raudenbush, S. W., & Earls, F. (1997). Neighborhoods and violent crime: A multilevel study of collective efficacy. *Science, 277*(5328), 918–924.

Sampson, R. J., & Sharkey, P. (2008). Neighborhood selection and the social reproduction of concentrated racial inequality. *Demography, 45*(1), 1–29.

Sampson, R. J., & Wilson, W. J. (1995). Toward a theory of crime, race, and urban inequality. In J. Hagan & R. D. Peterson (Eds.), *Crime and inequality* (pp. 37–54). Stanford, CA: Stanford University Press.

Sampson, R. J., & Winter, A. S. (2018). Poisoned development: Assessing childhood lead exposure as a cause of crime in a birth cohort followed through adolescence. *Criminology, 56*(2), 269–301.

Savolainen, J., Applin, S., Messner, S. F., Hughes, L. A., Lytle, R., & Kivivuori, J. (2017). Does the gender gap in delinquency vary by level of patriarchy? A cross-national comparative analysis. *Criminology, 55*(4), 726–753.

Schmitt, D. P., Realo, A., Voracek, M., & Allik, J. (2008). Why can't a man be more like a woman? Sex differences in Big Five personality traits across 55 cultures. *Journal of Personality and Social Psychology, 94*(1), 168–182.

Schnittker, J., & John, A. (2007). Enduring stigma: The long-term effects of incarceration on health. *Journal of Health and Social Behavior, 48*(2), 115–130.

Secretary of Health and Human Services (SHHS). (2000). *Special report to the US Congress on alcohol and health.* June 2000. Available at https://pubs.niaaa.nih.gov/publications/10report/10thspecialreport.pdf.

Segert, J., & Nathan, A. (2018). Understanding ownership and privacy of genetic data. *Harvard University, The Graduate School of Arts and Sciences.* November 28, 2018. Available at http://sitn.hms.harvard.edu/flash/2018/understanding-ownership-privacy-genetic-data/.

Semenza, D. C., Meldrum, R. C., Jackson, D. B., Vaughn, M. G., & Piquero, A. R. (2020). School start times, delinquency, and substance use: A criminological perspective. *Crime & Delinquency, 66*(2), 163–193.

Sharkey, P. (2018). *Uneasy peace: The great crime decline, the renewal of city life, and the next war on violence.* New York: W. W. Norton.

Shaw, C. R., & McKay, H. D. (1942). *Juvenile delinquency and urban areas.* Chicago: University of Chicago Press.

Sheldon, S., Diamond, N. B., Armson, M. J., Palombo, D. J., Selarka, D., Romero, K., . . . Levine, B. (2018). Assessing autobiographical memory. In E. A. Phelps & L. Davachi (Vol. Eds.), *Stevens' handbook of experimental psychology and cognitive neuroscience* (vol. 1, pp. 363–396). New York: Wiley.

Sherman, L. (1997). Family-based crime prevention. In L. W. Sherman, D. Gottfredson, D. MacKenzie, J. Eck, P. Reuter, & S. Bushway, *Prevention crime: What works, what doesn't, what's promising.* A report to the United States Congress. Washington, DC: National Institute of Justice.

Sherman, L. W., Gartin, P. R., & Buerger, M. E. (1989). Hot spots of predatory crime: Routine activities and the criminology of place. *Criminology, 27*(1), 27–56.

Sherman, L. W. & Strang, H. (2007). *Restorative justice: The evidence.* London: Smith Institute.

Shonkoff, J. P., Phillips, D. A., & National Research Council. (2000). The developing brain. In National Research Council (US) and Institute of Medicine (US) Committee on Integrating the Science of Early Childhood Development, J. P. Shonkoff, & D. A. Phillips (Eds.), *From neurons to neighborhoods: The science of early childhood development.* Washington, DC: National Academies Press.

Silver, E. (2006). Understanding the relationship between mental disorder and violence: The need for a criminological perspective. *Law and Human Behavior, 30*(6), 685–706.

Simon, R. J. (1975). *Women and crime.* Lexington, MA: Lexington Books.

Simons, R. L., & Lei, M. K. (2013). Enhanced susceptibility to context: A promising perspective on the interplay of genes and the social environment. In C. Gibson & M. D. Krohn (Eds.), *Handbook of life-course criminology* (pp. 57–67). New York: Springer.

Simons, R. L., Lei, M. K., Beach, S. R., Brody, G. H., Philibert, R. A., & Gibbons, F. X. (2011). Social environment, genes, and aggression: Evidence supporting the differential susceptibility perspective. *American Sociological Review, 76*(6), 883–912.

Skardhamar, T., Savolainen, J., Aase, K. N., & Lyngstad, T. H. (2015). Does marriage reduce crime? *Crime and Justice, 44*(1), 385–446.

Smith, D. A., & Paternoster, R. (1987). The gender gap in theories of deviance: Issues and evidence. *Journal of Research in Crime and Delinquency, 24*(2), 140–172.

Smits, A. H., Ziebell, F., Joberty, G., Zinn, N., Mueller, W. F., Clauder-Münster, S., . . . & Michon, A. M. (2019). Biological plasticity rescues target activity in CRISPR knock outs. *Nature Methods, 16*(11), 1087–1093.

Sniekers, S., Stringer, S., Watanabe, K., Jansen, P. R., Coleman, J. R., Krapohl, E., . . . & Amin, N. (2017). Genome-wide association meta-analysis of 78,308 individuals identifies new loci and genes influencing human intelligence. *Nature Genetics, 49*(7), 1107–1112.

Sowell, E. R., Peterson, B. S., Thompson, P. M., Welcome, S. E., Henkenius, A. L., & Toga, A. W. (2003). Mapping cortical change across the human life span. *Nature Neuroscience, 6*(3), 309–315.

Springer, K. W., Sheridan, J., Kuo, D., & Carnes, M. (2007). Long-term physical and mental health consequences of childhood physical abuse: Results from a large population-based sample of men and women. *Child Abuse & Neglect, 31*(5), 517–530.

Steffensmeier, D., Zhong, H., & Lu, Y. (2017). Age and its relation to crime in Taiwan and the United States: Invariant, or does cultural context matter? *Criminology, 55*(2), 377–404.

Steffensmeier, D. J., Allan, E. A., Harer, M. D., & Streifel, C. (1989). Age and the distribution of crime. *American Journal of Sociology, 94*, 803–831.

Steinberg, L. (2005). Cognitive and affective development in adolescence. *Trends in Cognitive Sciences, 9*(2), 69–74.

Steinberg, L. (2010). A dual systems model of adolescent risk-taking. *Developmental Psychobiology, 52*(3), 216–224.

Steinberg, L. (2014). *Age of opportunity: Lessons from the new science of adolescence.* Boston: Houghton Mifflin Harcourt.

Stergiakouli, E., Martin, J., Hamshere, M. L., Heron, J., St Pourcain, B., Timpson, N. J., . . . & Davey Smith, G. (2017). Association between polygenic risk scores for attention-deficit hyperactivity disorder and educational and cognitive outcomes in the general population. *International Journal of Epidemiology, 46*(2), 421–428.

Stevens, J. E. (2012). The adverse childhood experience study—the largest, most important public health study you never heard of—began in an obesity clinic. *Aces Too High News.* October 3, 2012. Available at https://acestoohigh .com/2012/10/03/the-adverse-childhood-experiences-study-the-largest -most-important-public-health-study-you-never-heard-of-began-in-an-obe sity-clinic/.St-Onge, M. P., Mikic, A., & Pietrolungo, C. E. (2016). Effects of diet on sleep quality. *Advances in Nutrition, 7*(5), 938–949.

Stohr, M. K., Walsh, A., & Hemmens, C. (2013). *Corrections: A text/reader* (2nd ed.). Thousand Oaks, CA: Sage.

Stone, R., & Rydberg, J. (2019). Parenthood, maturation, and desistance: Examining parenthood transition effects on maturation domains and subsequent reoffending. *Journal of Developmental and Life-Course Criminology, 5*(3), 387–414.

Stretesky, P. B., & Lynch, M. J. (2004). The relationship between lead and crime. *Journal of Health and Social Behavior, 45*(2), 214–229.

Sukhodolsky, D. G., Kassinove, H., & Gorman, B. S. (2004). Cognitive-behavioral therapy for anger in children and adolescents: A meta-analysis. *Aggression and Violent Behavior, 9*(3), 247–269.

Sundram, F., Deeley, Q., Sarkar, S., Daly, E., Latham, R., Craig, M., . . . & Murphy, D. G. (2012). White matter microstructural abnormalities in the frontal lobe of adults with antisocial personality disorder. *Cortex, 48*(2), 216–229.

Sutherland, E. H. (1947). *Principles of criminology.* New York: J. B. Lippincott.

Sutin, A. R., Stephan, Y., & Terracciano, A. (2016). Perceived discrimination and personality development in adulthood. *Developmental Psychology, 52*(1), 155–163.

Sweeten, G., Piquero, A. R., & Steinberg, L. (2013). Age and the explanation of crime, revisited. *Journal of Youth and Adolescence, 42*(6), 921–938.

Sykes, G., & Matza, D. (1957). Techniques of neutralization: A theory of delinquency. *American Sociological Review, 22*(6), 664–670.

Taylor, D. (2014). *Toxic communities: Environmental racism, industrial pollution, and residential mobility.* New York: New York University Press.

Thatcher, R. W., Lester, M. L., McAlaster, R., Horst, R., & Ignasias, S. W. (1983). Intelligence and lead toxins in rural children. *Journal of Learning Disabilities, 16*(6), 355–359.

The Osborne Association. 2018. The high costs of low risk: The crisis of America's aging prison population. May 2018. Available at http://www.osborneny.org /resources/the-high-costs-of-low-risk/the-high-cost-of-low-risk/#:~:text =While%20new%20reports%20and%20articles,US%20prison%20history %20that%20any.

Tibbetts, S. G., & Piquero, A. R. (1999). The influence of gender, low birth weight, and disadvantaged environment in predicting early onset of offending: A test of Moffitt's interactional hypothesis. *Criminology, 37*(4), 843–878.

Tielbeek, J. J., Johansson, A., Polderman, T. J., Rautiainen, M. R., Jansen, P., Taylor, M., . . . & Viding, E. (2017). Genome-wide association studies of a broad spectrum of antisocial behavior. *JAMA Psychiatry, 74*(12), 1242–1250.

Tittle, C. R., Villemez, W. J., & Smith, D. A. (1978). The myth of social class and criminality: An empirical assessment of the empirical evidence. *American Sociological Review, 43*(5), 643–656.

Tittle, C. R., Ward, D. A., & Grasmick, H. G. (2003). Self-control and crime/ deviance: Cognitive vs. behavioral measures. *Journal of Quantitative Criminology, 19*(4), 333–365.

Toby, J. (1957). Social disorganization and stake in conformity: Complementary factors in the predatory behavior of hoodlums. *Journal of Criminal Law, Criminology, and Police Science, 48*, 12.

Tomasi, D., & Volkow, N. D. (2012). Laterality patterns of brain functional connectivity: Gender effects. *Cerebral Cortex, 22*(6), 1455–1462.

Tremblay, R. E., Japel, C., Perusse, D., McDuff, P., Boivin, M., Zoccolillo, M., & Montplaisir, J. (1999). The search for the age of 'onset' of physical aggression: Rousseau and Bandura revisited. *Criminal Behaviour and Mental Health, 9*(1), 8–23.

Tremblay, R. E., Nagin, D. S., Seguin, J. R., Zoccolillo, M., Zelazo, P. D., Boivin, M., . . . & Japel, C. (2004). Physical aggression during early childhood: Trajectories and predictors. *Pediatrics, 114*(1), e43–e50.

Turner, J. H. (2013). Neurology and interpersonal behavior: The basic challenge for neurosociology. In D. D. Franks & J. H. Turner (Eds.), *Handbook of neurosociology*. Dordrecht, Netherlands: Springer.

Tuvblad, C., & Baker, L. A. (2011). Human aggression across the lifespan: Genetic propensities and environmental moderators. In R. Huber, D. L. Bannasch, & P. Brennan (Eds.), *Advances in genetics* (vol. 75, pp. 171–214). Cambridge, MA: Academic Press.

Tyler, T. R. (1990). *Why people obey the law*. New Haven, CT: Yale University Press.

Tyler, T. R. (2003). Procedural justice, legitimacy, and the effective rule of law. *Crime and Justice, 30*, 283–357.

Tyler, T. R. (2004). Enhancing police legitimacy. *The Annals of the American Academy of Political and Social Science, 593*(1), 84–99.

Uggen, C., & Massoglia, M. (2003). Desistance from crime and deviance as a turning point in the life course. In J. T. Mortimer & M. J. Shanahan (Eds.), *Handbook of the life course*. Boston, MA: Springer.

Unnever, J. D., & Gabbidon, S. L. (2011). *A theory of African American offending: Race, racism, and crime*. New York: Taylor & Francis.

Upswell.org. (n.d.). https://upswellarchive.org/speaker/eddie-bocanegra/.

Urban, N. B., Kegeles, L. S., Slifstein, M., Xu, X., Martinez, D., Sakr, E., . . . & Abi-Dargham, A. (2010). Sex differences in striatal dopamine release in young adults after oral alcohol challenge: A positron emission tomography imaging study with [11C] raclopride. *Biological Psychiatry, 68*(8), 689–696.

U.S. Census. 2020. Historical marital status tables. December 2020. Available at https://www.census.gov/data/tables/time-series/demo/families/marital.html.

Vaske, J., Galyean, K., & Cullen, F. T. (2011). Toward a biosocial theory of offender rehabilitation: Why does cognitive-behavioral therapy work? *Journal of Criminal Justice, 39*(1), 90–102.

Vaske, J. C. (2017). Using biosocial criminology to understand and improve treatment outcomes. *Criminal Justice and Behavior, 44*(8), 1050–1072.

Vaske, J. C., & Boisvert, D. L. (2015). Stress and antisocial behavior. In M. DeLisi (Ed.). *The Routledge International Handbook of Biosocial Criminology* (pp. 128–143). New York: Routledge.

Vaughn, M. G. (2016). Policy implications of biosocial criminology: Toward a renewed commitment to prevention science. *Criminology & Public Policy, 15*, 703–710.

Vaughn, M. G., & DeLisi, M. (2018). Criminal energetics: A theory of antisocial enhancement and criminal attenuation. *Aggression and Violent Behavior, 38*, 1–12.

Viau-Colindres, J., Axelrad, M., & Karaviti, L. P. (2017). Bringing back the term "intersex." *Pediatrics, 140*(5), e20170505.

Vrijkotte, T. G., Van Doornen, L. J., & De Geus, E. J. (2000). Effects of work stress on ambulatory blood pressure, heart rate, and heart rate variability. *Hypertension, 35*(4), 880–886.

Walsh, A. (2000). Evolutionary psychology and the origins of justice. *Justice Quarterly, 17*(4), 841–864.

Walsh, A., & Vaske, J. C. (2015). *Feminist criminology through a biosocial lens*. Durham, NC: Carolina Academic Press.

Walsh, A., & Yun, I. (2014). Epigenetics and allostasis: Implications for criminology. *Criminal Justice Review, 39*(4), 411–431.

Warr, M. (1998). Life-course transitions and desistance from crime. *Criminology, 36*(2), 183–216.

Warr, M. (2002). *Companions in crime: The social aspects of criminal conduct*. New York: Cambridge University Press.

Warr, M., & Stafford, M. (1991). The influence of delinquent peers: What they think or what they do? *Criminology, 29*(4), 851–866.

Weisburd, D., Bushway, S., Lum, C., & Yang, S. M. (2004). Trajectories of crime at places: A longitudinal study of street segments in the city of Seattle. *Criminology*, *42*(2), 283–322.

Weisburd, D., Eck, J. E., Braga, A. A., Telep, C. W., Cave, B., Bowers, K., . . . & Yang, S. M. (2016). *Place matters*. New York: Cambridge University Press.

Weisburd, D., & Piquero, A. R. (2008). How well do criminologists explain crime? Statistical modeling in published studies. *Crime and Justice*, *37*(1), 453–502.

Wertz, J., Caspi, A., Belsky, D., Beckley, A. L., Arseneault, L., Barnes, J. C., . . . & Moffitt, T. E. (2018). Genetics and crime: Integrating new genomic discoveries into psychological research about antisocial behavior. *Psychological Science*, *29*(5), 791–803.

West, D. J. (1982). *Delinquency, its roots, careers, and prospects*. Cambridge, MA: Harvard University Press.

Wilson, J. Q., & Herrnstein, R. (1985). *Crime and human nature*. New York: Simon and Schuster.

Wilson, M., & Daly, M. (1997). Life expectancy, economic inequality, homicide, and reproductive timing in Chicago neighbourhoods. *BMJ: British Medical Journal*, *314*(7089), 1271–1274.

Wilson, W. J. (1987). *The truly disadvantaged: The inner city, the underclass, and public policy*. Chicago: University of Chicago Press.

Wilson, W. J. (2009). *More than just race: Being black and poor in the inner city*. New York: Norton.

Winick, M. (1969). Malnutrition and brain development. *Journal of Pediatrics*, *74*(5), 667–679.

Wright, J., Beaver, K., Delisi, M., & Vaughn, M. (2008). Evidence of negligible parenting influences on self-control, delinquent peers, and delinquency in a sample of twins. *Justice Quarterly*, *25*(3), 544–569.

Wright, J. P., & Beaver, K. M. (2005). Do parents matter in creating self-control in their children? A genetically informed test of Gottfredson and Hirschi's theory of low self-control. *Criminology*, *43*(4), 1169–1202.

Wright, J. P., & Boisvert, D. (2009). What biosocial criminology offers criminology. *Criminal Justice and Behavior*, *36*(11), 1228–1240.

Wright, J. P., Moore, K., & Newsome, J. (2016). Molecular genetics and crime. In A. Walsh & K. M. Beaver (Eds.), *The Ashgate research companion to biosocial theories of crime* (pp. 105–126). New York: Routledge.

Wolfe, S. E., Nix, J., Kaminski, R., & Rojek, J. (2016). Is the effect of procedural justice on police legitimacy invariant? Testing the generality of procedural justice and competing antecedents of legitimacy. *Journal of Quantitative Criminology*, *32*(2), 253–282.

Wolfgang, M. E., & Ferracuti, F. (1967). *The subculture of violence: Towards an integrated theory in criminology*. London: Tavistock Publications.

Yehuda, R., Cai, G., Golier, J. A., Sarapas, C., Galea, S., Ising, M., . . . & Buxbaum, J. D. (2009). Gene expression patterns associated with posttraumatic stress disorder following exposure to the World Trade Center attacks. *Biological Psychiatry, 66*(7), 708–711.

Yehuda, R., Daskalakis, N. P., Bierer, L. M., Bader, H. N., Klengel, T., Holsboer, F., & Binder, E. B. (2016). Holocaust exposure induced intergenerational effects on FKBP5 methylation. *Biological Psychiatry, 80*(5), 372–380.

Yehuda, R., Engel, S. M., Brand, S. R., Seckl, J., Marcus, S. M., & Berkowitz, G. S. (2005). Transgenerational effects of posttraumatic stress disorder in babies of mothers exposed to the World Trade Center attacks during pregnancy. *Journal of Clinical Endocrinology & Metabolism, 90*(7), 4115–4118.

Yehuda, R., & Lehrner, A. (2018). Intergenerational transmission of trauma effects: Putative role of epigenetic mechanisms. *World Psychiatry, 17*(3), 243–257.

Young, C. A., Haffejee, B., & Corsun, D. L. (2017). Developing cultural intelligence and empathy through diversified mentoring relationships. *Journal of Management Education, 42*(3), 319–346.

Zimmerman, G. M., & Posick, C. (2016). Risk factors for and behavioral consequences of direct versus indirect exposure to violence. *American Journal of Public Health, 106*(1), 178–188.

Zimmet, P., Shi, Z., El-Osta, A., & Ji, L. (2018). Epidemic T2DM, early development and epigenetics: Implications of the Chinese famine. *Nature Reviews Endocrinology, 14*(12), 738–746.

Zimring, F. E. (2007). *The great American crime decline.* New York: Oxford University Press.

Index

The letter f following a page number denotes a figure. The letter t following a page number denotes a table.

Chad Posick is an Associate Professor of Criminal Justice and Criminology at Georgia Southern University. He is the coauthor of *The Criminal Brain: Understanding Biological Theories of Crime*, Second Edition, and *Great Debates in Criminology*.

Michael Rocque is an Associate Professor of Sociology at Bates College. He is the author of *Desistance from Crime: New Advances in Theory and Research* and the coauthor of *The Criminal Brain: Understanding Biological Theories of Crime*, Second Edition, and *Great Debates in Criminology*.

J. C. Barnes is a Professor in the School of Criminal Justice at the University of Cincinnati and the coauthor of *Criminological Theory: A Brief Introduction*, Fourth Edition. He is an Associated Investigator with the Dunedin Multidisciplinary Health and Development Study, which is run out of the University of Otago in New Zealand.